THE URANTIA BO

URANTIA®

URANTIA FOUNDATION
533 WEST DIVERSEY PARKWAY
CHICAGO, ILLINOIS 60614
U.S.A.

URANTIA®

THE URANTIA BOOK WORKBOOKS

VOLUME I

Foreword and Part I

This series of workbooks originally was published in the 1950s and 1960s to assist those early students who wanted to pursue an in-depth study of *The Urantia Book*. The workbook creators recognized that the materials were imperfect and were far from being definitive works on these subjects. Current students may be able to make more exhaustive analyses due to advances in knowledge and computerization of the text that are available today. Nevertheless, we recognize the enormous effort that went into this attempt to enhance understanding of *The Urantia Book* by some of its earliest students. We think these materials will be of interest to many and are therefore republishing them for their historic and educational value.

FIRST PRINTING 2003

THE URANTIA BOOK WORKBOOKS
VOLUME I
FOREWORD AND PART I

The Urantia Book Workbooks

Volume I: Transcripts of Lecture and Discussion of the Foreword
              and An Analytic Study of Part One of *The Urantia Book*
Volume II: Science in *The Urantia Book*
Volume III: Topical Studies in *The Urantia Book* and A Short Course in
              Doctrine
Volume IV: The Teachings of Jesus in *The Urantia Book*, The Life of
              Jesus Compared to the four Gospels

ISBN:
0-942430-99-9

PUBLISHED BY URANTIA FOUNDATION
Original Publisher since 1955
533 Diversey Parkway
Chicago, Illinois 60614 U.S.A.
Telephone: +1 (773) 525-3319
Fax: +1 (773) 525-7739
Website: http://www.urantia.org
E-mail: urantia@urantia.org

Information

URANTIA Foundation has Representatives in Argentina, Belgium, Brazil, Bulgaria, Colombia, Ecuador, Estonia, Greece, Indonesia, Korea, Lithuania, México, Norway, Perú, Senegal, Spain, Uruguay, and Venezuela. If you require information on study groups, where you can obtain *The URANTIA Book*, or a Representative's telephone number, please contact the office nearest you or the head office in Chicago, Illinois.

International Offices:

Head Office

533 West Diversey Parkway
Chicago, Illinois 60614 U.S.A.
Tel.: +(773) 525-3319
Fax: +(773) 525-7739
Website: www.urantia.org
E-mail: urantia@urantia.org

Canada—English

PO Box 92006
West Vancouver, BC Canada V7V 4X4
Tel: +(604) 926-5836
Fax: +(604) 926-5899
E-mail: urantia@telus.net

Finland / Estonia / Sweden

PL 18,
15101 Lahti Finland
Tel./Fax: +(358) 3 777 8191
E-mail: urantia-saatio@urantia.fi

Great Britain / Ireland

Tel./Fax: +(44) 1491 641-922
E-Mail: urantia@easynet.co.uk

Australia / New Zealand / Asia

Tel./Fax: +(61) 2 9970-6200
E-mail: urantia@urantia.org.au

Canada—French

C. P. 233
Cap-Santé (Québec) Canada G0A 1L0
Tel.: +(418) 285-3333
Fax: +(418) 285-0226
E-mail: fondation@urantia-quebec.org

St. Petersburg, Russia

Tel./Fax: +(7) 812-580-3018
E-mail: vitgen@peterlink.ru

Other books available from URANTIA Foundation:

The URANTIA Book	hard cover		ISBN 0-911560-02-5
The URANTIA Book	leather collector ($7^5/_8$" x $5^3/_4$")		ISBN 0-911560-75-0
The URANTIA Book	small hard cover ($8^7/_{16}$" x $5^1/_2$")		ISBN 0-911560-07-6
The URANTIA Book	paperback	($8^7/_{16}$" x $5^1/_2$")	ISBN 0-911560-51-3
The URANTIA Book	gift-box leather ($8^7/_{16}$" x $5^1/_2$")		ISBN 0-911560-08-4
The URANTIA Book	softcover*	($8^7/_{16}$" x $5^1/_2$")	ISBN 0-911560-50-5
Le Livre d'URANTIA	hard cover	French	ISBN 0-911560-05-X
Le Livre d'URANTIA	soft cover	French	ISBN 0-911560-53-X
El libro de URANTIA	paperback	Spanish ($8^7/_{16}$" x $5^1/_2$")	ISBN 1-883395-02-X
El libro de URANTIA	hard cover	Spanish ($8^7/_{16}$" x $5^1/_2$")	ISBN 1-883395-03-8
URANTIA-kirja	hard cover	Finnish	ISBN 0-911560-03-3
URANTIA-kirja	soft cover	Finnish	ISBN 0-911560-52-1
Книга Урантии	hard cover	Russian* ($8^7/_{16}$" x $5^1/_2$")	ISBN 0-911560-80-7
Het URANTIA Boek	hard cover	Dutch	ISBN 0-911560-54-6
유란시아서	hard cover	Korean	ISBN 0-911560-40-8
The URANTIA Book Concordance	English Index		ISBN 0-911560-00-9
URANTIA-kirja Hakemisto	Finnish Index		ISBN 0-911560-04-1
The URANTIA Book	Audio	English*	ISBN 0-911560-30-0
The URANTIA Book	CD ROM	English, Finnish, French	ISBN 0-911560-63-7
The URANTIA Book Workbooks			
Forward and Part I	Paperback	English	ISBN 0-942430-99-9
Science	Paperback	English	ISBN 0-942430-98-0
Topical and Doctrinal Study	Paperback	English	ISBN 0-942430-97-2
Jesus	Paperback	English	ISBN 0-942430-96-4

INTRODUCTION

Much has already been written regarding the study groups called "The Forum" and "The Seventy". Therefore I will try to confine my remarks more closely to the compiling and printing of several workbooks by Dr. William Sadler to be used in conjunction with *The Urantia Book*.

"The Forum" was the larger of the two groups and met on Sunday afternoons. The Wednesday night group was much smaller, studied in more depth, and was called "The Seventy" as that was the number of its members. Both met at the home of Dr. Sadler at 533 Diversey Parkway in Chicago. Doctor and some others in the group felt that something concrete was needed to train teachers for the future. Workbooks would help the teachers to form classes in the state or country in which they lived and use then to understand and present the concepts and new ideas from the Book in a uniform manner.

For several years members of the Wednesday night group were asked to prepare topical papers and teach the contents to the others in the group thus giving them experience in teaching. Dr. Sadler and his son, Bill, also taught the members of the group the information contained in the Papers of *The Urantia Book*. From the information Dr. Sadler taught at these classes the workbooks were developed for use by the group and for future teachers of the revelation.

The titles of the workbooks were:
Urantia Doctrine;
The Theology of *The Urantia Book*, Part I, Part II, and Part III;
Worship and Wisdom;
The Short Course in Doctrine,
 Summary Of The Theology Of *The Urantia Book*;
Science in *The Urantia Book* Volume I (with the collaboration of Alvin Kulieke);
    and
The Teachings Of Jesus.

Dr. Sadler possessed a great intellect, which may be one of the reasons he was selected by the Contact Commission to be the recipient of the *Urantia Papers*. He was able to understand and present, in a form that is understandable for others, many of the more difficult concepts and information in *The Urantia Book*. This is a great advantage for students who may be teaching these concepts in the future. The reprinting of these study aids will help many students of *The Urantia Book* gain a more comfortable understanding of the more difficult teachings in the book and an insight into Dr. Sadler's plan for instructing the future teachers of the revelation.

What a legacy has been left to us!

Katharine

Katharine Lea Jones Harries

AN ANALYTIC STUDY

OF

PART ONE OF *THE URANTIA BOOK*

TRANSCRIPT OF A LECTURE
AND DISCUSSION OF *THE FOREWORD*

by
William Sadler, Jr.

Presented June 12, 1961

TRANSCRIPTS OF
LECTURE AND DISCUSSION
OF "THE FOREWORD" BY
WILLIAM SADLER, JR.*
6/12/61

Well, I want to tell you something, this is, in my life, a very historic occasion and one of very deep gratification because in my entire experience with this Blue Book, this is the first time any group of human beings has ever *asked* to have the Foreword discussed.

Well honey, we're glad to be the first !

I have taught the Foreword under various stages of compression. I've used a kind of an intellectual (Alimite) gun to force it down people. I've done a strip-tease with the Foreword. I've made it ridiculously simple and um... I've always had a captive audience, but you folks actually *asked* to talk about the Forward, and, and um... well, all I can say is, in terms of the Bible, "This hour has come". I'd like to do this *this*, if I may, would you let me, would you let me try to give you a feeling for the Foreword first, and would you hold detailed questions until we've just taken an overview of the Foreword?

I would like to communicate to you my feeling for the *intent* which is behind the Foreword. The, the Foreword starts out with an apology, it says that our language isn't very good (and indeed it isn't) and it says, uh... we want to help you understand. You see, the *secondary* purpose of *The Urantia Book* is the illumination of the human mind. It's *primary* purpose is the salvation of human souls, but the Book makes an intellectual appeal because the Book is in English, therefore it's got to enter our consciousness through mind. The Foreword tips its hat, in two paragraphs, to the human desire to start from man and proceed to God. You'll recall in one of the papers where they first talk about Trinity Teacher Sons, they tell why they wrote the Book the way they did, starting from God and proceeding outward and downward to man. They point out that if you start from man and go to God...uh...this might be a certain way of grasping fact, but you, the truth would elude you. You don't start with conse-quences, you start with causes, you start with sources, and so they start this Book talking about God, but there are two paragraphs here (that start on page 1 at the bottom) in which very quickly accede to the human yearning to start

---

from the simple and proceed to the complex. In the last two paragraphs on page 1 they very quickly start with, *Our world* and go right into *Paradise* and then they add a few comments: "Your world is one of many similar planets which make up the local universe of Nebadon. This, with similar creations, makes up the Superuniverse of Orvonton, from whose capitol, Uversa, our commision hails. Orvonton is one of the seven evolutionary superuniverses of time and space which circle the never-beginning, never-ending creation of divine perfection- the central universe of Havona. At the heart of this eternal and central universe is the stationary Isle of Paradise, the geographic center of infinity and the dwelling place of the eternal God."

I submit that's quite a paragraph, isn't it? In just a, in just 8 or 9 lines of type, they start here and take you swiftly into the center of all things. This is their concession to the human desire to start from the simple and go into the complex. I think it's very significant that the Forward starts with a discussion of diety and divinity. Diety, they define, as a word which is larger than the word God, because God means a *personal aspect* of diety. Diety can be other-than personal, as well as personal. The first half of section 1 in the Forward is nothing more nor less than a discussion of *how* diety functions and they give us seven levels on which diety functions. These levels vary from the quiet to the active and they encompass all of the, all of the known, comprehensible functions of diety. Diety can be very quiet. Diety can also plan, and that means that there is a potential, a plan which will be fulfilled, a plan that will be consumated. Diety can be fraternal as in the case of Father, Son and Spirit. Diety creates and spreads itself out over creation. Diety engages in creativity in time as well as instantaneous creativity, because evolution is simply creativity in time and evolution simply means that creatures go in partnership with diety. When a seraphim is created, she has nothing to say about her status, she simply is born as a full-grown seraphim, but human beings have everything to say about their status, as finaliters. The evolutionary process is no different than the creative process, except the act of creation is slowed down, broken into many stages and steps, and the creature has the possibility of going into a partnership with the Creator and of being co-creator of himself as he is to be. I think of the creative and the evolutionary aspects of diety as the *outgoing* aspects of diety and I think of the supreme and the ultimate aspects of diety as the *in-gathering* of the consequences of creation and evolution. When all finite evolution is summed up, it consolidates in Supreme Diety and this is a concept that's quite new in *The Urantia Book*. It's quite foreign to orthodox Christian theology, it is not only foreign to western philosophy. The concept of a finite God is encoun- tered in western philosophy, but usually when you encounter that concept, it is to the exclusion of an infinite God. Only in this Book do I find the two concepts associated. In the evolutionary Supreme Being, the Universal Father who inhabits eternity and pervades infinity, is escaping from the terrible limitation of absolutes. Through the Supreme Being, the Universal Father vicareously can have the experienc of having an origin, of having a time of growth, of knowing what it is to struggle. How could an infinite God know struggle, except through a finite expression of that infinite God? As you see, God's love, His purpose, His energies, broadside throughout the finite level, in creation and evolution, then consider a bringing back together of all these things, and *that* is the supreme function of diety. And in the same sense, on the super-finite level we have the *ultimate* function of diety, because what the Supreme is to the finite, the Ultimate is to the super-finite, to the absonite, not absolute, but more than finite. This paper, this section goes on to discuss briefly what is finite, what is absonite, what is absolute, and I think the simplest way of looking at it is to consider time and space. If we're *in* time and space, we're *finite*. Those beings who are *above* time and space, but understand time and space, deal with it, they're *absonite*. An absolute being is timeless and spaceless. I could think of a practical illustration there. Jesus' personalized thought adjuster is a timeless being, a timeless entity, and you'll recall that when the Master put the command of all celestial forces into the keeping of His personalized adjuster, this adjuster warned Him, he said…" now I'll make sure that you don't move about the planet, I understand space," but he said "I want to warn You, if You want to do something which merely needs an abridgement of time, I can't help you there, because I'm not conscious of time." This thought adjuster does not transcend time, this thought adjuster is timeless. Time has no meaning to the thought adjuster. This section goes on to discuss divinity, and it points out that there are many different kinds of divinity, qualities of divinity, but that the one thing which is characteristic of divinity is it is the *cement* that holds all the acts of diety together. If something is related to diety in any way, shape or form, it manifests qualities of divinity. Elsewhere in the Papers, the comprehensible elements of divinity are defined as truth, beauty and goodness. We are told that these are unified in living personalities, as love, mercy and ministry.

Elsewhere we are told that God is love, we're told that mercy is love applied, and that ministry is mercy in action. An effort is made in the second half of this first section to open up our thinking in terms of the quality of divinity, and for the first time you encounter the permutation of three. There are seven different aspects of divinity portrayed here, and if you'll stop and consider, this is the same pattern you encounter in the Seven Master Spirits. They point out that divinity may be perfect, relative or imperfect, and then they let these associate, and you wind up with seven different combinations, and I think if you think of 3 in relation to 7, you'll find this pattern more than once. Perfect in all respects,

imperfect in none. Perfect in some respects, relative in other respects, imperfect in none. Perfect, relative, and imperfect, all in association. Relative
perfection in all aspects, imperfect in none. Relative perfection in all aspects,
imperfect in none. Relative and imperfect in association, imperfect in all
aspects. I would say in human beings you have an association of the perfect and
the imperfect. The thought adjuster would disclose perfection of divinity, and a
human being would be a rather completely imperfect entity, wouldn't he? You
would have Alpha and Omega associated in man.

Having discussed diety and divinity, this Forward then goes on to talk about
God. When we consider God, we are considering an *aspect* of diety, the personal
qualities of diety. How can we best understand that diety can be other than
personal? Well, the Universal Father is the lord of gravity as well as the source
of love. To use the word God loosely now, God has a different attitude toward
the physical universe as compared with His sons and daughters in time and
space. God could hardly love a spiral nebula, could He?

The physical, the material level of cosmic reality. They talk about force, energy,
and power, and these are stages in the *emergence* of what we would recognize as
physical reality. Force is the *beginning*, energy is a stage of *emerging*, and power ia
a stage of *having emerged*. This ties in with their later discussion starting with
space potency, going on down through primordial force, (puissant) energy,
gravity energy, and universe power. Ah, you might say that, uh, in terms of, in
terms of liquid water (this is good symbolization), when you look up into the
sky and you don't see the water vapor up there at all, all you see is the blue sky
with the sun shining, this would be like *force*. Now when it, when it turns cold
and (you) see the clouds form, this would be like *emergent energy* and then when
it starts to rain you've got *universe power*, now you can feel the, the wetness.
Does, does that help? Force would be intangible, energy, you know you, you'd
sense it, but you wouldn't get your hands on it until it rained, then you could
feel it.

They point out that mind always means *somebody* is doing *something*, there's a
ministration if there's mind. Mind never is generated out of matter, mind is put
in to matter. And they talk about pattern, which is a very, a very interesting bit
of discussion here. They point out that pattern is a very real thing but it's hard
to put your hands on. Ah… we're very unhappy if we have unfortunate pattern
we call that being homely, being ugly. The whole beauty industry is built around
the improvement of the human pattern. Our forms are patterns. The spiral
nebula is a pattern. A triangle is a pattern. And the reason that these patterns
appear is because the universe is full of energy; material, spiritual, mindal. And
the universe has personalities in it and personalities are *always trying to order* the

manifestation of energy. So patterns are always appearing. Elsewhere in the Papers, they speak of the forms of ascenders as being patterns which become increasingly responsive to the purpose and action of the inner personality, and I've long suspected that one of the main reasons we'll have for trying to grow in grace on the Mansion Worlds is, if we are ugly on the inside we will jolly well look ugly on the outside, and the only "Helena Rubenstein" you can visit is the house-cleaning of your own soul, and when you begin to be good on the inside, you will begin to look beautiful on the outside. This is even true in (nil), as you write... as the hand of experience writes on your face, uh... the blank pages take on the aspect of your personality. I put it, in my words, we can't avoid wrinkles, but we have a choice as to which kind, the frowning kind, or the smiling kind. You can choose which kind of wrinkles that you choose, that you want to wind up with.

The next 4 sections of the Foreword are a discussion of Experiential Diety, and here they use the word *experiential* in contrast to the word *existential*. Let's see what the word experience means. It means that, it's something that you learn by living through and because of this, you grow in wisdom, you grow in judgement, you grow in capacity. This is utterly foriegn to the nature of God, isn't it? How could God *grow* by any technique, because God *is infinite*? How could God learn anything? God forsees. How could anything take the Father by suprise? Nothing could. God is beyond experience, isn't He? His nature shuts Him off from all things experiential directly. He might grow, He might experience vicareously, in thought adjusters, but never directly, and as it is with the Father, so it is with the Son and the Spirit. These beings are *existential* dieties, They are *beyond* experience. They are without beginning or ending of days. The Father's infinity could hardly increase, could it? If He starts out as infinite, what can be added to it? Now, the Supreme Being, the Sevenfold, the Ultimate, and God the Absolute are experiential dieties. Let's leave God the Sevenfold for the cogent. The Universal Father is engaged in augmenting diety, having started with 3, He is adding 3, and all of these expressions of diety are experiential. They have origins, historic origins. They have beginnings. They know growth. They know setbacks if you please. As the Supreme Being is growing in time and space, I would say, the Lucifer Febellion is like a cancer taking place within the Supreme, and if you'll recall, they isolated the system of Satania much as white leucocytes would wall off an infection in the human body. The Supreme Being is finite diety, is growing diety. The Supreme Being compensates God for the lack of experience of never having been finite. Through the Supreme, God can know what it would be like to have an origin and to grow. The Supreme Being compensates man for his inability ever really to understand an Infinite God. We're told that God is the *first truth* and the *last fact*. We first feel God's love and then we seek to understand Him, but that quest will never end. There are only two beings who understand God and that's the Eternal Son and the Infinite Spirit. They *can* because They have infinite comprehension capacity. We will never understand God, but we will someday understand the Supreme Being, because He has an origin. He has a growth. He has a destiny. He can achieve completion, even as man has an origin, a growth, and can achieve the fufillment of destiny in the Corps of the Finality. The Supreme Being is God as He can be understood by finite creatures. The Supreme Being is not the personalization of the Universal Father, But the Supreme Being *is* the finite equivalent of the personalization of the Paradise Trinity. The Trinity is not a person but when we want to say "What would the Trinity be like if the Trinity were a person and were finite?", *this* is the Supreme Being. He who has seen the Supreme, has seen the equivalent of the finite personalization of the Paradise Trinity.

What we say about the Supreme Being in relation to the finite universe we could say about God the Ultimate in relation to the Master Universe. This is the personification of the Trinity in relation to the Master Universe and as comprehensible by beings that are more than finite, and some day that will include us. I make this comparison between, the Papers make this comparison between Jesus and the Supreme Being. As Jesus is the bridge over which men moves from the human level to the finding of God, so the Supreme Being someday will be the bridge over which finite creatures will move to those levels that lie beyond the finite of creature experience, the absonite levels. God the Absolute. They don't say much about God the Absolute, but I once paraphrased those 2 short paragraphs and it took, as I recall, 6 typewritten pages to paraphrase them and break them, down into what,…what these compact words mean. This statement, these statements about God the Absolute are like *anchovies*, the flavor is packed *in* very tight. You don't eat anchovies in large quantities. You can dilute these paragraphs with much, much, English, and you still have intriguing concepts. The trouble with God the Absolute is that God the Absolute is both experiential and existential and the chances are that our dealings with God the Absolute lie on beyond the whole Master Universe. I can see an end to the Supreme. I can see an end and destiny in the Ultimate, although it's almost incomprehensible, but I can see *only* a beginning to God the Absolute, I can see no end.

Going back to God the Sevenfold and to the present days. If you look on page 11, you'll see that this is a diety association. This is seven levels of diety in action and in time and space, and I strongly suspect that God the Sevenfold will go on functioning after the present universe age in outerspace. Perhaps in slightly modified associations, but in principle, this is *God in action* in time and space.

These are the beings that we encounter on the paradise ascent, starting with Jesus, going on up through the rulers of Orvonton, the Master Spirit of our Superuniverse and then successively, The Spirit, The Son and the Father. God the Sevenfold breaks down into three levels. I always think of the Sevenfold as in 3 principle subdivisions one, two, and three are the Supreme Creators, (They're so defined in the Papers), They are not infinite, They're sub-infinite, They're sub-absolute, They're the folks that are out here working in time and space. They're the Master Spirits, The Ancients of Days, The Creator Sons, and we should include the Creative Spirits with the Creator Son. The last three are the 3 dieties of Paradise, and in between the Supreme Being is growing. As the first 3 levels collaborate with the last 3 levels, this is the essence of the growth of the power of the Supreme Being, and as we participate in this adventure, we make our contribution. I always think of it as when you… let's say that a spiritual act… let's compare it to a physical act because we can understand a physical act, and let the physical act consist of the lifting of a 10 pound, or 50 pound weight. What you get is the developement of muscles, moral muscles perhaps, in the lifting of the weight, but as you lift the weight, your feet push down, don't they? And that's what the Supreme Being gets, is the downthrust of all our liftings. These repercuss in Him if they're of spiritual character.

Section 11 is a very simple section dealing with the three Absolutes. Um… it's simple, because you can read it without understanding any of it whatsoever. These three Absolutes are, in a sense, the potentials out of which future things are drawn, but that's an over-simplification. These three Absolutes also function throughout all time and space, transcendent time and space, etceteras. Now, here's what makes Their function very difficult to comprehend: Let's consider a child in a given situation, he looks at a green apple and he has hunger and so he eats without any thought of the consequences of the bellyache. This is a, this is an… an act… this is a stimulus and response and a consequence, without judgement, without foresight, without anything. An adult looks at the green apple, it looks succulent, the adult forecasts the consequences of eating green apples and decides to pass it up because the adult doesn't want the bellyache. The adult is not reacting to the stimulus of the present, is he? Yes, his salivary glands may react, his mouth may water, but his reaction has to do with future time, does it not? And with the consequences of his acts. Michael, when He was here on earth as Jesus, lived a life from day to day, He looked ahead, He exibited rare foresight. When He was pressed to do something prematurely, He said "But my time has not yet come", no one ever stampeded Him. He was always looking ahead, He was reacting to consequences and to effects, just as the adult looks ahead as compared with the child. These Absolutes react in a *timeless* fashion. When this Absolute, when any Absolute reacts, this Absolute reacts in terms of the eternal past, the eternal present, and the eternal future. Therefore the reaction of an Absolute can never be understood within any frame this side of infinity. Does this make sense? The child couldn't understand why the adult wouldn't eat the green apple, the Twelve did not understand why Jesus did *not do* certain things, the universe administrators are just as mystified by the actions and transactions of the Three Absolutes. Nobody this side of the Paradise Dieties, I think, *comprehends* what these Absolutes are doing because *one of them* mechanizes everything, another one… uh…activates everything, and the third One unifies mechanization and activation. That *is* the function of the universe.

They say don't, don't look upon these Absolutes as antecedent to God. They're not. Don't look upon these Absolutes as being independent of the Trinity. They're not, although the Trinity deals with some of Them only indirectly, but deals with one of Them directly. When the Trinity… when the Paradise Trinity functions in a *total sense*, this *is* the function of the Diety Absolute, and through the Universal Absolute this causes responses in the Unqualified Absolute.

Over on page 15…

Bill?

Yes?

To go over this, one mechanizes, one activates, one…

The Universal Absolute *mechanizes*, the Diety Absolute *activates*, the Universal Absolute *correlates* these 2, unifies these 2. In the full function of the Universal Absolute, you might as well say there's only one Absolute. Page 15 has some of the most difficult English in the Papers, and if we will forget what it says there, and try and get the flavor of the meaning, we can simply say this; The thing that makes it possible to have God and man in the same universe, is the Universal Absolute, who, like Sampson, holds up the temple and keeps the infinity of God from crushing the imperfection of man. The Universal Absolute's function is *to maintain the room* in which things can be imperfect in the *same* universe with a perfect and omnipotent Diety. The Universal Absolute is the prop which God has set up *under* the room in which He is willing to *tolerate* imperfection in time. Were it *not* for the Universal Absolute the suggestion is, there wouldn't be any room, God would fill all things. I will give you my personal opinion of the Universal Absolute. The Universal Absolute is a *symbol* indicating our inability to find the infinite, God as infinite.

This Foreword closes with a discussion of the Trinities, there are three of them. They point out that the Paradise Trinity is the *existential* Trinity, the other 2 are *experiential* Trinities. The Paradise Trinity has no origin. The other 2 Trinities have an historic origin, a time of coming into being, a time of coming into full function. The Trinities happen, I think because of divinity. When God separates things, they've got to reunite in some way. When He achieves threefold personalization as Father, Son, and Spirit, the Trinity became inevitable. This seperation could exist *only* if there were a *unification*, because diety is one. There could be a threefold personalization *only* if the three dieties were unified in some fashion. This sets a pattern which is followed as reality is expressed on the finite level, all those who participate in this finite expression and *perfecting* of the finite, find themselves, in essence, reunified as a trinity, as the first experiential trinity, the Trinity Ultimate. Many beings are involved, but, I visualize this as the union of the diety of three groups of beings; The Supreme Creators, The Transcendentlers (the Architects of the Master Universe) and The Supreme Being. This is not the union of over a million personalities, this is a union, again, of three dieties. All of the Supreme Creators add up to some form of diety manifestation, this is, this is a consequence of Their success. It's not difficult for me to visualize the diety expression of the Corps of the Architects of the Master Universe, and the union of these two with the Supreme Being, not as a person, but as diety, constitutes the First Experiential Trinity, The Trinity Ultimate, and this is the trinity which will *supplement* the acts of the Paradise Trinity in the exploration of the Master Universe and the consequence of the full developement of the Master Universe is the formation of the Second Experiential Trinity (The Trinity Absolute), and the union of all three constitutes The Trinity of Trinities. And that's what the Foreword means to me.

That was a wonderful explanation.

Thank you Bill, you sound good.

Crowd noise and conversation

The question put is, "How can the Universal Absolute be diety ?". Well first of all, we know that It's defined as diety. On page 15, paragraph 1, 2, 3, *4*, it's spoken of, The Universal Absolute is spoken of as "the *potential* of the static-dynamic Diety functionally realizable…etc", uh…"This incomprehensible aspect of Diety may be static, potential, and associative ", now those are the first three levels of Diety function. I want to go elsewhere for help because this is a rough one to try to answer.

Yes it is.

The ah....

(crowd conversation)... It's back on 2 I think Bill.

Over on page 1154, we can get a little help. On 1154 they expand their discussion in the Foreword on the subject of reality, when they're talking about the metamorphosis of the I AM, self distribution of the I AM. Uh...

Is that Diety and reality ?

Yeah, 1154 paragraph 2. It says "In following the chronological portrayal of the origins of reality, there must be a postulated theoretical moment of 'first' volitional expression and 'first' repercussional reaction within the I AM." In other words, this is before the circle starts to separate. In our attempts to portray the genesis and generation of reality, this stage may be concieved as the self-differentiation of the Infinite One from the infinitude. The Infinite One being... uh ... pre-God, the infinitude being a pre-Unqualified Absolute. We've got the Infinite One and the infinitude, but the postulation of this dual relation-ship must always be expanded to a Triune concept by the recognition of the *eternal continuum* of the infinity, the I AM. To me, J.B., the Universal Absolute is a kind of a functional symbolization of the continuation of the Infinite, and when you start with that single circle of reality, this *is* Diety, this is not non-diety. Diety takes precedence over non-diety. Non-diety comes into existence only because Diety has withdrawn Itself. Question ?

No, now I know.

That's the best explanation I can give you. When you think of the 3 circles linked together, that middle circle symbolizes the original circle, and as such, would be Diety. The original circle is not non-diety.

No, that's understandable.

You get non-diety because of the removal of something, this produces non-diety by subtraction, but they're, they're still united. Now you can either, you can express this in two ways. Let me draw you another concept symbol... *[noise of drawing on blackboard]* Here I've got 3 circles linked and I've got all my 3 links in the chain surrounded by one circle. We can't find the large circle, but we can symbolize it by considering the *middle circle* of the 3-chain-link. That's the best explanation I can offer you. I think this, I think if you could ever finalize God the Absolute, I think you'd have *one* Absolute, and then I think the Universal Absolute would become revealed as the Concealed Infinite, but I don't think the Universal Absolute will ever cease to exist, because this would mean we would have reached the end of eternity and the outer edge of infinity, and those are self-contradictory statements.

Visualize the Trinity of Trinities, got 3 Trinities on the bottom level, you've got 3 Experiential Dieties on the next level, but one of them is not complete, and as long as God the Absolute is incomplete, the third level is the Universal Absolute, but if you could ever complete God the Absolute, this would absorb all three Absolutes and would experientialize all three, and then I think on the third level you have the Infinite.

You confused me on a higher plane than I was before!

But at least you're going up, James.

I 'm still confused.

Well, I, I offer this, I offer this with great humility but if, if, if this is not the explanation, then I have none to offer, it's the best I can do. That's a rough question.

Bill, have you ever described, I hope you have some time to describe the separation of the circles, this one and two?

Say that again Bert...

Have you ever described the separation of the circles when they're separated, as one and a two? I mean and.

Yes, yes, yes...

Good!

The *and* itself is a reality. Or I've used the expression : one *and* another, and the, the *and* itself is a reality. Yes.

See, see J.B. didn't ask "*Why* is the Universal Absolute?" he said "Why is the Universal Absolute diety?"

Yes, I understand.

I can understand this association and unification factor, but I can't hardly concieve how it can be Diety.

Well Frank can see by not being Diety, that Diety might be the answer.

Well you see free will moved clear out in the Diety Absolute when it left the Unqualified. Didn't stop.

Right!

All right, I know that!

This, this Universal Absolute is, is pretty mysterious. The uh... I'll, I'll have my ignorance better unified when I do my 30th appendix to the story. I haven't done it yet. Question?

> *Bill, I do have a question and this don't [sic] relate to everything we've been working on. Uh... you said a while ago, (to reinforce my mind) but I don't know why I'm asking. It had to do when,... the first separation from...uh...Absolute Diety. Which separated from the other? And that seems awfully important to me.*

All right, the question is, "Which moved away from what ?".

> *Yes.*

Uh, Diety moved.

> *Not the Unqualified?*

No, the Unqualified Absolute was left behind, because the principle, the potential of, *for* volition *is* the essence of the concept of Diety.

> *Diety had to move, the other one couldn't move...*

The Unqualified Absolute is a *reactor* not an *initiator*. The Unqualified Absolute is the *sneezer* not the taker of snot.

> *That's awful important, you know, I didn't know why Bill, but I understand now.*

I think it is important. The Unqualified Absolute what's was left behind when Diety moved. Now please remember all of this is symbolization.

> *I'll buy that.*

You can, you can argue that this is simultaneous, you can argue it for sequence, and it just makes just as much sense to say that it's happening today as that it ever did happen or that it will happen, or better still, *it is an always happening.* You see we're using time language in eternity. Here, in reading these Papers, uh, make allowance for the *by-and-large.* Now, a statement like this might be made in the Papers: Human beings, the experience of human beings is characterized by birth and death. That's a pretty reasonable statement, isn't it? But it's not 100% true because *fusion* might take the place of death, but that's so nearly 100% true that it might be made in the Papers as virtually an absolute statement. It's near absolute. We know of 2 people who've probably fused *and* there are undoubtably more, because in, in the Papers on thought adjusters, it says, " *Most* of the adjusters who have taken their subjects to fusion were experienced on your world". Well, that suggests to me more than 2. The only two I could put my finger on, would be Enoch and Elijah.

I don't know how much to make doubt about it.

That's right, Bert was pointing out that it says in the, last night the, it says the…uh, they're talking about absonites, They're beginningless and endless, but God the Ultimate has a beginning. It doesn't say though, *all absonites* are beginningless or endless, it says the absonite level is *characterized* by this. Just as mortal life is characterized by birth and death. Had Jesus been an ordinary person, he would never have died, he'd of fused. About the time He was baptized in the Jordan, and they had to take His adjuster away from Him to stop fusion.

I'm glad you said that. I've never been able to understand why His adjuster stood away from Him.

Same reason, uh, Wilma, on a planet settled in light and life, when a human being is scheduled for fusion, you know they warn them ahead of time. He can plea for a stay of execution. He's about halfway through an important job, and they grant him this privilege but then they detach the adjuster and he works just as Jesus did.

It worked out that, in the continuation of the growth of the soul which we are not cognisant of the growth, and you get on the ladder way up there and you have completed the soul's growth to the point of fusion, but you're not conscious of it.

No that's right, but you can get a stay of execution. You see Jesus, Jesus' life has certain parallels in worlds settled in light and life. A human being might go on and function 5 years as a post-fusion human being, and then, ah… report to the Morontia Temple, all his friends would be there like a commencement excercise, the adjuster would enter the soul and Whambo!, the pyrotechnics take place and off he is. And what a nice way to go.

Bill, we had a question on extra-divine, and uh… to explain your symbol of the 2 inches and the 1600 miles.

All right. The term extra-divine would refer, I suspect, to the Unqualified Absolute, is that correct ? Let me check this usage. Page 14 paragraph 6, "The Unqualified Absolute is non-personal, extradivine and undeified." Divinity is the characteristic unifying quality of Diety. This is not Diety, hence the Unqualified Absolute discloses no aspects of divinity.

OK… extra there, does not mean greater than?

No, outside of, outside of Divinity! Yes you could, well it sounds better to say extra-divine than un-devine. Un-divine could, *has* a connotation of evil. The Unqualified Absolute is not evil but is not in any way related to Divinity, per se.

Now the function of the 3 Absolutes is related to Divinity because the *mechanizing function* of the Unqualified is unified by the Universal Absolute with the *activating function* of the Diety Absolute. So the total Absolute is not extra-divine, only *this* aspect of the Absolute. Page 4 paragraph 15, no, this is page 14...*page 15* paragraph 6...*paragraph 4*. One...two...three...paragraph 4 page 15...one...two...three...four. I can't find extra-divine in paragraph 4.

It's over here on 14.

Maybe it's in 6, let me try...no...I think that would be my *interpretation* of the word exrta-divine...a much better choice than the word *undivine*.

It's like five steps...

It's *not* antagonistic to Divinity...

No, but it's outside of...

But it's outside of...

...and obviously does not connote 'greater than.'

Yeah... see, this Absolute is not personal, has no Divinity, is not a Creator and you can't understand it. You can't use fact, truth, experience, revelation, philosophy or super-philosophy (absonity), to understand it. And that's why I... I shudder when I glibly explain it. *[Sound of Laughter]* There's a question here about...ah... 2 inches versus 1600 miles, where we're talking about...that... that must be the *firehouse*, is that right ?

Yeah, that's the first floor.

Well I'm using space to symbolize time.

Say that again, I'm [words uncertain] *good yardstick.*

I'm using, I'm using space to symbolize time and since, uh... our time calculations are, uh... are even looser than our space calculations, cause we have no,...We have to assume a constant rate, uh... it doesn't mean much, but I, what I'm saying here is this, ... in considering our firehouse...remember? we build a 3 story firehouse, we put a center pole down the middle where the firemen slide down, and the purpose of that center pole is to symbolize God who is contactable on any level of the firehouse, it's the same God, the only thing that's changed is you. We said if the first story is 2 inches high, then the second story is 1600 miles high and the third story has no roof, which is to say, if, creative expansion through 2 inches produces the Supreme Being, it takes 1600 miles to produce God the Ultimate, and you can *start* God the Absolute but *there is no roof*. You can't finish God the Absolute, it's a good illustration.

God does not create universal brotherhood, universal brotherhood *eventuates out of the fact* of God's Universal Fatherhood, you cannot have one without the other.

The word *God* has more than one meaning in these Papers, the word *God* is used with seven different meanings. We are familiar with the first three, God the Father, God the Son, and God the Spirit. We're not familiar with God the Supreme, this is the emerging diety of the finite level of existence. This is evolutionary diety. This is God in time, not God in eternity. This is God in space, not God in infinity. God the Supreme is a consequence of the acts of infinite diety. God the Sevenfold is an association of diety. Our encounter with God the Sevenfold is in the bestowal of Jesus, a very real encounter. When Jesus said, "He who has seen He has seen the Father", He spoke *as God* and *for God* and this is the truest illustration that we can apprehend concerning the function of God the Sevenfold. God the Sevenfold is God *anywhere* in time and space. God *in action*, in the *imperfect* evolutionary domains. To us, the only God that we can comprehend is in the human bestowal of Jesus, and this is God the Sevenfold in action. God reaching out from Paradise to fellowship any creature at any level of existence, even mortal creatures at the lowest level of existence. What God the Supreme is to the finite level, God the Ultimate is to the super-finite, the absonite level, that level which, (always like the *ham* in a sandwich, if the lower piece of bread is finite and the upper piece of bread is absolute and infinite, then the ham would be absonite, transcendental seperating the finite from the absolute.) God the Absolute would be the final expression of diety. God the Absolute would be the final experiential or comprehensible expression of the Father, as the Eternal Son is the existential expression of the Father.

Existential meaning, that which comes into being by the inherent acts of God. Experiential meaning, that which creatures have had a hand in, hence, could understand. If God the Absolute could ever, ever appear in fact and in completion, then through God the Absolute we might understand God the Father as infinite. This tells me that God the Absolute will never complete His growth, because we will *never* understand, the Father is infinite, we'll merely grow in that understanding.

The third section deals with the First Source and Center. I'm intrigued with the fact that there, they speak of the First, Second, and Third Sources and Centers, but there are only 2 sections in these Papers which use those captions. They discuss the First Source and Center, then I believe, over in Paper 9, they discuss the Third Source and Center. You see, God the Father and God the Spirit are quite alike, and They are both quite different from God the Son. The Father and the Spirit are personal, as is the Son, but They are also everything else besides being personal. They have many, other-than-personal characteristics. The Son is personal and *only* personal, that's why the Son can't fragment Himself as both the Father and the Spirit can. You can't fragment a personality, and the Son can find nothing in His diety to fragment, because there is nothing in His diety which is *not* personal. He is the full, personal expression of God. The Father and the Spirit are equally personal, but They are also much that is, other-than-personal, hence, They can fragment Themselves, and so you have Father-fragments and you have Spirit-fragments. Some fragments, you will recall, come from the Creator Sons, not from the Eternal Son. Son fused mortals derive their spirit endowment not from the Eternal Son but from the Creator Son of their local universe.

In this third section we are, for the first time, introduced to the 7 absolutes of infinity. And we're… we're told about the relationship which the First Source and Center has to the 7 absolutes. And I think the easiest way to think about these 7 absolutes is to think of them in terms of matter, mind, and spirit. The Second Source and Center is the source of spirit, the Third Source and Center is the source of mind, not that there's not also spiritual ministry there. The Paradise Source and Center, the Eternal Isle, is the source of all things material, and the controller of all things material. And then the easiest way to think of these 3 absolutes is, as the reservoirs out of which, the matter, the mind, and the spirit of the evolving present and the unexpressed future is coming. From the Unqualified Absolute come the evolving universes, From the Diety Absolute come the spirit beings which are being created and will be created, from the Universal Absolute, perchance, They draw upon from mind. I'm not so sure about the last one but I'm pretty sure about the first 2. But I think it's a good convenient way of looking at this. Example; When a local universe Mother-Spirit creates seraphim, they appear in what is it, unit formation? 100 and some odd thousand of them ? It's a large number of seraphim! They don't come from nothing, they come from something. When a cloud appears in the sky, that cloud does not come from nothing, that cloud was there in the form of invisible water vapor before a change in temperature made it visible. These seraphim that are created were potential in the universe, before the Creative Spirit, by Her creative action, transformed them from a potential to an actual. The unborn of the next generation are potential in the germ plasm of the present generation of human beings, and if they *weren't* potential, they jolly well couldn't ever become actual, could they? This section makes an unqualified statement: "There are 7 Absolutes of Infinity, but the First Source and Center is *primal* in relation to total reality." This is not polytheism we're studying, this is monotheism. There is only one Infinite Being, others share His infinity and His absoluteness, but *none* takes precedence over the First Source and Center. God, the Universal Father, is the personality of the First Source and Center. Then they discuss how God is related to the universe, and we see that God is not directly related to the universe except in *one* aspect. God is related to creation, to the universes, through, His 6 associated Absolutes, *except* in one particular, He is the direct Father of *every* personality in existence. All personalities derive *that* quality of being *from* the Universal Father, and they are linked to the Father by the personality circuit. The other 6 Absolutes do not *participate* with the Father in this bestowal of personality, with one minor exception, the Infinite Spirit (the Third Source and Center) has the Father's proxy (He's the Father's attorney-in-fact) and He can act for the Father, but again this is the delegation of creative power. This section goes on to talk about reality, and they point out that the maximum reality which we can understand is a finite God, and let's face it, we want God to have a beginning, don't we? A beginning-less God is really beyond our comprehension. The only reason we accept an un-beginning God is because it's ridiculous to have a beginning, because if He has a beginning, who's His father? Who's His grandfather? Who's His great-grandfather? We have the choice between an uncaused cause or an endless series. Do you see that? And the endless series of course is ridiculous. The Greeks tried it, back at Zeus, they had Cronus and back of him they had someone else, but eventually you give up and you simply start with the Uncaused Cause. This section goes on to point out that we need, conceptually we need, a beginning, and though there never was a beginning, they're gonna give us one, in concept, but they warn us this is *not* reality. To God, to diety, *prior* to any self distribution, they give the name, the I AM , and they say, "This is a philosophic concept, this is *not* a reality". And the most helpful thing I can suggest to you, to deal with that, is this; we use the number 0 in all our mathematics but you have never seen *nothing*, have you? You can see one of something, or one and a half or two, but you've never seen a zero of anything, have you? And yet we think in terms and it's a, it's a most convenient concept in mathematics. Zero is a valid concept but zero is not a factual reality, only a concept of reality. Are you with me? The term, I AM, is just a valuable a *thinking tool* as the term zero but neither are factual. Nevertheless, they qualify, they say, "Now look, the I AM may be a theoretical concept in the philosophic concession, but the Infinite is not, the Universal Father *is* the Infinite." I think of the term First Source and Center as this; when you get down to the level of the Seven Absolutes and you want to isolate out the Infinite, it *is* the First Source and Center. This is the Infinite as manifest on the level of the Seven Absolutes. Just as when you want to say, "What is the personality of the First Source and Center ?" the answer is God. What name do we give to that personality?…The Universal Father. That is the name of our choosing. How could He have a name? He's nameless. In shorthand here, they tell you how the I AM distributed Himself. They simply tell you, and this again, these are valid concepts but these are not factual realities. They simply say that... I'm gonna use the word *God* to describe (pre-God) because it's a simpler way of telling the story, they simply say that God seperated Himself from total reality and if He hadn't done that there would have been no room in which anything could take place because how would you squeeze something in where God filled all things? God, as it were, contracted Himself and He can do this because He has will. What He contracted Himself into is the essence of diety, at the heart of which is will, and what He left behind is the essence of non-diety, non-will. One of the greatest criticisms I ever read of the Book of Genesis was written by a Zoroastrian theologian, uh...about 250 A.D., it's in the (Palavi) Texts, and this Zoroastrian, in criticizing Genesis says, "God was not alone, because when God commanded "Let there be light!", in order for that command to have effect, there must also have been present an *Obeyer of Commands*" and I borrow that term from the old Zoroastrian theologian. The Unqualified Absolute is the obeyer of commands, when diety takes snuff, the Unqualified Absolute sneezes. Now, when God separates Himself from that which is not diety, He is still Himself to that which is not diety. This linkage is the function of the Universal Absolute, the conjoiner of the non-diety Absolute from the Diety Absolute, and I think 3 links, linked together, is an excellent symbol for that relationship. God still fills all diety, and I think of God as contracting within diety while at the same time He expands to continue to fill all diety. I think of God as *separating* Himself from the Son, of *conjoining* Himself *with* the Son, of *constituting* the Trinity, as a thing that happened simultaneously, so that instead of one of these circles, you know the 3 circles, just being full of God, this circle is now a tri-concentric circle, it is full of the Trinity, and in so doing, God achieves companionship. He seperates Himself from absolute personality, and in so doing He becomes the Father of the Absolute Person, who thereby becomes His Son, and if He can become Father of the Absolute Person. He can become Father of any person. He ceases to be the Absolute Person but becomes the Universal Father of the Absolute Person and of all other persons. At the same time that He does this, when He expresses Himself absolutely as a person, He expresses Himself absolutely as a non-person, and this is the origin of the Isle of Paradise, or to anthropomorphize it, Paradise is the *absolute machine* which God built for the same reason that men build machines, to perform repetitive acts. The physical governing of the physical universes is a repetitive act, and God devised a flawless machine to do this job for Him. Why should He personally attend to it when a machine, an absolute machine, can do the job? They tell us that reality, in section 4 is... they're trying to point out that all is not spirit. These Papers make some startling statements, they say for example, "God is spirit but Paradise is not." They point out that our direction God-ward is spirit-ward, so that as we consider matter, mind, and spirit, the spiritual is the more real to us because our growth towards reality follows a spiritual route. This is truth, this is not however, fact. Energy, physical energy is just as real as spiritual energy, but it doesn't have as much meaning or as much value to human beings. They point out here that reality can be deified or not deified. This planet is hardly deified reality, is it? But finaliters have partaken of divinity and are a part of deified reality, creature-parts of deified reality. They go on to point out that things may be either actual or potential. We are actual people, children yet un-born are potential people, are they not? And of course you can have something in between. A good illustration of something which is neither actual nor potential, the brotherhood of man. Is it real? Well, read any newspaper and you can determine that it's not really here, is it? It is a *becoming* reality, isn't it? It's in the gray area, the zone of becoming. Are human beings real? Yes and no. Until they've fused with their thought adjusters, they're not truly real in the universe, are they? We're simply *becoming* citizens of the universe. Is a child an adult? Well, no, and yet he's not, not an adult, he's a becoming adult, or have you coped with teenagers? This section closes with a discussion of not-spirit reality. It discusses the Isle of Paradise, where they point out that Paradise is an absolute reality derived from diety, but it is not diety. And I think, I think the, the best way of looking at Paradise is, it is the *Absolute Machine* which God built. And we can understand that, because we build machines to do jobs. Somewhere in here, it's not this particular context, it says. "Paradise is not conscious as man could ever understand the meaning of such a term." Paradise, is some way, is a *knowing* reality. Paradise is not mind-less, but it does not have mind as we could *ever* understand the meaning of that word. You think of Paradise, you should think of Paradise in two ways. Paradise is a place, the dwelling place of God, at the center of all things. It is our, it is our final destination in our quest for God. On Paradise we will find God, and figura-tively speaking, we shall stand before Him, face-to-face. Paradise also has a *function* in the universes. As the Son draws all things spiritual, as the Third Person draws all things intellectual, so Paradise draws all things material. Paradise is the central governing power of the Material Universe of Universes. Section 5 talks about personality realities and it points out that personality comes from God and that all, all reality that is linked with personality is associable. Pre-personal fragments, super-personal beings, are all contactable and associable with personality and personal beings. This is a part of diety reality, in contrast to the *not-personal* which can never be associated with a person. Man has no fellowship with a rock but man can have fellowship with an adjuster, a seraphim, or a transcendentler, given enough time to have contact with transcendentlers, and they would be super-personal beings. They sum up, at the end of this section, the functioning entity of a human being; body, mind, spirit, and soul. The body, our life mechanism. The mind, which we think with and confuse ourselves with. The spirit, which invades the mind, just as sperm invades the womb, and the soul is the embryo that comes into origin as a result of that cosmic conception. The human mind is the material womb of the soul. The spirit that comes from the Father is the invader, and when that invasion takes place, in about the 5th year of mortal life, something *new* begins to grow, and this is the embryonic soul that evolves within the womb of the mind, and this is the soul which has the capacity to survive death. And they point out that personality is none of these things, that personality is not matter, not mind, not spirit. Personality is a fourth reality in the cosmos. Personality is that which comes from God the Father, not the Son, not the Spirit, unless the Spirit acts for the Father. Then they define Morontia, because the soul is Morontia, the soul is neither matter nor spirit. And the best definition I know of Morontia is; it is a fabric, the (warp) of which is physical, the (woof) of which is spiritual.

Uh, uh, you said it wrong there...

Well it doesn't make any difference... because the soul is Morontia, one goes one way, and one, the other.

I was looking at it, I wouldn't be that smart, I was looking in at it.

Or you might say that matter and spirit will not mix. They don't ordinarily, any more than oil and water will mix, but in the presence of *soap*, oil and water will emulsify. Morontia is an emulsification of the oil of matter and the water of spirit.

Section 6 deals, in a sense, as a continuation of their discussion of Paradise. As they have talked about personality realities in section 5, they talk about non-personal realities in section 6. They try to define some terms that they're going to use in talking about this would require an exhaustion of infinity and the completion of eternity. Now in terms of time calculation and agility of... abba, you brought the baby,... and I'll give it to you in time...

END OF TAPE

ANALYTIC STUDY OF
PART I OF *THE URANTIA BOOK*

A Note on Usage of this Section

The paragraph numbering system used in this text differs slightly from the method currently used by Urantia Foundation in its contemporary publications. This is because it was written before the notation of citations from *The Urantia Book* became standardized. Rather than change this scheme, we have left it as is to reflect this volume's historical status. Also, since this volume is a paragraph-by-paragraph examination of Part I, paragraphs were often grouped by concept rather than by format as is the current standard. To reference paragraphs from this volume, please note these variations between Urantia Foundation's citation scheme and that employed by Dr. Sadler in these early workbooks:

1.   While Urantia Foundation refers to an incomplete paragraph at the top of a page as paragraph 0, Dr. Sadler counted those as paragraph one.

2.   Each item in a numbered list that follows a colon or elaborates on a previous paragraph is, in the current scheme, counted as a separate paragraph. However, Dr. Sadler counted these together as one paragraph.

See page 135 of *The Urantia Book* for an example of these differences. The opening paragraph, rather than being paragraph zero, is paragraph one. The workbook discussion of the text of this paragraph is included with that of the last paragraph of the previous page. The numbered paragraphs at mid-page, for the purposes of more coherent study, are included with the line that precedes them and are counted as one paragraph.

Concerning quotations from other religous texts (The Bible, The Vedas etc.), quotations themselves are *italicized* and the source references are in **bold** typeface. A listing of the abbreviations used for the books of The Bible follows on the next page.

A final note – the sections in each paper titled **"INTRODUCTION"** refer to that portion of text in each paper that comes before the first section title. In the individual table of contents on the page preceding the study of each paper in this workbook, we have numbered the introduction section as item zero.

We hope this information will help you in your study of this material and that the work itself will deepen your understanding of the teachings of *The Urantia Book*.

.

BIBLICAL ABBREVIATIONS USED IN THIS SECTION

The Old Testament

Gen .... The Book of Genesis

Ex .... The Book of Exodus

Lev .... The Book of Leviticus

Num ...... The Book of Numbers

Deut ...... The Book of Deuteronomy

Josh .... The Book of Joshua

Judges .... The Book of Judges

Ruth ...... The Book of Ruth

1 Sam ..... The First Book of Samuel

2 Sam ..... The Second Book of Samuel

1 Kings ... The First Book of Kings

2 Kings ... The Second Book of Kings

1 Chron .. The First Book of Chronicles

2 Chron .. The Second Book of Chronicles

Ezra .... The Book of Ezra

Neh .... The Book of Nehemiah

Esther .... The Book of Esther

Job .... The Book of Job

Ps .... The Book of Psalms

Prov ...... The Book of Proverbs

Eccl .... Ecclesiastes

Song ...... The Song of Songs

Isa .... The Book of Isaiah

Jer .... The Book of Jeremiah

Lam .... Lamentations

Eze .... The Book of Ezekiel

Dan .... The Book of Daniel

Hos .... The Book of Hosea

Joel .... The Book of Joel

Amos ..... The Book of Amos

Obad ..... The Book of Obadiah

Jon .... The Book of Jonah

Nah .... The Book of Nahum

Hab .... The Book of Habakkuk

Zeph ...... The Book of Zephaniah

Hag .... The Book of Haggai

Zec .... The Book of Zechariah

Mal .... The Book of Malachi

The New Testament

Matt ...... The Gospel According to Matthew

Mark ...... The Gospel According to Mark

Luke ...... The Gospel According to Luke

John ...... The Gospel According to John

Acts .... The Acts of the Apostles

Rom ...... The Epistle to the Romans

1 Cor ..... The First Epistle to the Corinthians

2 Cor ..... The Second Epistle to the Corinthians

Gal .... The Epistle to the Galatians

Eph .... The Epistle to the Ephesians

Phil .... The Epistle to the Philippians

Col .... The Epistle to the Colossians

1 Thess ... The First Epistle to the Thessalonians

2 Thess ... The Second Epistle to the Thessalonians

1 Tim ..... The First Epistle to Timothy

2 Tim ..... The Second Epistle to Timothy

Tit .... The Epistle to Titus

Phmon ... The Epistle to Philemon

Heb .... The Epistle to the Hebrews

Jas .... The Epistle of James

1 Peter ... The First Epistle of Peter

2 Peter ... The Second Epistle of Peter

1 John .... The First Epistle of John

2 John .... The Second Epistle of John

3 John .... The Third Epistle of John

Jude ...... Jude

Rev .... Revelation

PAPER 1
The Universal Father

PAPER 1
The Universal Father

1. **THE FATHER'S NAME**
2. **THE REALITY OF GOD**
3. **GOD IS A UNIVERSAL SPIRIT**
4. **THE MYSTERY OF GOD**
5. **PERSONALITY OF THE UNIVERSAL FATHER**
6. **PERSONALITY IN THE UNIVERSE**
7. **SPIRITUAL VALUE OF THE PERSONALITY CONCEPT**

INTRODUCTION

I. *REFERENCE*: Page 21, ¶1 – "The Universal Father is..."

COMMENT

1. *The Urantia Book* starts out with a positive assumption—"The Universal Father is the God of all creation." No arguments are presented to prove the reality of God. Jesus pursued this same method—he seemed to take it for granted that people believed in God.

2. The threefold function of Gods:

   A. Creator.
   B. Controller.
   C. Upholder.

3. The next step is a direct appeal to the authority of a sacred book—the Old Testament. Here appears a composite quotation apparently derived from five Old Testament passages.

   A. **2 Kings 19:15.** *"Thou art the God, thou alone."*
   B. **Deut. 4:35.** *"The Lord is God, there is no other besides him."*
   C. **Neh. 9:6.** *"Thou hast made heaven, the heaven of heavens...and thou preservest all of them."*
   D. **Ps. 33:6.** *"By the word of the Lord the heavens were made."*

4.   **Note:** The authors of *The Urantia Book* seem to have their own versions of the world's sacred books. Scriptural quotations in *The Urantia Book* many times differ from all of our versions of the Bible. This fact is enough to invalidate the doctrine of the verbal inspiration of the Bible.

5.   Note the highly condensed and telescopic character of *The Urantia Book*—five texts in one.

6.   In the opening paragraph of this Urantia revelation appears this recognition of the teachings of a sacred book. This is a clear declaration that this is not a *new religion*. These Old Testament writers are called prophets—the highest designation of a religious teacher.

7.   *The Urantia Book* presents a modernization of language—abandonment of the solemn style.

II. *REFERENCE*: Page 21, ¶2 - "The myriads of planetary systems..."

COMMENT

1.   Urantia is not the only inhabited world in the universe, and there are multiple types of intelligent creatures who can love God and be loved by God.

2.   The introduction of "universe of universes" refers to the superuniverse.

3.   The quotation is from **Isa. 45:18**. *"For thus says the Lord, who created the heavens...who formed the earth and made it...he did not create it a chaos, he formed it to be inhabited."*

III. *REFERENCE*: Page 21, ¶3 - "The enlightened worlds..."

COMMENT

1.   Enlightened worlds—worlds free from rebellion—all worship God.

2.   In the third paragraph of *The Urantia Book* is introduced the vast plan and purpose of the Paradise Deities—the perfection plan of mortal ascension to Paradise.

3.   The highest mortal ambition is to know God, find him, and become more and more like him.

4.   The quotation is found in **Matt. 5:48**. *"You, therefore, must be perfect, as your heavenly Father is perfect."*
     Compare this text with **Luke 6:36**. *"Be merciful, even as your Father is merciful."* And with **1 Peter 1:16**. *"You shall be holy, for I am holy."*
     (See also Lev. 11:44.)

5. Note the introduction of the following ideas:
   A. Man's free will.
   B. Cosmic evolution.
   C. Fascination of the eternal struggle.
   D. A transcendent goal.
   E. Man's organic evolutionary nature.

6. We comprehend the divine nature and *recognize* the Father. We do not fully comprehend the Father.

7. God's mandate is supreme. Man's ambition is supreme. These things take place on the finite—experiential—level, not on the infinite.

8. To find God implies search, effort, adventure, and *time*.

IV. *REFERENCE*: Page 22, ¶1 - "This magnificent and universal injunction..."

COMMENT

1. Divinity is a quality of many levels. Even man can attain such perfection on the supreme level. Such a goal should be:

   A. Our first duty.
   B. Our highest ambition.

2. This perfection of divinity is man's final and certain destiny. This perfection pertains to finite levels of supremacy.

V. *REFERENCE*: Page 22, ¶2 - "Urantia mortals..."

COMMENT

1. Mortal perfection in the Corps of the Finality consists in:
   A. Perfection of self-realization, integration, and unification of personality.
   B. Mind attainment—intellectual maturity on finite levels.
   C. Divinity of will—eternal choices have been made.
   D. Motivation is settled and secure.
   E. God-consciousness is complete, even if knowledge of God is not.

2. This perfection does not embrace:
   A. Universal knowledge of the cosmos—things material.
   B. Unlimited development of mind—absonite intellectual grasp.
   C. Finality of spiritual experience.

    D.   Completed association with one's fused Adjuster.

    E.   The attainment of God the Ultimate.

V. REFERENCE: Page 22, ¶3 - "This is the true meaning..."

COMMENT

The true meaning of the perfection achievement:

1.   It is the supreme mortal urge.

2.   It beckons man "onward and inward"—true conception of the cosmos.

3.   It is a long and fascinating struggle.   ·

4.   The goal: Higher and higher levels of—

    A.   Spiritual values.

    B.   True universe meanings.

1. THE FATHER'S NAME

I. *REFERENCE*: Page 22, ¶4 - "Of all the names..."

COMMENT

1.   First Source and Universe Center—adequately descriptive of Creator, Controller, and Upholder.

2.   First Father—then our Father.

3.   Here at the outset is portrayed Jesus' gospel—the fatherhood of God and the brotherhood of men.

4.   How we regard God depends on personal relationship.

II. *REFERENCE*: Page 22, ¶5 - "The Universal Father..."

COMMENT

1.   The Father never imposes: A. Arbitrary recognition. B. Formal worship. C. Slavish service.

2.   We should, in our own hearts, recognize, love, and worship him.

    (**Note**: All this inhibits state religions and all authoritarian churches.)

3.   God refuses to coerce or compel spiritual free will.

    A.   Human will is sovereign only on the spiritual level.

    B.   Question—Is nonspiritual will free?

    C.   Discussion of determinism. (Interrelations of heredity, environment, and education.)

4.   "Dedication" is our only true gift.

5.   *"In God, man lives, moves, and has his being."* This is from Paul's sermon on Mars' hill, at Athens. **Acts 17:22-34.** This is the first New Testament citation to appear in *The Urantia Book.*

6.   Reality of true worship consists in this dedication of human will to the doing of the Father's will.

7.   Note definition of God—love-dominated—utterly controlled by LOVE.

8.   God is a person—he experiences "satisfactions." He hungers for love and is satisfied by worship.

9.   The will acts—choosing, deciding.

10.   Worship may embrace many qualities, but its *reality* is a dedicated will.

III. *REFERENCE:* Page 22, ¶6 - "When you have once become..."

COMMENT

1.   In order to find a proper name for God, you must:

    A.   Become God-conscious.

    B.   Discover the majestic Creator.

    C.   Realize the indwelling divine presence.

    D.   So yield that the Adjuster becomes a controller.

    E.   Experience the enlightenment of revelation—personal and epochal.

    F.   Benefit by bestowal of the Paradise Sons.

2.   In worship—the important thing is not the words employed, but the genuine personal relationship.

IV. *REFERENCE:* Page 23, ¶2 - "Near the center..."

COMMENT

1.   Remoteness from Paradise influences the name whereby universe personalities designate God.

2.   It is proper to employ many and varied names to express differing concepts of Deity.

V. *REFERENCE*: Page 23, 13 – "On those worlds where…"

COMMENT

1. On bestowal worlds God's name should portray personal relationships, tender affection, and fatherly devotion.

2. The far-flung meaning of Father: Earthly Father, System Sovereign, Most Highs, Creator Sons, Ancients of Days, Supreme Being, Paradise Father.

3. As we personally know God and love him, it becomes "our Father."

VI. *REFERENCE*: Page 23, ¶4 – "On a planet of sex creatures…"

COMMENT

1. On a sex planet "Father" is an expressive and appropriate word for God.

2. "Father value" is determined by the character of parenthood on the planet.

3. The important thing is not God's name, but: Do you know him? Do you aspire to be like him?

4. The prophets called him the "everlasting God—who inhabits eternity."

   Gen. 21:33. *"Abraham…called there on the name of the Lord, the Everlasting God."*

   Isa. 57:15. *"Thus says the high and lofty One who inhabits eternity, whose name is Holy."*

DISCUSSION OF GOD'S NAME

1. Yahweh was in use before the times of Moses.

2. There was an evolutionary growth in the concept of Deity from Abraham's days to the later prophets—like Isaiah. There is a great difference between God as depicted in the book of Judges and the God portrayed in the gospel of John.

3. Jesus talks about different concepts of God—see p. 1598 in *The Urantia Book*.

   A. **Yahweh** - God of the Sinai clans.
   B. **El Elyon** (the Most High) - God of Abraham and Melchizedek.
   C. **El Shaddai** - Egyptian Deity.
   D. **Elohim** - God of the Paradise Trinity. The Creator in Genesis.
   E. **The Supreme Yahweh** - God of latter-day Israel.
   F. **The Father in heaven** - God of Jesus' gospel.

4. God's name as revealed in the incarnation of Michael. **See p. 1965.**

"I am the bread of life.
"I am the living water.
"I am the light of the world.
"I am the desire of all ages.
"I am the open door to eternal salvation.
"I am the reality of endless life.
"I am the good shepherd.
"I am the pathway to infinite perfection.
"I am the resurrection and the life.
"I am the secret of eternal survival.
"I am the way, the truth, and the life.
"I am the infinite Father of my finite children.
"I am the true vine; you are the branches.
"I am the hope of all who know the living truth.
"I am the living bridge from one world to another.
"I am the living link between time and eternity."

2. THE REALITY OF GOD

I. *REFERENCE*: Page 23, ¶5 - "God is primal reality..."

COMMENT

1. As a reality God is primal in the spirit world, truth in mind spheres, and overshadows all in the material world. He is personality to created intellegences, and to the universe is the First Source and Center.

2. But God is neither manlike nor machinelike.

3. The First Father is:

    A. Universal spirit.
    B. Eternal truth.
    C. Infinite reality.
    D. Absolute personality.

II. *REFERENCE*: Page 23, ¶6 - "The eternal God is..."

COMMENT

1. The eternal God is more than: reality idealized, the universe personalized, supreme desire of man, mortal quest objectified, mere concept, power-potential of righteousness, synonym for nature, natural law personified, man's concept of supreme values, psychological focalization of spiritual meanings, the noblest work of man.

2. God may be any or all of these concepts in the minds of men, but he is more—he is: A. A transcendent reality, B. A saving person, C. A loving Father to all who enjoy spiritual peace and crave survival.

- 47 -

III. *REFERENCE*: Page 24, ¶2 – "The actuality of the existance..."

COMMENT

Actuality of God is demonstrated in human experience by the indwelling Adjuster as disclosed by three experiential phenomena:

1. Intellectual capacity for knowing God—God-consciousness.
2. The spiritual urge to find God—God-seeking.
3. The personality craving to be like God.

Note: The presence of the Adjuster is disclosed by *experience*—not by theology.

IV. *REFERENCE*: Page 24, ¶3 – "The existence of God..."

COMMENT

1. Knowing God is wholly a matter of personal religious experience.
2. The concept of a personal God is wholly compatible with:
   A. Logic—science.
   B. Philosophy.
   C. Theology.

V. *REFERENCE*: Page 24, ¶4 – "Those who know God..."

COMMENT

1. We know God because we have experienced the fact of his presence.
2. The existence of God is demonstrated only in the human experience of God-consciousness.
3. The Adjuster doing all this is God's free gift to man.

VI. *REFERENCE*: Page 24, ¶5 – "In theory you may think..."

COMMENT

1. In theory you may think of God as a Creator:
   A. He is the personal creator of Paradise and the perfect central creation.
   B. The universes of time and space are created by his Creator Sons.
2. The Universal Father is not the creator of our universe—Nebadon. His Son Michael created it.

Note: First mention of Michael.

MICHAEL

A. Mentioned ten times in Old Testament as a name of some person, group, or family.

B. Mentioned five times in the Bible as a superhuman being.

    (1) **Dan. 10:13.** *"The prince of the kingdom of Persia withstood me twenty-one days; but Michael, one of the chief princes, came to help me."* **(Marginal reading Authorized Version— "the first chief prince.")**

    (2) **Dan. 10:21.** *"But I will tell you what is inscribed in the book of truth: there is none who contends by my side against these except Michael, your prince."*

    (3) **Dan. 12:1.** *"At that time shall arise Michael, the great prince who has charge of your people…At that time your people shall be delivered, every one whose name shall be found written in the book."*

        Then follows a description of a *special* resurrection: *"And many of those who sleep in the dust of the earth shall awake."* **(Dan. 12:2)**

    (4) **Jude v.9.** *"But when the archangel Michael, contending with the devil, disputed about the body of Moses, he did not presume to pronounce a reviling judgment upon him, but said, 'The Lord rebuke you.'"*

    (5) **Rev. 12:7:** *"Now war arose in heaven, Michael and his angels fighting against the dragon; and the dragon and his angels fought."*

C. The name Michael signifies: "Who is like God."

    In the rabbinic writings Michael is frequently mentioned in connection with the history of Moses. The devil claimed the body of Moses because of the murder of the Egyptian. **(See Ex. 2:11-13.)**

3. Although the Father does not personally create the evolutionary worlds, he does:

A. Control many of their universal relationships.

B. Have a hand in certain of their energy, mind, and spirit manifestations.

4. God created the Paradise universe and, with the Eternal Son, created all other universe Creators. This is the introduction of the dual origin of the Creator Sons.

VII. *REFERENCE*: Page 24, ¶6 - "As a physical controller..."

COMMENT

1. As a physical controller, God functions through the "patterns" of Paradise and by means of the "absolute gravity" of Paradise.

2. Otherwise God functions:

    A. *As mind*—in the Deity of the Infinite Spirit.
    B. *As spirit*—in the person of the Eternal Son.

3. None of the interrelations of the Father with his co-ordinates precludes his *direct* action on all levels of creation.

4. By means of his fragmentized spirit the Father maintains intimate contact with his creature children.

3. GOD IS A UNIVERSAL SPIRIT

I. *REFERENCE*: Page 25, ¶1 - "'God is spirit.'"

COMMENT

1. **John 4:24**. *"God is spirit, and those who worship him must worship in spirit and truth."*

    This was spoken to Nalda, the Samaritan women at Jacob's well near Sychar. **(p. 1614)**

2. God is:

    A. Universal spiritual presence.
    B. Infinite spiritual reality.
    C. Sovereign—eternal God and immortal.
    See 1 Tim. 1:17. *"To the king of ages, immortal, invisible, the only God, be honor and glory forever and ever."*

3. While we are the offspring of God, there is great danger of misunderstanding what is meant by being created in the "image of God."

    A. Paul preaching on Mars' hill—after saying "in him we live and move and have our being"—added:

    "As even some of your poets have said, 'For we are indeed his offspring.' Being then God's offspring, we ought not to think that the Deity is like gold, or silver, or stone, a representation by the art and imagination of man." **Acts 17:28,29**.

    (This is the first quotation from non-Biblical sources.)

B. Created in his image.

Gen. 1:26. *"Then God said, 'Let us make man in our image, after our likeness.'"* **Question:** Whom was God talking to? The Old Testament starts out with a proclamation of the Trinity.

Gen. 9:6. *"Whoever sheds the blood of man, by man shall his blood be shed; for God made man in his own image."*

Col. 3:10. *"And have put on its new nature, which is being renewed in knowledge after the image of the creator."*

C. **Mystery Monitors.** First introduction of this term. They are also called: Thought Adjuster. Thought Controller. Thought Changer. Divine Presence. Pilot Light. Better Self. Fragment of God. Prisoner of Hope. Delegated Spirit of human indwelling.

D. Personality—gift of the Father—is also a part of the "image of God."

4. Spirit beings are real, even though they have not flesh and blood.

II. *REFERENCE:* Page 25, ¶2 - "Said the seer of old..."

COMMENT

1. **Job 9:11.** *"Lo, he passes by me, and I see him not; he moves on, but I do not perceive him."*

Note: The book of Job is Babylonian, one of the oldest parts of the Old Testament. **See Jesus' marvelous discussion of Job in Paper 148, P. 1662.**

2. We may observe the works of God, but we may not visualize the divine presence. The Thought Adjusters are invisible.

III. *REFERENCE:* Page 25, ¶3 - "The Universal Father..."

COMMENT

1. The Father is not invisible because he is hiding, but because our materialistic handicaps and limited spiritual endowments prevent our seeing him. **See Ex. 33:20.** *"'You cannot see my face; for man shall not see me and live.'"*

2. Man cannot approach the spiritual luminosity of the Father's presence. **See 1 Tim. 6:16.** He *"alone has immortality and dwells in unapproachable light, whom no man has ever seen or can see."*

3. But it is not necessary to see God with the eyes of the flesh in order to discern him by the faith-vision of the spiritualized mind.

IV. *REFERENCE*: Page 25, ¶4 - "The spirit nature..."

COMMENT

1. The Father and the Son are equal in spirit nature.

2. The Father and the Son share their spirit nature with the Conjoint Actor.

   Note: First mention of Conjoint Actor.

3. God's spirit is:

   A. In and of himself—absolute.
   B. In the Son—unqualified.
   C. In the Spirit—universal.
   D. In and by all of them—infinite.

V. *REFERENCE*: Page 25, ¶5 - "God is a universal spirit..."

COMMENT

1. God is a universal spirit-person.

2. *Absonite* intervenes between finite and infinite just as morontia functions between the material and the spiritual.

3. Only the levels of infinity are absolute; only on absolute levels is there finality of oneness between matter, mind, and spirit.

VI. *REFERENCE*: Page 25, ¶6 - "In the universes..."

COMMENT

1. God the Father is, in potential, the overcontroller of energy, mind, and spirit.

2. Outside of Paradise, God is contactable only by means of his fragmented entities—"the will of God abroad in the universes."

3. **Note**: Plural fragmented entities. They are the will of God. In man, will is inseparable from personality.

4. WILL here means way, plans, method, purpose—not decision and choice. Illustration:

   A. It is my will to teach this class—DECISION.
   B. It is also my will that you be diligent students—my wish, hope, PLAN.

5. Only by means of these Father fragments does God deal directly with the personalities of evolutionary mortals.

   Note: If God's presence were personal it would transcend and therefore negate the creature personality. God respects and holds inviolate every personality in his circuit.

6. The indwelling spirit *fosters* the evolution of the surviving soul. The immortal soul has both material and spirit parents.

7. The material minds of evolutionary creatures attain divinity by choosing to do the will of the Father in heaven.

   A. Perfection is achieved by experience—"experiential transformations."

   B. Transformations produce inevitable spiritual attainment—as a *result* of our choosing to do the will of God.

VII. *REFERENCE*: Page 26, ¶1 - "In the inner experience..."

COMMENT

1. The human mind can only survive as a result of those transformations of being spirit taught—and eventually spirit led.

2. The evolution of human mind from material to spirit levels is attended by the creation of the immortal soul—a morontia reality.

   Note: First mention of **morontia**.

3. If mind becomes subservient to matter—it must suffer extinction.
   Question: In event of extinction, what becomes of mind and personality? Survival in the Supreme—but not as a separate personality.

4. Spirit-dominated mind becomes identified with the divine spirit and attains eternity of existence.

DISCUSSION OF MORONTIA

1. For full consideration of morontia, see Paper 48, "The Morontia Life," p. 541.

2. "*Morontia* is a term designating a vast level intervening between the material and the spiritual. It may designate personal or impersonal realities, living or nonliving energies. The warp of morontia is spiritual; its woof is physical." p. 9.

3. The mortal part of man which survives is called the "morontia soul."

4. Surviving mortals are resurrected as first-stage morontians.

5. From first-stage morontia to first-stage spirit you successively have 570 changes in morontia bodies.

6. The morontia career continues throughout our ascension of the local universe.

7. Morontians enjoy the ministry of both the reversion directors and the celestial artisans."

8. Mota is the advanced philosophy of the morontia life.

VIII. REFERENCE: Page 26, ¶2 - "I come forth..."

COMMENT

1. The author of this paper is a Divine Counselor—a Trinity-origin being. He asserts that he personally knows the Universal Father and testifies to the spirit nature and loving attributes of the Paradise Father.

2. God's attributes are best revealed in the Eternal Son—and the Paradise "grandsons."

3. These quotations are from:
   A. **1 John 4:8.** *"For God is love."*
   B. **John 4:24.** *"God is spirit."*(**See also 2 Cor. 3:17.** *"Now the Lord is the Spirit, and where the Spirit of the Lord is, there is freedom."*)
   (Discuss pantheism. God is personal as well as spirit. A personal spirit—a spirit personality.)

4. THE MYSTERY OF GOD

I. REFERENCE: Page 26, ¶3 - "The infinity of the perfection..."

COMMENT

1. The infinity of God's perfection makes him an eternal mystery.

2. The phenomenon of the indwelling Adjuster is:
   A. The greatest of all mysteries.
   B. A universal mystery.
   C. The mystery of mysteries.

II. REFERENCE: Page 26, ¶4 - "The physical bodies..."

COMMENT

1. The physical bodies of mortals are the temples of God. This is **1 Cor. 3:16.** *"Do you not know that you are God's temple and that God's Spirit dwells in you?"*(**See also 1 Cor. 6:19.**)

   Again: 2 Cor. 6:16. *"For we are the temple of the living God."*

Paul is quoting from the Old Testament—**Ex. 29:45**. *"And I will dwell among the people of Israel, and will be their God."*

Lev. 26:11. *"And I will make my abode among you."*

2. Observations on these quotations:

   A. Paul alters the text so as to impart new meanings. He changes "dwell among you" to read "dwell in you."

   B. This constitutes *re-interpretation*. In this way doctrine is modified by editorializing translation.

   C. *The Urantia Book* does this same thing. Paul supplies New Testament precedent for such a practice.

   Note: John Calvin objected to this Biblical editorializing.

3. Even though the Creator Sons come close to us—"draw all men to themselves"—God is nearer us in the presence of the Adjusters.

4. This statement of Jesus is found in **John 12:32**. *"And I, when I am lifted up from the earth, will draw all men to myself."* In the next verse John says: *"He said this to show by what death he was to die."* The Urantia Book would differ with John.

5. "Stand at the door and knock." This is **Rev. 3:20**. *"Behold, I stand at the door and knock; if any one hears my voice and opens the door, I will come in to him and eat with him, and he with me."*

III. *REFERENCE*: Page 26, ¶5 - "When you are through..."

COMMENT

1. When we finish our "shakedown" trip on Urantia—our body returns to the dust and the Adjuster returns to God.

   This is an Old Testament quotation. **Eccl. 12:7**. *"And the dust returns to the earth as it was, and the spirit returns to God who gave it."*

2. This is a direct identification of the Thought Adjuster with the spirit nature of man.

3. The Adjusters are on loan for the time being—but it is intended that they become "one with us."

IV. *REFERENCE*: Page 26, ¶6 - "We are constantly confronted..."

COMMENT

1. We are ever confronted with this mystery of God.

2. We are nonplused by the endless unfolding of this truth of: infinite goodness, endless mercy, matchless wisdom, superb character.

V. *REFERENCE*: Page 26, ¶7 - "The divine mystery..."

COMMENT

1. Note the differences between the levels of the finite and the infinite.

2. Mortal capacity of spiritual receptivity is indicated by one's ability to grasp the qualities of truth, beauty, and goodness.

3. Truth, beauty, and goodness is not a Biblical concept. It is the sum and substance of later Greek philosophic idealism.

4. This is its first recognition by *The Urantia Book*, and the second quotation of Greek teachings.

DISCUSSION OF TRUTH, BEAUTY, AND GOODNESS

1. Truth, beauty, and goodness are man's comprehension of divinity. p. 3, 27.

2. We may discern beauty in the physical world, truth in the intellectual values, but goodness is found only in the spiritual world of religious experience. p. 40.

3. "Health, sanity, and happiness are integrations of truth, beauty, and goodness as they are blended in human experience." p. 43.

4. "The Hebrews based their religion on goodness; the Greeks on beauty; both religions sought truth. Jesus revealed a God of love, and love is all-embracing of truth, beauty, and goodness." p. 67.

5. Every God-knowing creature possesses the potential of unlimited self-expression of unified self-realization by achievement of God-likeness —experiential blending in experience of eternal truth, universal beauty, and divine goodness. p. 507.

6. See a whole section on truth, beauty, and goodness. p. 646.

7. God answers prayer by giving man:

   A. Increased revelation of truth.
   B. Enhanced appreciation of beauty.
   C. Augmented concept of goodness. p. 1002.

8. It is the mission of socialized religion to magnify the lures of truth, beauty, and goodness. p. 1092.

9. Spirituality enhances the ability to:

   A. Discover beauty in things.
   B. Recognize truth in meanings.
   C. Discover goodness in values. p. 1096.

10. We believe truth, admire beauty, and reverence goodness—but we do not worship them. p. 1114.

11. The Father-life is predicated on truth, sensitive to beauty, and dominated by goodness. p. 1175.

12. We should base human life on the highest consciousness of truth, beauty, and goodness, and co-ordinate these divine qualities by wisdom, worship, and faith. p. 1206.

13. The morontia soul, permeated by truth, beauty, and goodness is indestructible. p. 1219.

14. The Supreme Being is:

    A. Beauty of physical harmony.
    B. Truth of intellectual meaning.
    C. Goodness of spiritual value. p. 1278.

15. Love divested of truth, beauty, and goodness is:

    A. A sentiment.
    B. A philosophic distortion.
    C. A psychic illusion.
    D. A spiritual deception. p. 2096.

VI. *REFERENCE*: Page 27, ¶2 - "To every spirit being..."

COMMENT

1. God gives everything possible of himself to every creature in the universe of universes.

2. God is no respecter of persons. See **Acts 10:34**. *"And Peter opened his mouth and said: 'Truly I perceive that God shows no partiality.'"* This was Peter's opening statement to Cornelius, who had sent to Joppa for him.

   See also: Deut. 10:17. Job 34:19. Rom. 2:11. Gal. 2:6. 1 Pet. 1:17.

3. The divine presence with any child of the universe is limited only by the creature's capacity of spiritual receptivity.

VII. *REFERENCE*: Page 27, 13 - "As a reality..."

COMMENT

1. As a reality in human spiritual experience, God is not a mystery.

2. But when the material mind attempts to comprehend spiritual realities, mystery appears.

3. The philosophic miracle of recognizing the Infinite by the finite is only achieved by the faith-grasp of the God-knowing mortal.

5. PERSONALITY OF THE UNIVERSAL FATHER

I. *REFERENCE*: Page 27, ¶4 - "Do not permit..."

COMMENT

1. This text is **Ps. 94:9**. *"He who planted the ear, does he not hear? He who formed the eye, does he not see?"*

    See also Prov. 20:12. *"The hearing ear and the seeing eye, the Lord has made them both."*

2. God is a personality—notwithstanding that his infinity places him beyond our comprehension.

II. *REFERENCE*: Page 27, ¶5 - "God is much more..."

COMMENT

1. God is more than personality—even more than a superpersonality.

2. Our concept of infinite personality is limited to our finite idea and ideal of personality.

3. While we know that God must be much more than our concept of personality, we equally know that he cannot be anything less than an eternal and infinite personality.

III. *REFERENCE*: Page 27, ¶6 - "God is not hiding..."

COMMENT

1. God is not hiding from any of his creatures.

2. God is unapproachable because he "dwells in a light which no material creature can approach." This is **1 Tim. 6:16**. *"Who alone has immortality and dwells in unapproachable light, whom no man has ever seen or can see."*

3. The immensity and grandeur of the divine personality is beyond the grasp of the evolutionary mortal mind.

4. God encompasses the material universe. This first part of the quotation is **Isa. 40:12**. *"Who has measured the waters in the hollow of his hand and marked off the heavens with a span, enclosed the dust of the earth in a measure and weighed the mountains in scales and the hills in a balance?"*

    The second part comes from **Isa. 40:22**. *"It is he who sits above the circle of the earth, and its inhabitants are like grasshoppers; who stretches out the heavens like a curtain, and spreads them like a tent to dwell in."*

5. "Lift up your eyes." This is **Isa. 40:26**. *"Lift up your eyes on high and see: who created these? He brings out their host by number, calling them all by name; by the greatness of his might, and because he is strong in power not one is missing."*

6. In a measure, God's visible creation enables us to understand something of his invisible nature. **See Rom. 1:20**. *"Ever since the creation of the world his invisible nature, namely, his eternal power and deity, has been clearly perceived in the things that have been made."*

7. But it is even better understood through the revelation and ministrations of his Sons.

IV. *REFERENCE*: Page 28, ¶2 - "Even though material mortals..."

COMMENT

1. By faith we should recognize the love of God which provides for our eternal spiritual progression.

   This is the nearest to **John 3:16**. *"For God so loved the world that he gave his only Son,"* etc. (**This passage is not in** *The Urantia Book*.)

2. He "delights in his children." This quotation is not found in the Bible. May be derived from either **Prov. 8:31**. *"And delighting in the sons of men,"* or **Isa. 62:4**. *"You shall be called My delight."*

3. Question: May not this quotation be from the Apocrypha? No. It has been checked.

   Note: Quotation marks seem to be used in the book *only* when quoting from the sacred books of the great world religions.

4. Why do they never quote from the Apocrypha—since they do not recognize verbal inspiration?

5. The writers of *The Urantia Book* try always to associate the old with the new.

6. Jesus always said: "I came not to destroy the law and the prophets, but to fulfill." (**See Matt. 5:17**.)

V. *REFERENCE*: Page 28, ¶3 - "In the local creations..."

COMMENT

1. God the Father is residential only on Paradise.

2. Out in time and space, we mortals see God best in the person of the Creator Sons—more especially when they are on bestowal missions.

3. Said Jesus: "He who has seen me has seen the Father." **See John 14:9**.

VI. *REFERENCE*: Page 28, ¶4 - "The natures of..."

COMMENT

1. While the Paradise Creator Sons do not encompass all of the absoluteness of the First Source and Center, the Universal Father is in every way divinely present in these Creator Sons.

2. The Father and his Sons are one.

3. These Michael Sons are the pattern for all local universe personalities.

4. The Bright and Morning Star. **See Job 38:7.** *"When the morning stars sang together, and all the sons of God shouted for joy."* **(See Rev. 2:28; 22:16.)**

5. *The Urantia Book* makes use of Biblical names, such as angels, Ancients of Days, etc. Note the multiple Sons of God.

6. Discussion of progressive evolution.

    A. **Darwin law.** Variations and natural selection. Darwinism tells how species survive—not how they originate.
    B. **DeVriesian mutations.** This theory explains the origin of species.
    C. *The Urantia Book* validates the theory of DeVries—the *sudden* appearance of new species.

7. Discuss creative vs. accidental evolution. Evolution is supervised, purposive, and progressive.

VII. *REFERENCE*: Page 28, ¶5 - "Without God..."

COMMENT

God is personality. Little wonder that man cannot define or comprehend personality.

VIII. *REFERENCE*: Page 28, ¶6 - "Notwithstanding that God is..."

COMMENT

1. God is: Eternal Power. Transcendent Ideal. Glorious Spirit. Majestic Presence. And infinitely more.

2. Nonetheless, he is truly and everlastingly:

    A. A perfect Creator personality.
    B. A person who can know and be known.

  C. One who can love and be loved.
  D. One who can befriend us.
3. The source of the following quotations has not been located: "know and be known" and "love and be loved."
4. The *friend of God* is not in quotes, but must refer to Abraham—**see Jas 2:23.** *"Abraham…was called the friend of God."*

IX. *REFERENCE*: Page 28, ¶7 – "As we see…"

COMMENT

1. In spite of all these amazing manifestations of God—it remains that he is a true person.
2. God probably maintains personal connections through the personality circuit and in case of evolutionary mortals through the Thought Adjusters.

X. *REFERENCE*: Page 28, ¶8 – "The idea of…"

COMMENT

The personality of God and the unity of Deity are the ministry of revelation and the earmarks of religious maturity.

XI. *REFERENCE*: Page 29, ¶1 – "Primitive religion had…"

COMMENT

1. Primitive religion had many gods fashioned in the image of man.
2. Revelation validates the personality of God which is:
    A. Merely possible in the scientific postulate of a first cause.
    B. Only provisionally suggested in the philosophic idea of Universal Unity.
3. In the spiritual world personality is identical with reality and the unity of God.
4. To deny the personality of the First Source and Center leaves one only the choice of two philosophic dilemmas:
    A. Materialism.
    B. Pantheism.
5. **Materialism.** The theory that matter is the only ultimate reality. The brain is the reality of the psychic process.

    Atomism. The universe is wholly material.

    Many materialists prefer to call themselves **naturalists.** This is the theory that nature is the totality of spatial-temporal objects—the only reality.

Mechanists believe that physics and chemistry can account for all of the cosmos.

6. **Pantheism.** The doctrine that the universe as a whole is God. God is but the combined forces and laws of the cosmos. Extreme *mysticism*—"the divine one is the only true reality."

7. Varied meanings:

    A. Pantheism—All is God.
    B. Theopantism—God is all.
    C. Cosmotheism (Monism)—Ascription of divinity to the cosmos.
    D. Acosmism—Denial of the existence of a universe apart from God.

XII. *REFERENCE*: Page 29, ¶2 - "In the contemplation..."

COMMENT

1. It is not necessary for personality to have a corporeal body. This is true for both man and God.

2. This error of corporeality shows in two extremes:

    A. In materialism, man ceases to exist because he loses his body.
    B. In pantheism, God is not a person because he has no body.

3. Progressing personality functions in a union of mind and spirit.

XIII. *REFERENCE*: Page 29, ¶3 - "Personality is not..."

COMMENT

1. Personality stands for the totality of the infinite nature and divine will shown in eternity and universality of divine expression. God expresses himself through his personality.

2. It is the revelation of God to the universes.

XIV. *REFERENCE*: Page 29, ¶4 - "God, being eternal..."

COMMENT

1. God, being eternal, universal, absolute, and infinite, does not grow in knowledge nor increase in wisdom.

2. While God does not acquire experience, as finite man might comprehend, he does enjoy continuous expansions of self-realization.

3. These expansions are comparable to the acquirement of new experience by finite creatures.

XV. *REFERENCE*: Page 29, ¶5 - "The absolute perfection..."

COMMENT

1. The Father participates in the personality struggle of every Adjuster-endowed creature in the cosmos.

2. Every ascending mortal—every progressing spirit being—is a part of the Father's ever-expanding self-consciousness of ceaseless self-realization.

XVI. *REFERENCE*: Page 29, ¶6 - "It is literally true..."

COMMENT

1. God shares our afflictions. This is **Isa. 63:9**. *"In all their affliction he was afflicted, and the angel of his presence saved them."* Compare with **Zech. 2:8**. *"For thus said the Lord of hosts...he who touches you touches the apple of his eye."*

2. In all your triumphs he triumphs with you. (Have been unable to locate this quotation.)

3. His prepersonal spirit is a part of you. This refers to the Adjuster.

4. The Isle of Paradise participates in all of the metamorphoses of the universe of universes.

5. The Eternal Son embraces all the spirit impulses of all creation.

6. The Conjoint Actor encompasses all the mind expression of the expanding cosmos.

7. The Universal Father shares all personality experiences.

8. This is all true, because *"in him we live and move and have our being."* **Acts 17:28**.

    Note: The word "all" in the quotation in *The Urantia Book*. Explanation: Different versions. Perhaps quoted from memory. Editorialization.

6. PERSONALITY IN THE UNIVERSE

I. *REFERENCE*: Page 29, ¶1 - "Human personality is..."

COMMENT

In general, things finite and temporal are but the shadow of infinite and eternal realities. (Greek philosophy—Plato)

II. *REFERENCE*: Page 30, ¶1 - "God is to science..."

COMMENT

1. God is:
   A. To science a cause.
   B. To philosophy an idea.
   C. To religion a person.
2. God is:
   A. To the scientist a primal cause.
   B. To the philosopher a hypothesis.
   C. To the religionist an experience.
3. Man's concept of God's personality will remain inadequate until he is embraced by the Father on Paradise.

III. *REFERENCE*: Page 30, ¶2 - "Never lose sight..."

COMMENT

1. God and man view personality from the diverse positions of the finite and the infinite.
2. Again: man possesses the lowest type of personality—God the highest.
3. Personality, both human, and divine, is best understood by the study of the bestowal life of Jesus.

IV. *REFERENCE*: Page 30, ¶3 - "The prepersonal divine spirit..."

COMMENT

1. The prepersonal divine spirit (Thought Adjuster) is referred to as "which" and "it."
2. Personal religious experience is necessary for insight into the divine personality.

V. *REFERENCE*: Page 30, ¶4 - "Some degree of..."   ·

COMMENT

1. Love and affection are mutual experiences.
2. Consecration is demanded in this business of finding and comprehending God.

VI. *REFERENCE*: Page 30, ¶5 - "The more completely..."

Comment

1. The better we understand any and all personalities, the better we can understand God's personality—and vice versa.

2. You can argue about God, but experience with him is beyond controversy.

3. Your religious experience is not to convince unbelievers—but to edify believers.

VII. *REFERENCE*: Page 30, ¶6 - "To assume that..."

Comment

1. The fact that the universe can be known proves that it is mind made and mind managed.

2. If man's personality can perceive the universes, then there is personality concealed somewhere in the universe.

VIII. *REFERENCE*: Page 30, ¶7 - "God is spirit..."

Comment

1. God is a real spirit personality; man is potentially a spirit personality.

2. Jesus attained the full potential of spirit personality in human experience, therefore his life becomes man's most real and ideal revelation of the personality of God.

Note: The whole plan of human religious experience and eternal survival is presented in this first paper.

3. While the personality of God is only comprehended by personal religious experience, Jesus' earth life constitutes a perfect revelation of the personality of God in association with a human personality.

7. SPIRITUAL VALUE OF THE PERSONALITY CONCEPT

I. *REFERENCE*: Page 31, ¶1 - "When Jesus talked..."

Comment

1. Jesus' living God was a personal Deity.

2. Jesus, in discussing the living bread, said in **John 6:57**: *"As the living Father sent me, and I live because of the Father..."*

3. The personality concept of Deity:
   A. Facilitates fellowship.
   B. Favors intelligent worship.
   C. Promotes refreshing trustfulness.
4. You can have interaction between nonpersonal things, but not fellowship.
5. Personal communion can exist only between persons—albeit such communion can be assisted by an impersonal spirit—the Adjuster.

II. *REFERENCE*: Page 31, ¶2 - "Man does not achieve..."

COMMENT

1. Man's union with God is not like a drop of water which finds unity with the ocean.
2. Consider theosophy and the Hindu religions. The Oriental concept of salvation—the lost identity of the survivor—is much like the concept of the nonsurvivor as presented in *The Urantia Book*.
3. Diverse concept of the "Universe Oversoul" as taught by Hinduism and *The Urantia Book*.
4. Man attains divine union by intelligent, co-operative, and progressive conformity to the divine will. Both head and heart are involved.
5. These sublime relations can exist only between persons.

III. *REFERENCE*: Page 31, ¶3 - "The concept of truth..."

COMMENT

1. The concept of truth and even beauty might be entertained apart from personality—but never goodness.
2. Only persons can love and be loved.

IV. *REFERENCE*: Page 31, ¶4 - "We cannot fully understand..."

COMMENT

1. God exists changeless and perfect in an ever-changing, apparently law-limited, and imperfect universe.
2. We cannot understand this, but we can know it in our personal experience for we maintain identity and unity of will in spite of constant change.

V. *REFERENCE*: Page 31, ¶5 - "Ultimate universe reality..."

COMMENT

1. Ultimate reality is grasped only by the personal experience in conformity to the will of a personal God.

2. The personality of God is not validated by science, philosophy, or theology—but only by personal experience of the faith sons.

3. Note the use of "heavenly Father." This is an effort to avoid a break with the "heaven" concept. They break squarely with "hell."

VI. *REFERENCE*: Page 31, ¶6 - "The higher concepts..."

COMMENT

1. The higher concepts of universe personality imply: identity, self-consciousness, self-will, and the possibility for self-revelation.

2. All these imply fellowship with other and equal personalities as shown in the Deity association of the Paradise Trinity. Nathaniel used this concept to convince Rodan of the Trinity.

3. There is absolute unity in these Deity associations—"The Lord God is one." This is **Deut. 6:4.** *"Hear, O Israel: the Lord our God is one Lord."* This is a part of the prelude of the *first* Ten Commandments as recorded in **Deut. 5:6-21**. The *second* Ten Commandments are found in **Ex. 20:1-17. (See also Ex. 23:8-13; 34:14-22.)**

4. Deity indivisibility does not prevent God's bestowing his prepersonal spirit (the Thought Adjuster) upon man.

5. A human father's personality is not divided by the reproduction of offspring.

Note: Germ-plasm is pre-individual, but has full potential of the future individual.

VII. *REFERENCE*: Page 31, ¶7 - "This concept of indivisibility..."

COMMENT

1. Note concept of unity and individuality in reference to the Ultimate.

2. The First Source and Center is an infinity which unqualifiedly transcends all mind, all energy, and all spirit.

3. We can conceptualize God as:
   A. Father.
   B. Creator.
   C. Upholder.

D. Controller.

E. Trinity.

F. First Source and Center.

G. "I AM." Infinite, eternal, universal—ABSOLUTE.

VIII. *REFERENCE*: Page 31, ¶8 - "The fact of..."

COMMENT

1. The Paradise Trinity in no manner violates the truth of divine unity. In all universe reactions and in all creature relations, the three persons are one.

2. How three can be one is not wholly clear to even high celestial beings.

IX. *REFERENCE*: Page 32, ¶2 - "(Presented by a...)"

COMMENT

1. This author is a Divine Counselor, belonging to a group of Trinity-origin beings embracing:
    A. Trinity Teacher Sons.
    B. Perfectors of Wisdom.
    C. Divine Counselors.
    D. Universal Censors.
    E. Inspired Trinity Spirits.
    F. Havona Natives.
    G. Paradise Citizens.

2. This paper begins with "The Universal Father is the God of all creation..." and ends with "...the long mortal ascent to Paradise."

    We would have a transcendent and enlarged religion to give the world —a superb philosophy—if we had only this *one* paper. It is about all there.

3. "Ancients of Days." This is the first use of this name (found in Daniel) and the introduction to the superuniverse geography. The name of the local universe is used for the first time.

4. This is the first designation of these papers as a REVELATION.

5. The early introduction of such a far-flung terminology requires the FOREWORD to prevent confusion.

6. The author leaves no doubt as to his authority to present truth.

SPONSORSHIP OF THE URANTIA PAPERS

The Urantia Papers were sponsored by various personalities, but, as they are grouped into Parts, these major divisions were sponsored as follows:

PART I—THE CENTRAL AND SUPERUNIVERSES as a group of papers was "Sponsored by a Uversa Corps of Superuniverse Personalities, acting by authority of the Orvonton Ancients of Days." "These thirty-one papers...were sponsored, formulated, and put into English by a high commission consisting of twenty-four Orvonton administrators acting in accordance with a mandate issued by the Ancients of Days of Uversa..."

PART II—THE LOCAL UNIVERSE papers, twenty-five in number, were "...sponsored as a group by a commission of Nebadon personalities numbering twelve and acting under the direction of Mantutia Melchizedek." The Commission as a whole functioned "...by authority of Gabriel of Salvington."

PART III—THE HISTORY OF URANTIA embraces sixty-three presentations "...sponsored by numerous personalities...These papers were authorized by a Nebadon commission of twelve acting under the direction of Mantutia Melchizedek..." And as in Part II the sponsoring commission acted "...by authority of Gabriel of Salvington."

PART IV.—THE LIFE AND TEACHINGS OF JESUS are told in seventy-seven papers, and, excepting the first, were based on a narrative "...supplied by a secondary midwayer who was onetime assigned to the superhuman watchcare of the Apostle Andrew." The first paper is indited by a certain Melchizedek who states that he has been "assigned by Gabriel to supervise the restatement of the life of Michael when on Urantia and in the likeness of mortal flesh..." and further, that he is the "...director of the revelatory commission intrusted with this task..." The entire seventy-seven papers in Part IV as a group are "...sponsored by a commission of twelve Urantia midwayers acting under the supervision of [this] Melchizedek revelatory director."

PAPER 2
The Nature of God

PAPER 2
The Nature of God

1. **THE INFINITY OF GOD**
2. **THE FATHER'S ETERNAL PERFECTION**
3. **JUSTICE AND RIGHTEOUSNESS**
4. **THE DIVINE MERCY**
5. **THE LOVE OF GOD**
6. **THE GOODNESS OF GOD**
7. **DIVINE TRUTH AND BEAUTY**

INTRODUCTION

I. *REFERENCE*: Page 33, ¶1 – "Inasmuch as man's..."

COMMENT

1. Since God is a person, it is permissible to study his nature—character. Note that character and nature are used synonymously.

2. Jesus' life in the flesh is the best revelation of God's nature—but *not* necessarily of the divine attributes.

3. The divine nature can also be better understood by man when he regards himself as a child of this God-Father.

II. *REFERENCE*: Page 33, ¶2 – "The nature of God..."

COMMENT

1. While the nature of God can be studied in supreme ideas and supernal ideals, it is better revealed in the religious life of Jesus of Nazareth.

2. Jesus portrayed his Father's character both before and after he attained full self-consciousness of divinity.

3. When did Jesus attain the full self-consciousness of divinity? Answer: Probably on Mt. Hermon prior to his baptism, following his year of solitary wanderings.

4. But there are two points to bear in mind:

    A. *Technically* this event was signalized at the time of his baptism by John in the Jordan.
    B. *Full consciousness* of divinity (not self-consciousness) came to Jesus during the 40 days following his baptism.

Note: On the sixth mansion world—"The union of the evolving immortal soul with the eternal and divine Adjuster is signalized by the seraphic summoning of the supervising superangel for resurrected survivors and of the archangel of record for those going to judgment on the third day; and then, in the presence of such a survivor's morontia associates, these messengers of confirmation speak: 'This is a beloved son in whom I am well pleased.'...

"Immediately upon the confirmation of Adjuster fusion the new morontia being is introduced to his fellows for the first time by his new name and is granted the forty days of spiritual retirement from all routine activities wherein to commune with himself and to choose some one of the optional routes to Havona and to select from the differential techniques of Paradise attainment." p. 538.

5. The incarnated life of Michael serves as the background for the attempt to illuminate the human concept of the nature of God.

DISCUSSION OF THE NEW NAME

1. **See Isa. 56:5**. *"I will give them an everlasting name."*

2. **Rev. 2:17**. *"To him who conquers I will give... a white stone, with a new name written on the stone which no one knows except him who receives it."*

3. **Rev. 3:12**. *"He who conquers...I will write on him the name of my God ...and my own new name."*

4. **Rev. 14:1**. *"On Mount Zion stood...a hundred and forty-four thousand who had his name and his Father's name written on their foreheads."*

Note: This new name might well be the name of the fused Adjuster. Before fusion they are registered by number. After fusion the new personality—Adjuster fused with the surviving soul—may be known by this new name.

III. *REFERENCE:* Page 33, ¶3 - "In all our efforts..."

COMMENT

1. The limited capacity of the human mind greatly handicaps all efforts to enlarge the concept of the nature of God.

2. The revelation of God is curtailed by the limitations of language and the lack of material suitable for illustration and comparison.

3. All efforts to enlarge the concept of God would be well-nigh futile except for the fact that:

   A. Mortal mind is indwelt by the spirit of the Universal Father.
   B. Mind is pervaded by the Truth Spirit of the Creator Son.
   C. There is also present the Holy Spirit of the local universe Mother Spirit.

4. The human mind is thus subject to the spiritual endowment of the Father, Son, and Spirit.

5. **Note:** The Father's Spirit *indwells* the mind; the Son's spirit *pervades* the mind. Note dictionary definition of pervade: "To penetrate, to traverse, to pass, flow, or spread through; to permeate, hence to be diffused throughout."

6. Depending on this threefold spirit ministry, the author of this paper undertakes the portrayal of the nature of God to the mind of man.

7. The indwelling and pervading spirits are spoken of as being in the *heart* of man. Heart and mind seem to be used interchangeably. In common usage, heart refers more to the emotions; mind to intellectuality.

1. THE INFINITY OF GOD

I. *REFERENCE:* Page 33, ¶4 - "'Touching the Infinite...'"

COMMENT

1. **Job 37:23.** *"The Almighty…we cannot find him."*

    Ps. 77:19. *"Thy way was through the sea, thy path through the great waters; yet thy footprints were unseen."*

    Note change of Almighty to Infinite.

2. The first part of the second quotation is **Ps. 147:5.** *"Great is our Lord, and abundant in power; his understanding is beyond measure."*

    The second part of the second quotation is **Ps. 145:3.** *"Great is the Lord, and greatly to be praised, and his greatness is unsearchable."*

3. Again we note this combination of Scriptures to form a single quotation.

4. The blinding light of the Father's presence is such that to his creatures he apparently "dwells in the thick darkness."

    This is taken from Solomon's prayer at the dedication of the temple. See **1 Kings 8:12.** *"Then Solomon said, 'The Lord has set the sun in the heavens, but has said that he would dwell in thick darkness.'"*

5. This may refer to the "cloud" which was supposed to cover the "mercy seat" in the "Most Holy Place" of the Jewish sanctuary. **See Lev. 16:2.** *"And the Lord said to Moses, 'Tell Aaron your brother not to come at all times into the holy place within the veil, before the mercy seat which is upon the ark, lest he die; for I will appear in the cloud upon the mercy seat.'"*

See also Ps. 18:11. *"He made darkness his covering around him."*

6. His thoughts and plans are unsearchable, and "he does great and marvelous things without number."

   This is **Job 5:9**. *"Who does great things and unsearchable, marvelous things without number."* **See also Ps. 139:14.** *"I praise thee, for thou art fearful and wonderful. Wonderful are thy works! Thou knowest me right well."*

7. God is beyond our comprehension. **See Job 36:26.** *"Behold, God is great, and we know him not; the number of his years is unsearchable."*

8. God is greater than the universe of universes. **See 1 Kings 8:27.** *"But will God indeed dwell on the earth? Behold, heaven and the highest heaven cannot contain thee; how much less this house which I have built!"*

Note: Introduction of the concept of plural heavens—idea of diverse levels of heaven.

9. Unsearchable judgments and ways past finding out. **See Rom. 11:33.** *"O the depth of the riches and wisdom and knowledge of God! How unsearchable are his judgments and how inscrutable his ways."*

II. *REFERENCE:* Page 34, ¶2 - "'There is but one God...'"

COMMENT

This entire paragraph consists of quotations.

1. There is but one God—the Infinite Father and faithful Creator. This is a composite reference:

   1 Cor. 8:6. *"Yet for us there is one God, the Father, from whom are all things and for whom we exist."*

   1 Pet. 4:19. *"Therefore let those who suffer according to God's will do right and entrust their souls to a faithful creator."*

2. The Creator is the universal disposer, supreme soul, and primal mind.

   This is a composite quotation from the Hindu sacred books. In the versions consulted, the passages read:

   "He is the Creator, He is the Disposer." **Atharva Veda 13.4.3.12.20.**

   "The last source of every soul." **Beihad-Aranyaka Upanishad, 3.9.1.10.**

   "Verily there is one Supreme Soul." **Bhagavata Purana, 11.18.32.**

"The Primal Lord of Heaven." **Bhagavad Gita, 10.12.13.15.16.**

"He is the cause of creation." **Vishnu Purana, 1.1.35.**

"The great Controller makes no mistakes. He is resplendent in majesty and glory." This quotation is derived from two sources:

A. *"Great heaven makes no mistakes."* **Shi King, 3.3.3.12.8-10.**

B. *"But the face of the Lord shall abide, resplendent with majesty and glory."* **Koran 57:3.**

"The Creator God is wholly devoid of fear and enmity. He is immortal, eternal, self-existent, divine, and bountiful." This passage is from Sikhism: *"There is but one God, whose name is true, the Creator, devoid of fear and enmity, immortal, unborn, self-existent, great, and bountiful."* **Jopji—Preamble.**

"How pure and beautiful, how deep and unfathomable is the supernal Ancestor of all things." This is from Taoism: *"How pure and still is the Supreme Being! How deep and unfathomable is the supernal ancestor of all things."* **Tao-Teh-King 4.2.1.**

"The Infinite is most excellent in that he imparts himself to men. He is the beginning and the end, the Father of every good and perfect purpose." This is also a quotation of double origin:

A. *"It is only the Supreme that excels in imparting himself to men, and enabling them to achieve merit."* **Tao-Teh-King 41.3.**

B. This section is from Zoroastrianism. *"As the beginning and the end, the Father of good purpose."* **Yasna 31.8.**

"With God all things are possible; the eternal Creator is the cause of causes." This seems to be a double origin quotation:

A. **Matt. 19:26.** *"But with God all things are possible."*

B. A Hindu passage: *"This universe has sprung from the Lord. In him it is established. He is the cause of creation."* **Vishnu Purana 1.1.35.**

Question: Do the midwayers have a single book of composite origin? They do seem to have their own versions of the Old Testament and New Testament.

III. *REFERENCE*: Page 34, ¶3 - "Notwithstanding the infinity..."

COMMENT

1. The eternal and infinite God is self-conscious of his perfection and power.

2. God is the only person in the universe (aside from his divine co-ordinates) who really knows himself in all aspects.

IV. *REFERENCE*: Page 34, ¶4 - "The Father constantly..."

COMMENT

1. God perfectly regulates the differential of his self-distribution.

2. God is self-conscious of his infinity.

3. God is not a cosmic accident; neither is he an experimenter.

4. Subordinate Deities may adventure and experiment, but the Father pursues an eternal purpose and knows the end from the beginning.

V. *REFERENCE*: Page 34, ¶5 - "No thing is new to God..."

COMMENT

1. There is nothing new to God—he is never surprised.

2. "He inhabits the circle of eternity."

Note: A circle is about the only concept of eternity that the human mind could even begin to comprehend.

While this statement is not in quotes, it suggests a number of scriptures, such as:

Isa. 40:22. *"It is he who sits above the circle of the earth."*

Job 22:14. *"Thick clouds enwrap him, so that he does not see and he walks on the vault of heaven."*

3. He is without beginning or end of days. While this is not quoted, it suggests **Isa. 46:10.** *"Declaring the end from the beginning and from ancient times things not yet done, saying, "My counsel shall stand, and I will accomplish all my purpose.""*

   The statement "without beginning or end of days" is found in **Heb. 7:3.** *"Has neither beginning of days nor end of life."* It is spoken of Melchizedek.

4. He is the great and only I AM.

Note: In Paper 3 the I AM concept is fully presented as a philosophic attempt to help the finite mind comprehend some of the transactions of infinity and eternity.

VI. *REFERENCE*: Page 34, ¶6 - "The Universal Father..."

COMMENT

It is the infinity of God that prevents direct personal communication with finite beings—except through the Thought Adjusters.

VII. *REFERENCE*: Page 34, ¶7 - "And all this necessitates..."

COMMENT

The infinity of God necessitates making special arrangements for communicating with his creatures:

1. The Paradise Sons—who often bestow themselves in the likeness of the creatures themselves.

2. The ministering personalities of the Infinite Spirit—and the daughters of the Infinite Spirit.

3. The Thought Adjusters.

Note: A child may not be God-conscious when the Adjuster comes, upon the first moral decision, but the potential is there.

VIII. *REFERENCE*: Page 35, ¶2 - "In these ways..."

COMMENT

1. And in many other ways does God attenuate his infinity in order that he may draw near his universe children.

   Definition of attenuate: "To lessen the amount, force, or value; to make less complex, to weaken."

2. Through personalities which are less and less absolute, God draws nearer and nearer his children of the far-flung universes.

IX. *REFERENCE*: Page 35, ¶3 - "All this he has done..."

COMMENT

1. God's universal activities in no way detract from his infinity, eternity, or primacy.

Note: This is a relationship in reality with which we are not familiar as concerns material things. But parents know that they may go on loving (without restraint) successive children without any consciousness of depleting their parental love—not even to lessen it.

2. And all these things are true—even though mortal minds may fail of comprehension.

X. *REFERENCE*: Page 35, ¶4 - "Because the First Father..."

COMMENT

1. The infinite plans and eternal purposes of the First Father are beyond our finite grasp.

Compare **Eph. 3:10,11. (King James Version)** *"To the intent that now unto the principalities and powers in heavenly places might be known by the church the manifold wisdom of God, according to the eternal purpose which he purposed in Christ Jesus our Lord."*

2.   While we only glimpse the Father's purpose, we know that his infinity lovingly embraces all of our finity.

XI. *REFERENCE*: Page 35, ¶5 – "Divinity and eternity..."

COMMENT

1.   Divinity and eternity God shares with many, but infinity only with his Trinity associates.

2.   Infinity of personality must embrace all finitude of personality; hence the saying, "In Him we live and move and have our being." (Direct quotation from Paul at Athens—**see Acts 17:28**.)

3.   The Thought Adjuster is a part of infinity.

2. THE FATHER'S ETERNAL PERFECTION

I. *REFERENCE*: Page 35, ¶6 – "Even your olden prophets..."

COMMENT

1.   The use of the word "circular" in describing the nature of God gives us something we can visualize—no beginning and no end—a symbol of eternity.

2.   God inhabits the present moment. "Present moment" is an excellent symbol. There is no past or future to God.

3.   The life of the Father is eternal life. This seems to be **John 5:26**. *"For as the Father has life in himself, so he has granted the Son also to have life in himself."*

4.   It is the Father who gives life to all. **See Acts 17:25**. *"Since he himself gives to all men life and breath and everything."*

5.   The integrity of God is changeless. **See Mal. 3:6**. *"For I the Lord do not change."*

6.   He is the Father of lights and in him there is no variableness or shadow of turning. This sounds like **Jas. 1:17**. *"Every good endowment and every perfect gift is from above, coming down from the Father of lights with whom there is no variation or shadow due to change."*

7.   He declares the end from the beginning. His counsel stands while he executes his eternal purpose.

Two texts are involved:

A. **Isa. 46:10**. *"Declaring the end from the beginning and from ancient times things not yet done, saying, 'My counsel shall stand, and I will accomplish all my purpose.'"*

B. **Eph. 3:11**. *"This was according to the eternal purpose which he has realized in Christ Jesus our Lord."*

8. Thus are the plans and purposes of God eternal, perfect, and forever changeless.

II. *REFERENCE*: Page 35, ¶7 - "There is finality..."

COMMENT

1. There is finality in what the Father does—it abides. **See Eccl. 3:14.** *"Whatever God does endures for ever; nothing can be added to it, nor anything taken from it."*

2. The Father repents of nothing, and a thousand years to him are but as yesterday. **Ps. 90:4**. *"For a thousand years in thy sight are but as yesterday when it is past, or as a watch in the night."*

3. Mortal man can never understand the perfection of divinity and the magnitude of eternity.

III. *REFERENCE*: Page 36, ¶2 - "The reactions of..."

COMMENT

1. The reactions of a changeless God may seem to vary as the result of cosmic changes, but this is only apparent.

2. Underneath the superficial, there functions the changeless purpose of the eternal God.

IV. *REFERENCE*: Page 36, ¶3 - "Out in the universes..."

COMMENT

Perfection is absolute on Paradise, but relative in the evolutionary universes. While varying perfection, the Trinity does not attenuate it.

V. *REFERENCE*: Page 36, ¶4 - "God's primal perfection..."

COMMENT

1. There is nothing assumed about God. He is final, complete, and perfect. There is nothing lacking in the divine nature.

2. The whole scheme of existence seems centered in the plan of elevating will creatures to the heights of sharing God's perfection.

3. God is neither self-centered nor self-contained. He bestows himself on all self-conscious creatures.

DISCUSSION: Man is self-conscious, animals are not. The superanimal traits of men:

1. Self-consciousness.
2. Sense of humor. (Retroactive and prophetic memory)
3. Imitative ability. (Parrots and monkeys)
4. Ability to abstract. To learn new truth from truth already known. (Mind circuit)
5. Constitutive endowments. (Adjutant spirit of wisdom)
6. Worship. (Adjutant spirit of worship)
7. Personality. WILL.
8. Thought Adjuster, Spirit of Truth, etc.

VI. *REFERENCE*: Page 36, ¶5 – "God is eternally..."

COMMENT

1. God cannot know imperfection as a personal experience, but he does share the consciousness of imperfection as it is experienced by his finite children.
2. Through the divine presence the Father participates in man's evolutionary experience.

VII. *REFERENCE*: Page 36, ¶6 – "Human limitations..."

COMMENT

Evil is not a part of the divine nature, but man's experience with evil is certainly a part of God's experience with and in all of his finite will creatures.

3. JUSTICE AND RIGHTEOUSNESS

I. *REFERENCE*: Page 36, ¶7 – "God is righteous..."

COMMENT

1. This first quote is **Ps. 145:17**. *"The Lord is just in all his ways, and kind in all his doings."*
2. The next is **Eze.14:23**. *"'And you shall know that I have not done without cause all that I have done in it, says the Lord God.'"*
3. The third text is **Ps. 19:9**. *"The ordinances of the Lord are true, and righteous altogether."*
4. The last quote is from **2 Chron. 19:7**. *"'For there is no perversion of justice with the Lord our God, or partiality, or taking bribes.'"*

II. *REFERENCE*: Page 36, ¶8 - "How futile to make..."

COMMENT

1. How foolish to expect God to violate his own laws; to try to escape the results of violating natural laws or the divine mandates. **See Gal. 6:7.** *"Do not be deceived; God is not mocked, for whatever a man sows, that he will also reap."*

2. But all justice may be tempered with mercy. Wisdom is the arbiter between justice and mercy. Discuss: Prayer—intercession—mediators—sacrifice.

   Note: Cosmic bookkeeping is not mechanized. It is both merciful and WISE.

3. The greatest punishment for wrong-doing is loss of personal existence. See **Obad. 16.** *"They shall drink and stagger, and shall be as though they had not been."*

4. Deliberate sin destroys personality survival values.
   A. Man is created in the local universe.
   B. Endowed from Paradise.
   C. Extinguished from the superuniverse.

5. HELL is simply ignored in *The Urantia Book.*

6. Sin is really cosmic suicide.
   A. Choosing not to ascend.
   B. Sin-identification.

7. Factual disappearance of personality is always delayed until justice is fully ordained. The records are kept straight.

III. *REFERENCE*: Page 37, ¶2 - "Cessation of existence..."

COMMENT

1. Cessation of existence is usually decreed at dispensational adjudications. See **Dan. 7:9,10.** *"Thrones were placed and one that was ancient of days took his seat;...the court sat in judgment, and the books were opened."*

2. What technique is employed to execute the extinction mandate?
   A. Executioners of the conciliating commissions?
   B. Does expulsion from the personality circuit disrupt individuality?
   C. Does withdrawal of mercy collapse the cosmic unreality?

    D.   Is the liquidation effected by the Supreme Being's seizure of all surviving realities?

3.   We are indicted on the sphere of nativity, convicted in the local universe, confirmed and executed by the superuniverse.

IV. *REFERENCE*: Page 37, ¶3 - "When this sentence..."

COMMENT

1.   The sin-identified soul becomes as though it had not been. **Note:** The penalty—punishment for sin—is eternal death, not eternal fire—hell.

2.   The wages of sin is death—oblivion—there is no resurrection from such a death.

3.   Reality factors of a "lost soul" go back to the cosmic potential whence they emerged. Reality is conserved, but sin is not a cosmic reality.

4.   Personality and the Adjuster survive, but forever apart from the former individual of temporary association.

5.   The shadowy mortal being is dissolved and resolved into its cosmic potentials by the transformations of time and the metamorphoses of space.

6.   The nonsurviving mortal suffers annihilation—all experiential spirit values survive in the continuing Adjuster.

V. *REFERENCE*: Page 37, ¶4 - "In any universe contest..."

COMMENT

1.   In a universe contest between levels of reality, the higher personality will triumph over the lower.

2.   Divinity equals reality. The more divine you are, the more real you are.

3.   Undiluted evil and willful sin are automatically suicidal.

4.   Such unrealities exist only because of mercy—tolerance pending the justice-determining mechanisms of the tribunals of righteous adjudication.

VI. *REFERENCE*: Page 37, ¶5 - "The rule of..."

COMMENT

1.   Creator Sons create, foster, rehabilitate, and lovingly promote the Paradise ascension of their mortal children.

2. When these Creator Sons fail to effect survival of their children, the final decrees of dissolution are executed by the forces of the Ancients of Days.

DISCUSSION OF JUSTICE

1. Divine justice is a Trinity function. "Justice is inherent in the universal sovereignty of the Paradise Trinity." p. 114.

2. Trinity judges.

   "The Ancients of Days and their Trinity-origin associates mete out the just judgment of supreme fairness to the seven superuniverses." p. 115.

3. Justice and mercy.

   "That which mercy cannot rehabilitate justice will eventually annihilate." p. 241.

4. Jesus discusses justice on p. 1469 of the Urantia Book.

5. Some Bible texts.

   Ps. 89:14. *"Righteousness and justice are the foundation of thy throne."*

   Rev. 19:1,2. *"Salvation and glory and power belong to our God, for his judgments are true and just."*

   Ps. 119:75. *"I know, O Lord, that thy judgments are right."*

   1 Chron. 16:14. *"He is the Lord our God; his judgments are in all the earth."*

   Rom. 11:33. *"How unsearchable are his judgments."*

   Prov. 21:3. *"To do righteousness and justice is more acceptable to the Lord than sacrifice."*

4. THE DIVINE MERCY

I. *REFERENCE*: Page 38, ¶2 - "Mercy is simply justice..."

COMMENT

1. Mercy is justice modified by wisdom based on the knowledge of:
   A. Natural weaknesses.
   B. Environmental handicaps.

2.   The scriptural references are:

Ps. 86:15. *"But thou, O Lord, art a God merciful and gracious."*   ·

Rom. 10:13. *"For, 'every one who calls upon the name of the Lord will be saved.'"*

Isa. 55:7. *"Let the wicked forsake his way, and the unrighteous man his thoughts; let him return to the Lord, that he may have mercy on him, and to our God, for he will abundantly pardon."*

Ps. 103:17. *"But the steadfast love of the Lord is from everlasting to everlasting upon those who fear him, and his righteousness to children's children."*

1 Chron. 16:34. *"O give thanks to the Lord, for he is good; for his steadfast love endures forever."*

Jer. 9:24. *"'I am the Lord who practice kindness, justice, and righteousness in the earth; for in these things I delight, says the Lord.'"*

Lam. 3:33. *"For he does not willingly afflict or grieve the sons of men."*

2 Cor. 1:3. *"Blessed be the God and Father of our Lord Jesus Christ, the Father of mercies and God of all comfort."*

II. *REFERENCE*: Page 38, ¶3 - "God is inherently kind..."

COMMENT

1.   Since God is inherently compassionate, it is never necessary to employ intermediaries to call forth his loving-kindness.

2.   Our need insures the full flow of the Father's mercy and saving grace.

3.   It is easy for God to forgive because he knows all about us.

4.   The better we know our neighbor, the easier it will be to forgive him —even love him.

III. *REFERENCE*: Page 38, ¶4 - "Only the discernment..."

COMMENT

1.   Infinite wisdom enables a righteous God to minister justice and mercy at the same time and in any given universe situation.

2.   The Father ministers final justice through triune groups:

A.   Central universe: Paradise Trinity and its agents.

B.   Superuniverses: Through the triune Ancients of Days.

    C.   Local universes: Referee trio of the conciliating commissions.

3.   God ministers mercy through:

    A.   The Eternal Son and his Sons.
    B.   The vast host of the personalities of the Infinite Spirit.
    C.   The local universe Mother Spirit and her ministering children.

4.   The Father's justice-mercy ministry is a wisdom-blend representing the WILL and LOVE of God.

5.   God is never torn by conflicting attitudes; he is not a victim of attitudinal antagonisms. (Only mortals are subject to schizophrenia.)

6.   God's all-knowingness directs his absolute free will in doing that which simultaneously satisfies the demands of his divine attributes and the infinite qualities of his eternal nature.

Note: God really has a free will. Man has only a relative and conditioned free will.

IV. *REFERENCE*: Page 38, ¶5 - "Mercy is the natural..."

COMMENT

1.   Mercy is the natural offspring of goodness and love. A Creator Father cannot withhold mercy from his universe children.

2.   Eternal justice and divine mercy combined constitute what man would call FAIRNESS.

V. *REFERENCE*: Page 38, ¶6 - "Divine mercy represents..."

COMMENT

1.   Mercy is the fairness technique of adjustment between the universe levels of perfection and imperfection.

2.   Mercy is Supreme justice adapted to the evolving finite; eternal righteousness modified for the welfare of the children of time.

3.   Mercy is not a contravention of justice—simply an understanding interpretation of justice in the interests of all concerned.

4.   Mercy is Paradise justice wisely and lovingly visited upon the creations of time and space in accordance with the sovereign free will of the Universal Father.

DISCUSSION OF MERCY

1. "Mercy is simply justice tempered by that wisdom which grows out of perfection of knowledge and the full recognition of the natural weaknesses and environmental handicaps of finite creatures." p. 38.

2. "Divine mercy represents a fairness technique of adjustment between the universe levels of perfection and imperfection." p. 38.

3. "Mercy is applied love." p. 75.

4. "The Spirit is a mercy minister." p. 92.

5. "They who would receive mercy must show mercy." p. 1639.

6. Mercy as presented in the Bible:

   Ps. 145.9. *"The Lord is good to all, and his compassion is over all that he has made."*

   Eph. 2:4. *"God, who is rich in mercy."*

   Hos. 2:19. *"I will betroth you to me...in mercy."*

   Matt. 5:7. *"Blessed are the merciful, for they shall obtain mercy."*

5. THE LOVE OF GOD

I. *REFERENCE*: Page 38, ¶7 - "'God is love'..."

COMMENT

1. This first reference is from **1 John 4:16.** *"God is love, and he who abides in love abides in God, and God abides in him."*

2. God's love is shown in the way he deals with the universe. **See Matt. 5:45**. *"So that you may be sons of your Father who is in heaven: for he makes his sun rise on the evil and on the good, and sends rain on the just and on the unjust."*

II. *REFERENCE*: Page 39, ¶2 - "It is wrong..."

COMMENT

1. The love of God is not influenced by sacrifices or intercessions. **See John 16:27.** *"For the Father himself loves you."*

2. It is God's love that sends the Thought Adjusters to indwell us.

3. God's love is universal. **Rev. 22:17.** *"And let him who is thirsty come, let him who desires take the water of life without price."*

4. God wants all to be saved. He is not willing that any should be lost.

    1 Tim. 2:4. *"Who desires all men to be saved and to come to the knowledge of the truth."*

    2 Peter 3:9. *"The Lord is not slow about his promise as some count slowness, but is forbearing toward you, not wishing that any should perish."*

III. *REFERENCE*: Page 39, ¶3 – "The Creators are..."

COMMENT

1. The Creator is the first to act to save the creature from the results of sin.

2. But even Fatherly affection must sometimes chasten us. **See Heb. 12:9,10**. *"We have had earthly fathers to discipline us and we respected them. Shall we not much more be subject to the Father of spirits and live? For they disciplined for a short time at their pleasure, but he disciplines for our good, that we may share his holiness."*

3. **See Isa. 63:9**. *"In all their affliction he was afflicted, and the angel of his presence saved them."*

4. God is an experiential participator in all of man's finite experience.

    Isa. 43:24. *"But you have burdened me with your sins, you have wearied me with your iniquities."*

    John 8:34. *"'Truly, truly, I say to you, every one who commits sin is a slave to sin.'"*

IV. *REFERENCE*: Page 39, ¶4 – "God is divinely kind..."

COMMENT

1. God is divinely kind to sinners. **Isa. 55:7**. *"Let the wicked forsake his way, and the unrighteous man his thoughts; let him return to the Lord, that he may have mercy on him, and to our God, for he will abundantly pardon."*

2. God destroys sin—blots it out. **Isa. 43:25**. *"'I am He who blots out your transgressions for my own sake, and I will not remember your sins.'"*

3. God loves us as a Father loves his son. **1 John 3:1**. *"See what love the Father has given us, that we should be called the children of God."*

V. *REFERENCE*: Page 39, ¶5 - "After all, the greatest evidence..."

Comment

1. The presence of our Thought Adjusters is the greatest evidence of the love of God.

2. Even though searching will not reveal God—you can know him in your own heart.

VI. *REFERENCE*: Page 39, ¶6 - "How unreasonable that..."

Comment

1. We can worship God in spite of the physical and spiritual gulf which separates us, because his spirit lives within us.

2. Paul taught the indwelling of the Father's spirit:

    1 Cor. 3:16,17. *"Do you not know that you are God's temple and that God's Spirit dwells in you? If any one destroys God's temple, God will destroy him. For God's temple is holy, and that temple you are."*

    1 Cor. 6:19. *"Do you not know that your body is a temple of the Holy Spirit within you, which you have from God?"*

    2 Cor. 6:16. *"For we are the temple of the living God."*

3. The Adjuster comes down from God to guide us back to God.

VII. *REFERENCE*: Page 39, ¶7 - "I find it easy..."

Comment

This is a Divine Counselor telling about his worship attitude.

VIII. *REFERENCE*: Page 39, ¶8 - "When I observe..."

Comment

1. The Divine Counselor has great affection for the valiant Creator Sons.

2. It is easy to love those who love us.

3. The Counselor thinks he would supremely love God even if he were divested of his absoluteness.

IX. *REFERENCE*: Page 40, ¶2 - "The Father's love..."

Comment

1. The more we experience of God and his love, the more we will love him.

2. God loves us *as* a father—not like a father.

X. *REFERENCE*: Page 40, ¶3 - "But the love of God..."

COMMENT

1. God's love is wise and farseeing.

2. God is love—but love is not God.

3. The Adjuster individualizes the love of God for each human soul.

XI. *REFERENCE*: Page 40, ¶4 - "At times I am almost..."

COMMENT

1. The human word LOVE is wholly inadequate to portray God's love.

2. We need fifty words to symbolize the range of affection extending from the lowest mortal love to the highest divine love.

3. If the revelators were not so averse to introducing new terms, I think they would have given us a new word for the divine affection—at least they do designate it *Fatherly* love.

XII. *REFERENCE*: Page 40, ¶5 - "When man loses sight..."

COMMENT

1. In losing sight of a personal God, the kingdom of God becomes merely the kingdom of good.

2. In God's dealings with his creatures love is the dominant characteristic.

3. Humanism leaves man in the plight of being a cosmic orphan.

DISCUSSION OF LOVE

1. Restrained justice proves the love of God. p. 616.

2. Love of God the Supreme.
   A. Divine love humanized.
   B. Human love divinitized.
   C. Combined love "suprematized."

3. We may admire beauty, but we love only persons. p. 31.

4. Jesus revealed a God of love—and love is all-embracing of truth, beauty, and goodness.

5. Planetary isolation does not interfere with God's love. p. 1259.

6. God's love is individualized for each creature.

7. God as a Father transcends God as a Judge. p. 41.

8. Jesus loves both as a Father and as a brother. p. 1573.

9. Jesus puts love in the place of fear. p. 1676.

10. Growth of love is unconscious. p. 1097.

11. The Revised Version uses the word "love" 26 times where the King James Version uses "charity."

12. Each day learn to love one more person. p. 1098.

13. Love is man's supreme motivation. p. 2096.

14. Some Bible references to God's love:

    1 John 4:16. *"God is love, and he who abides in love abides in God."*

    John 16:27. *"The Father himself loves you."*

    Jer. 31:3. *"I have loved you with an everlasting love."*

    Ps. 145:20. *"The Lord preserves all who love him."*

    1 John 4:19. *"We love, because he first loved us."*

    1 John 4:18. *"There is no fear in love, but perfect love casts out fear."*

6. THE GOODNESS OF GOD

I. *REFERENCE*: Page 40, ¶6 – "In the physical universe..."

COMMENT

1. Truth, beauty, and goodness.
    A. Beauty in the physical cosmos.
    B. Truth in the intellectual world.
    C. Goodness only in spiritual experience.
2. God could be absolute in philosophy, but in religion he must be good.
3. Man could fear God's greatness, but he loves God's goodness.
4. God's goodness is best revealed in the religious experience of his believing sons.

II. *REFERENCE*: Page 40, ¶7 - "Religion implies..."

COMMENT

1. Religion implies that the spiritual world is responsive to the needs of the human world.

2. Evolutionary religion may be ethical, but only revealed religion is moral.

3. Dictionary definitions:

    A. **Ethics**: Relating to moral action, motive, or character. Ethical emotions. Moral feelings, duties, or conduct. Precepts of morality.

    B. **Morals**: Moral principles, moral wisdom. Moral character, virtue, righteousness. Moral practice and action. Rectitude of life. Quality of right ideals or principles of human conduct.

4. Jesus upstepped the kingly morality of God to the higher morality of fatherly love.

III. *REFERENCE*: Page 41, ¶1 - "The 'richness of the goodness...'"

COMMENT

This paragraph consists of quotations:

Rom. 2:4. *"Do you not know that God's kindness is meant to lead you to repentance?"*

Jas. 1:17. *"Every good endowment and every perfect gift is from above, coming down from the Father of lights."*

Ps. 73:1. *"Truly God is good to the upright, to those who are pure in heart."*

Deut. 33:27. *"The eternal God is your dwelling place, and underneath are the everlasting arms."*

Ps. 103:8. *"The Lord is merciful and gracious, slow to anger and abounding in steadfast love."* **Note**: They use the first part of this verse, but reject the second part dealing with anger.

Ex. 34:6. King James Version. *"The Lord God, merciful and gracious, long-suffering, and abundant in goodness and truth."*

Ps. 34:8. *"O taste and see that the Lord is good! Happy is the man who takes refuge in him."*

Ps. 111:4. *"The Lord is gracious and merciful."*

Ps. 68:20. *"Our God is a God of salvation."*

Isa. 61:1. *"He has sent me to bind up the broken-hearted, to proclaim liberty to the captives."* **Note**: Jesus used this text in his Nazareth sermon.

The second part of this quote is from Sikhism. **Guri and Sarath, 38.** It reads: *"He is omnipotent, our own Lord, and our benefactor."*

Note: This is the first instance of the combination of a Bible passage with a quotation from another sacred book.

IV. *REFERENCE*: Page 41, ¶2 - "The concept of God..."

COMMENT

1.   The king-Judge concept of God fostered national morality, but afforded small comfort for the individual.

2.   The prophets proclaimed God as the father of Israel; Jesus revealed God as the father of the individual.

3.   Again, God loves not *like* a father, but *as* a father.

4.   Selflessness is the real nature of parental love.

V. *REFERENCE*: Page 41, ¶3 - "Righteousness implies that..."

COMMENT

1.   Righteousness implies that God is the source of the moral law of the universe, but this does not mean that such laws are in conflict with his fatherly love.

2.   Love gives and craves affection—fellowship.

3.   The atonement doctrine is an assault upon both the unity of Deity and the free-willness of God.

VI. *REFERENCE*: Page 41, ¶4 - "The affectionate heavenly Father..."

COMMENT

1.   God is not a divided personality. A mediator is not required to secure his favor.

2.   God as a father transcends God as a judge.

VI. *REFERENCE*: Page 41, ¶5 - "God is never wrathful..."

COMMENT

1.   God is not subject to anger, even though wisdom may restrain his love and justice condition his rejected mercy.

2. God's love of righteousness implies equal hatred for sin.

3. God is consistent—the divine unity is perfect.

VIII. REFERENCE: Page 41, ¶6 - "God loves the sinner..."

COMMENT

1. God loves the sinner and hates the sin. This is a philosophical idea. **Note**: God is a transcendent personality. A person can only love or hate other persons. Sin is not a person.

2. God loves the sinner—a person. Toward sin God has no personal attitude. Sin is neither spiritually real nor personal.

3. Only the justice of Deity takes cognizance of the existence of sin. The love of God saves the sinner; the law of God destroys the sin.

4. Mortal man may identify himself with the spirit Adjuster or with sin. The result: survival or extinction.

5. Unreality cannot exist forever in a progressively real spiritual universe.

IX. REFERENCE: Page 42, ¶1 - "Facing the world..."

COMMENT

1. In dealing with personality, God is a loving Father. Throughout the spiritual world he is a personal love.

2. Love identifies the volitional will of God.

3. The goodness of God is an expression of the divine free-willness— love, mercy, patience, forgiveness.

7. DIVINE TRUTH AND BEAUTY

I. REFERENCE: Page 42, ¶2 - "All finite knowledge..."

COMMENT

Finite knowledge is only relative. Information, even from high sources, is only relatively complete, locally accurate, and personally true.

II. REFERENCE: Page 42, ¶3 - "Physical facts are..."

COMMENT

1. Facts may be uniform, but truth is flexible. Evolving personalities can be certain only as regards their personal experience.

2. What may be true in one place may be only relatively true in another segment of creation.

III. *REFERENCE*: Page 42, 14 - "Divine truth, final truth..."

COMMENT

1. While final truth is uniform and universal, all revelations on the finite level are relative, partial, and limited by experience.

2. The eternally true decrees of the Deity are always adjusted to, and for, local situations on the finite level.

3. The comprehension of truth is segmental and limited by the capacity to perceive the infinite.

IV. *REFERENCE*: Page 42, ¶5 - "The false science..."

COMMENT

1. Materialism robs man of his divine parentage and his cosmic citizenship.

2. Partiality of truth (knowledge) may be both good and evil.

   Discussion of good and evil.

   A. The allegory of the tree of knowledge in Eden. See Gen. 3:1-8.
   B. Note the two accounts of creation: In Gen. 2:4-25 is found the shorter and more primitive account.
   C. In Gen. Chap. 1 is found the later and more detailed story. This account creates "man in the image of God"—male and female. Nothing is said about the "rib."
   D. The story of the Sabbath is sandwiched in between these two narratives.
   E. There is but one story of the "fall"—in Gen. 3.

3. Truth is beautiful because it is replete (not complete) and consistent.

V. *REFERENCE*: Page 42, ¶6 - "Philosophers commit..."

COMMENT

1. Abstraction misleads the philosopher into trying to understand the whole by examination of a part.

2. Creation is the better understood by looking for the creative design and purpose.

VI. *REFERENCE*: Page 42, ¶7 – "Intellectual self-consciousness..."

COMMENT

1. Truth can be known by its philosophic consistency and more certainly by the response of the Spirit of Truth.
2. Truth contributes to happiness because it can be enjoyed—lived.
3. Error disappoints because it is not real.
4. After all—truth is best known by its spiritual flavor.

VII. *REFERENCE*: Page 42, ¶8 – "The eternal quest..."

COMMENT

1. The universe strives for unification:
   A. The physical universe in Paradise.
   B. The intellectual universe in the God of mind.
   C. The spiritual universe in the Eternal Son.
2. Mortal man coheres in God the Father. Man's Thought Adjuster unifies with the Father.

VIII. *REFERENCE*: Page 43, ¶2 – "The discernment of..."

COMMENT

1. Beauty is an integration of reality. Divine goodness is ultimate beauty.
2. The charm of man's art consists in the harmony of its unity.

IX. *REFERENCE*: Page 43, ¶3 – "The great mistake..."

COMMENT

1. The mistake of Hebrew religion was the failure to associate the goodness of God with science and art.
2. The continuation of this has led modern man to turn away from concepts of isolated goodness.
3. Science, art, and philosophy could make religious morality more attractive to many modern minds.

X. *REFERENCE*: Page 43, ¶4 – "The religious challenge..."

COMMENT

1. The challenge is to those farsighted persons who will dare to construct a worthy philosophy of truth, beauty, and goodness.

2. Such a new vision of religion will attract the best in the human mind.

3. Truth beauty, and goodness become unified in God—who is love.

4. The author indicts our religion and challenges us to produce something better.

XI. *REFERENCE*: Page 43, ¶5 - "All truth..."

COMMENT

1. All truth is beautiful and good.

2. All beauty is true and good.

3. All goodness is true and beautiful.

4. Health, sanity, and happiness are integrations of truth, beauty, and goodness.

5. Such an experience represents the unification of energy systems, idea systems, and spirit systems.

XII. *REFERENCE*: Page 43, ¶6 - "Truth is coherent..."

COMMENT

1. The truth is coherent, beauty attractive, goodness stabilizing. Combined, they create a love which is conditioned by wisdom and characterized by loyalty.

2. The purpose of cosmic education is to overcome isolation by the reality of expanding experience.

3. Reality is finite on the human level, infinite on the eternal level.

PAPER 3
The Attributes of God

PAPER 3
The Attributes of God

1. **GOD'S EVERYWHERENESS**
2. **GOD'S INFINITE POWER**
3. **GOD'S UNIVERSAL KNOWLEDGE**
4. **GOD'S LIMITLESSNESS**
5. **THE FATHER'S SUPREME RULE**
6. **THE FATHER'S PRIMACY**

INTRODUCTION

I. *REFERENCE:* Page 44, ¶1 – "God is everywhere present..."

COMMENT

1. Presence and power are not passive. He *rules*. **Note:** Introduction of "circle of eternity."

2. We are related to God as a ruler, by and through Michael. God bestows life through Michael.

3. God's gift of eternal life is in his Sons. **See 1 John 5:11.** *"God gave us eternal life, and this life is in his Son."*

4. In our philosophy Creator Sons are plural; in our experience, singular.

5. Since God is eternal, his gift of life is eternal—that is, future eternal.

6. God's gift of eternal life can be accepted or rejected by free-will mortals.

7. The temporal personality comes to possess this eternal life by the technique of evolving an immortal soul through the joint parentage of:
   A. The human mind, and
   B. The divine Thought Adjuster.

8. These Creator Sons are the personal expression of God to the evolutionary worlds.

9. Without this eternal life, man lives and dies just like an animal.

10. Michael is the trustee of this eternal life—the channel between the infinite Source and the mortal bestowal.

11. Speaking of this life bestowal Jesus said:

    John 5:26. *"For as the Father has life in himself, so he has granted the Son also to have life in himself."*

John 10:28. *"And I give them eternal life, and they shall never perish."*

John 11:25. *"And Jesus said to her, 'I am the resurrection and the life.'"*

John 14:6. *"Jesus said to him, 'I am the way, and the truth, and the life; no one comes to the Father, but by me.'"*

II. *REFERENCE*: Page 44, ¶2 - "The highly personalized Sons..."

COMMENT

1. In actuality, God is our grandfather, Michael is our real father.

2. As a personality, God is our direct parent. And as a future finaliter—God is also our father through Adjuster fusion.

3. The Paradise Sons compensate for the invisibility of the Universal Father.

4. The circle of eternity contains the absoluteness and infinity of the Deities. "Circle of eternity"—a finite symbol of an infinite fact.

5. "Sectors of time" are segments of the eternity circle which has neither beginning nor end.

III. *REFERENCE*: Page 44, ¶3 - "Creatorship is hardly..."

COMMENT

1. When God acts he creates something. In this creation all of God's attributes are manifested.

2. But God does not create alone—other persons and forces function conjointly with the Father.

3. If one feature of the divine nature could be antecedent to his other attributes, it would be his creatorship.

4. The creatorship of Deity culminates in the universal truth of the Fatherhood of God.

5. To be a Father God must have children—we are his children. God as a Father transcends all other attributes.

1. GOD'S EVERYWHERENESS

I. *REFERENCE*: Page 44, ¶4 - "The ability of..."

COMMENT

1. This is God's omnipresence. Only God can be in numberless places at the same time.

2. These texts are found in:

Deut. 4:39. *"The Lord is God in heaven above and on the earth beneath: there is no other."*

Ps. 139:7. *"Whither shall I go from thy spirit? Or whither shall I flee from thy presence?"*

II. REFERENCE: Page 44, ¶5 – """I am a God at hand...."""

COMMENT

1. God is near at hand as well as afar off. **Jer. 23:23,24.** *"'Am I a God at hand, says the Lord, and not a God afar off? Can a man hide himself in secret places so that I cannot see him? says the Lord. Do I not fill heaven and earth?'"*

2. God is not just heaven and earth. He fills heaven and earth. God is all the time present in all parts and all hearts of his universe.

3. God is not only a power presence, but also a personal presence.

4. He is the fullness of him who fills all and in all. And he works all in all.

   This seems to be Paul in **Eph. 1:23.** *"Which is his body, the fulness of him who fills all in all."* **Note**: Some personality fills all and is in all. The Adjuster as contrasted with the Infinite Omnipresence.

5. This suggests self-existence—self-will. He not only is ALL—but he is also *in* all. This is a phenomena embracing both cause and effect—and all intervening interaction between cause and effect.

6. Paul further expresses this concept in **1 Cor. 12:6.** *"And there are varieties of working, but it is the same God who inspires them all in every one."*

7. But even the heaven of heavens cannot contain the personality of God. **See 1 Kings 8:27.** *"'Behold, heaven and the highest heaven cannot contain thee; how much less this house which I have built!'"* **Note**: Highest heaven—Paradise.

8. Note plural heavens. God cannot be limited to one place.

9. While it is true that God is all and in all, that is not *all* of God.

   A. God as First Source and Center is all. *Unqualified Absolute.*
   B. God as Creator-Father is in all. *Deity Absolute.*
   C. But that is not all of God. There is a potentiality of interrelatedness and co-ordination. *Universal Absolute.*

10. The Infinite can be finally revealed only in infinity—and that entails eternity.

11. The cause can never be fully revealed in effects. Causes are greater than effects, so the former can never be fully disclosed by the examination of the latter.

12. Primary causes are infinite. Secondary causes may be finite, but they are derived from infinite will.

13. The Creator is infinite—and the creation *potentially* infinite. The whole of causation is greater than all discoverable creation effects.

14. GESTALT. The parts derive their meaning from an attempted understanding of the whole. That is: Creation is best understood by worshipful contemplation of the Creator.

15. While God may partially be revealed through the cosmos, the cosmos can never contain or encompass the infinity of God.

III. *REFERENCE*: Page 45, ¶2 - "The Father's presence..."

COMMENT

1. The Father's presence patrols the master universe—not just the grand universe. **Note**: It is his presence—not his personality.

2. Patrol means to keep order—sustain—make secure for all concerned.

3. God the Father is not walking a beat—he has plenty of help.

4. Some factors of the Father's presence.

   A. Gravity presence. (Personality)
   B. Adjusters and other God-fragments.
   C. Spirit presence of the Eternal Son.
   D. Mind presence of the Infinite Spirit.
   E. Presence of the subordinate Creators.
   F. The Supreme and the Ultimate.
   G. The presence of the Absolutes.

5. God pervades the universe. **Ps. 19:6**. "*Its rising is from the end of the heavens, and its circuit to the end of them; and there is nothing hid from its heat.*" **Note**: *Light* in the King James version—*heat* in the Revised version. Remember: Light without heat.

6. Note the use of circuits.

   A. Gravity circuit.
   B. Mind circuit.
   C. Personality circuit.

IV. *REFERENCE*: Page 45, ¶3 – "The creature not only..."

COMMENT

This paragraph consists of six quotations from Sikhism:

1. *"As I behold creation, I am amazed and astonished. God is contained in the hearts of men. In may heart I hold God, who filleth every place."* **Hymns of Guru Nanak, Asa Ashtapadi: Macauliffe, Sikh Religion 1.301.**

2. **"God is concealed in every heart. His light is in every heart." Hymns of Guru Nanak, Rag Sorath: Macauliffe, Sikh Religion 1.330.**

3. *"Many millions search for God, and find him in their hearts."* **Hymns of Guru Arjan, Sukhmani: Ashtapadi 10.6. Macauliffe, Sikh Religion 3.330.**

4. *"I go searching for the friend; but the friend is with me."* **Sloks of Religion 6.413.**

5. *"Him whom I thought without me, I now find within me. When I found this secret, I recognized the Lord of the world."* **Kabir's Hymns, Acrostic 30: Macauliffe, Sikh Religion 6.186.**

6. This last quotation: *"The Father lives in the child. God is always with us. He is the guiding spirit of eternal destiny."* —I have been unable to locate.

Note: All passages in *The Urantia Book* which appear within quotes are from the sacred books of the world's living religions.

V. *REFERENCE*: Page 45, ¶4 – "Truly of the human race..."

COMMENT

1. Love can dominate us because God dwells within us.

   1 John 4:4. *"For he who is in you is greater than he who is in the world."*

   1 John 4:16. *"He who abides in love abides in God, and God abides in him."*

2. Even our wrong thinking torments our Thought Adjusters.

VI. *REFERENCE*: Page 45, ¶5 – "The omnipresence of God..."

COMMENT

1. Omnipresence is a part of God's infinite nature. Space is no barrier to Deity. If God is infinite he would have to be everywhere present.

2. But space is real. Wood is a barrier to light, but not to X rays.

3. The person of God dwells on Paradise. As such he is not observable elsewhere.

4. God's universe presence embraces manifold personalities and numerous influences.

5. It is not always possible to distinguish between the personal presence of God and the presence of his co-ordinates and subordinates.

6. But the Father is truly present in his personality circuit.

7. The divine co-ordinates:

   A. Eternal Son.
   B. Infinite Spirit.
   C. Isle of Paradise.
   D. The Absolutes.

8. Near co-ordinates:

   A. Creator Sons.
   B. Other Paradise Sons.
   C. The Seven Master Spirits.
   D. Local Universe Mother Spirits.
   E. Supreme Being.
   F. The Ultimate.
   G. God the Sevenfold.

VII. *REFERENCE*: Page 45, ¶6 – "The Universal Controller..."

COMMENT

1. God, the Controller, operates over the Paradise gravity circuits and in accordance with physical mass, because all things adhere and consist in him.

2. Paradise gravity acts on all material things—the pull of the ellipse.

3. Linear gravity acts only on the electronic level—attracting in straight lines.

4. The Controller is also present in the Unqualified Absolute—the potential of all uncreated universes.

5. Thus God pervades the universes of the past, present, and future.

6. He is the primordial foundation of all reality.

7. But God may project himself directly in the universe—as in the bestowal of the Adjusters.

VIII. *REFERENCE*: Page 45, ¶7 – "The mind presence of..."

COMMENT

As a mind presence, God is manifested to the universes:

1. The absolute mind of the Infinite Spirit.

2. The cosmic mind of the Master Spirits.

3. The adjutant mind of the local universe Mother Spirits.

IX. *REFERENCE*: Page 46, ¶1 – "The everywhere present..."

COMMENT

1. The spirit presence of the Father is co-ordinated with the spirit presence of the Eternal Son and the potential of the Deity Absolute.

2. But none of this prevents God's presence in the hearts of his children by means of the Adjusters.

3. God manifests himself in:

   A. Gravity circuit.
   B. Spirit circuit of Eternal Son.
   C. Mind gravity of Infinite Spirit:
      (1) Cosmic mind of Master Spirits.
      (2) Adjutants of Mother Spirits.
   D. Personality circuit.

X. *REFERENCE*: Page 46, ¶2 – "Concerning God's presence..."

COMMENT

1. The actualization of the Supreme Being is the indicator of the en masse presence of God in the universe.

2. This sort of presence has nothing to do with God's presence in the individual.

3. It is to conserve the divine presence that sin is quarantined and rebellion segregated.

4. Loyal majorities have a right to protect themselves from the alienating acts of wicked and rebellious minorities.

5. The injunction to love our neighbor as ourselves does not mean that we should allow him to impose upon us.

6. Moral and spiritual maladies should be quarantined, as well as physical contagion.

7. Civilization has a right to protect itself from the subversive influence of international gangsters.

XI. *REFERENCE*: Page 46, ¶3 - "While the Father..."

COMMENT

God's presnce with us is determined by:

1. Level of existence. Origin and order of being. Relation to Deity.

2. Whether or not we have Father fragments.

3. Our co-operation with these spiritual helpers.

XII. *REFERENCE*: Page 46, ¶4 - "The fluctuations of..."

COMMENT

1. Fluctuations of the divine presence are not due to changeableness in God, but rather to attitudinal changes on the part of his free-choosing children.

2. God is no respecter of persons or planets—man himself, and for himself, determines the divine presence.

3. God confers differential honor only on the personalities of God the Sevenfold.

    A. The Creator Son—Creative Spirit.
    B. The Ancients of Days.
    C. Seven Master Spirits.
    D. The Supreme Being.
    E. The Infinite Spirit.
    F. The Eternal Son.
    G. The Universal Father.

2. GOD'S INFINITE POWER

I. *REFERENCE*: Page 46, ¶5 - "All the universes know..."

COMMENT

1. All universes acknowledge God's sovereignty. **Rev. 19:6**. *"Then I heard what seemed to be the voice of a great multitude...crying, 'Hallelujah! For the Lord our God the Almighty reigns,'"*

2. The affairs of our world are supervised. **Dan. 4:35**. *"And he does according to his will in the host of heaven and among the inhabitants of the earth."*

3. God is the source of all power. **Rom. 13:1**. *"For there is no authority except from God."*

II. *REFERENCE*: Page 46, ¶5 - "Within the bounds..."

COMMENT

1. Within the bounds of consistency, all things are possible with God. The quotation is from Jesus' discussion about the camel going through the eye of a needle. **Mark 10:27.** *"With men it is impossible, but not with God; for all things are possible with God."*

2. But even things which are possible with God may not be probable. God could no doubt heal all diseases—cancer. But doctors must depend on what God *does* do, not on what he *can* do.

3. The long evolutionary process unfolds according to the eternal purpose. Why do we see so little of the divine plan?
   A. We are finite—we discover order, but discern little perfection.
   B. The purpose is eternal—we are time-conditioned. We cannot focus on an eternal project.
   C. The plan is universal—we are local in space.
   D. We are too finite to detect infinite wisdom in the eternal purpose.
   E. The plan is characterized by harmony—we are confused and distorted by sin and rebellion.
   F. It is not easy for the lowest order of intelligence to perceive the doings of the highest intelligence.
   G. We can only partially comprehend the Supreme—much less the Infinite.

4. There is but one law-giver. The laws of the cosmos are the habit of God.

5. God upholds the universes and swings them around their circuits.

III. *REFERENCE*: Page 47, ¶1 - "Of all the divine..."

COMMENT

1. Of all God's attributes, we best understand his omnipotence.

2. Aside from things spiritual, God is energy. All energy derives from the First Source and Center.

3. **Note:** The periodic law of chemistry.

4. Light without heat and other unknown forces are derived from Deity. (What holds atoms together?)

IV. *REFERENCE*: Page 47, ¶2 - "God controls all power..."

COMMENT

1. God controls all power—he makes a way for the lightning.

    A. God works through the Conjoint Actor and the Power Directors.
    B. **Job 28:26**. "When he made a decree for the rain, and a way for the lightning of the thunder."

2. **Note**: The decrees for water.

    A. Two gases—water.
    B. Three forms of water. Ice floats.

3. If energy were uncontrolled it would radiate into outer space.

4. The cosmic units swing on forever around their Paradise circuits.

V. *REFERENCE*: Page 47, ¶3 - "The omnipotence of..."

COMMENT

1. The Father dominates all energy—physical, mindal, spiritual—on the absolute level.

2. In infinity all energies are indistinguishable. Monota is nonspirit Paradise energy, but indistinguishable from Paradise spirit. Note: In a former edition of Webster the word *monota* appears as a footnote.

3. Creature mind—not originating on Paradise—is not directly dominated by the Universal Father. Mortal mind takes origin in the local universe.

4. God adjusts with mortal mind by means of the Thought Adjusters.

VI. *REFERENCE*: Page 47, ¶4 - "The Universal Father..."

COMMENT

1. God is not a transient force or fluctuating energy.

2. God is able to deal with all the emergencies of the cosmos: personality reactions, group antagonisms, animal propensities, mental and emotional conflicts, error, evil, and sin.

3. God deals with the cosmos according to:

    A. Dictates of eternal wisdom.
    B. Mandates of infinite judgment.

4.   Regardless of appearances, the power of God is not functioning like a blind force.

VII. *REFERENCE*: Page 47, ¶5 - "Situations do arise..."

COMMENT

1.   Things happen in the cosmos which appear to be emergency and make-shift rulings, but such is not the case.

2.   This superficial view of the universe results from:

A.   Limited range of viewpoint.
B.   Finiteness of comprehension.
C.   Circumscribed scope of survey.

3.   We fail to understand God's doings because of:

A.   Failure to recognize higher laws.
B.   Magnitude of God's character.
C.   Infinity of his attributes.
D.   Fact of his free-willness.

VIII. *REFERENCE*: Page 47, ¶6 - "The planetary creatures..."

COMMENT

1.   Because of the great differences in the creatures of the universe, it is difficult for these finite beings to comprehend the doings of an Infinite God.

2.   Said Jesus, just before leaving Urantia: *"I have overcome the world."* **John 16:33**. He did not say, I have understood or explained the world.

3.   Because of our misunderstanding, many of the doings of God may seem to be cruel and heartless. But they are not.

4.   God's doings are really wise, kind, and purposeful. They are for the highest good of the greatest number.

5.   The privileges of cosmic citizenship exact the price of subjection to the demands of cosmic welfare in its entirety.

6.   Sometimes the welfare of the part may appear to differ from the welfare of the whole. From God's viewpoint such differences do not exist.

IX. *REFERENCE*: Page 48, ¶2 - "We are all a part..."

COMMENT

1.   We are a part of the family of God, and must sometimes share in the family discipline. Compare: **Rom. 14:7**. *"None of us lives to himself."*

2. To mortals, many of the riddles of the universe are really the result of:

    A. The decisions of all-wisdom.

    B. Choosing of the infallible will.

    C. Decisions of a perfect personality for the highest good of all creation.

3. But many of the things which happen to us are caused by:

    A. Our own perverted choosing.

    B. Thoughtlessness and selfishness.

    C. Uncivilized cruelty.

    D. Out working of heredity.

    E. The evolutionary scheme.

    F. Social situations.

    G. Our political plight.

    H. Incompleteness of the Supreme.

X. *REFERENCE*: Page 48, ¶3 - "Thus it is..."

COMMENT

1. Our finite handicaps cause many of God's wise and kind acts to appear to be cruel and inconsiderate.

2. Our limitations cause us to pervert the motives and misunderstand the purposes of God's dealing with the universe.

3. But many things occur on an evolutionary world which are not the personal doings of God.

4. God is a divinely unified personality—he does not need to be adjudged by finite and mortal psychiatry.

XI. *REFERENCE*: Page 48, ¶4 - "The divine omnipotence..."

COMMENT

1. God's omnipotence is perfectly co-ordinated with all his other attributes.

2. God's power in the universe is ordinarily limited by three conditions—by his nature, by his will, and by his law.

XII. *REFERENCE*: Page 48, ¶5 - "God is unlimited..."

COMMENT

1. God is:

    A. Unlimited in power.

    B.   Divine in nature.

    C.   Final in will.

    D.   Infinite in attributes.

    E.   Eternal in wisdom.

    F.   Absolute in reality.

2.   But outside of Paradise and the central universe, everything pertaining to God is limited by:

    A.   The evolving presence of the Supreme,

    B.   the eventuating presence of the Ultimate.

and co-ordinated in the existential Absolutes of potentiality:

    A.   Deity Absolute.

    B.   Universal Absolute.

    C.   Unqualified Absolute.

3.   It is God's will that his presence be thus limited.

DISCUSSION OF INFINITUDE

1.   Notwithstanding God's eternity and infinity, he is absolute in volition. p. 59.

2.   Inability to attain the infinity of God should not prevent our enjoying him on the finite level. p. 1169.

3.   Bible texts:

Job 5:9. *"Who does great things and unsearchable, marvelous things without number."*

Job 36:26. *"Behold, God is great, and we know him not; the number of his years is unsearchable."*

Isa. 46:10. *"Declaring the end from the beginning and from ancient times things not yet done, saying, "My counsel shall stand, and I will accomplish all my purpose.""*

Matt. 19:26. *"But with God all things are possible."*

Dan. 4:35. *"And he does according to his will in the host of heaven and among the inhabitants of the earth."*

Job 42:2. *"I know that thou canst do all things, and that no purpose of thine can be thwarted."*

3. GOD'S UNIVERSAL KNOWLEDGE

I. *REFERENCE*: Page 48, ¶6 - "'God knows all things.'..."

COMMENT

1. God knows all things. **1 John 3:20.** *"God is greater than our hearts, and he knows everything."*

2. God's consciousness embraces the thought of all creation. **Note**:
   A. The mind circuit of the Infinite Spirit.
   B. The far-flung distribution of Thought Adjusters.

3. He knows about everything before it happens.

4. The divine entities (Adjusters) going out from him are a part of him.

5. He controls nature and is perfect in knowledge. **See Job 37:16.** *"Do you know the balancings of the clouds, the wondrous works of him who is perfect in knowledge."*

6. The eyes of the Lord are in every place. **Prov. 15:3.** *"The eyes of the Lord are in every place, keeping watch on the evil and the good."*

7. About the sparrows and the number of your hairs. **Matt. 10:29,30.** *"Are not two sparrows sold for a penny? And not one of them will fall to the ground without your Father's will. But even the hairs of your head are all numbered."* **(Regarding technique of counting hairs, see *The Urantia Book*, p. 419.)**

8. He knows all about astronomy. **Ps. 147:4.** *"He determines the number of the stars, he gives to all of them their names."*

II. *REFERENCE*: Page 49, ¶2 - "The Universal Father..."

COMMENT

1. The Universal Father is always conscious of all the worlds of all universes.

2. The rest of this paragraph is a series of quotations:

   Ex. 3:7. *"Then the Lord said, 'I have seen the affliction of my people who are in Egypt, and have heard their cry...I know their sufferings.'"*

   Ps. 33:13,14. *"The Lord looks down from heaven, he sees all the sons of men; from where he sits enthroned he looks forth on all the inhabitants of the earth."*

   Job 23:10. *"But he knows the way that I take; when he has tried me, I shall come forth as gold."*

Ps. 139:2,3. *"Thou knowest when I sit down and when I rise up; thou discernest my thoughts from afar. Thou searchest out my path and my lying down, and art acquainted with all my ways."*

Heb. 4:13. *"And before him no creature is hidden, but all are open and laid bare to the eyes of him with whom we have to do."*

Ps. 103:14. *"For he knows our frame; he remembers that we are dust."*

Matt. 6:8. *"Your Father knows what you need before you ask him."*

III. *REFERENCE*: Page 49, ¶3 – "God is possessed..."

COMMENT

1. God is universally self-conscious. He is infinitely conscious of his self-consciousness.

2. God could know everything in and of himself—but he elects to use a host of other beings.

3. The Infinite Spirit is also everywhere present.

IV. *REFERENCE*: Page 49, ¶4 – "We are not wholly..."

COMMENT

1. The authors are not sure that God foreknows sin. Even if he does, it does not abrogate man's free will.

2. God is never subject to surprise.

V. *REFERENCE*: Page 49, ¶5 – "Omnipotence does not imply..."

COMMENT

1. God cannot do the nondoable or an ungodlike act.

2. God does not know the unknowable.

3. But all such statements are not comprehensible to the mortal mind.

4. Note three Bible texts:

   1 John 3:20. *"For God is greater than our hearts, and he knows everything."*

   Heb. 4:13. *"And before him no creature is hidden, but all are open and laid bare to the eyes of him with whom we have to do."*

   Matt. 6:8. *"For your Father knows what you need before you ask him."*

4. GOD'S LIMITLESSNESS

I. REFERENCE: Page 49, ¶6 – "The successive bestowal..."

Comment

1. God's distribution of himself to the universes does not lessen his infinite attributes.

   Note: *Reside*—"To have an abiding place; to be present."
   Repose—"Freedom from that which excites or stirs up. Peace, calm, and tranquility."

2. The potential of God's nature and attributes is in no way lessened by the unstinted bestowal of himself upon his creation.

II. REFERENCE: Page 49, ¶7 – "The creation of..."

Comment

1. While each new creation calls for an adjustment of gravity, there remains the gravity potential to control even an infinite universe.

2. The endowment of an infinite creation would leave the Unqualified Absolute undiminished.

3. Regardless of his bestowals of energy and spirit, the infinite potential of God remains the same.

III. REFERENCE: Page 50, ¶2 – "And so with wisdom..."

Comment

1. The lavish bestowal of mind does not lessen the wisdom potential of Deity.

2. Enlargement of the universe does not diminish the infinite mind endowment of the personality of God.

IV. REFERENCE: Page 50, ¶3 – "The fact that he..."

Comment

1. There is no limit to the number of Adjusters which the Father can bestow upon his universe children.

2. While these prepersonal Monitors are volunteers, they are sent by a personal Father.

3. This reception of Adjusters creates an inconceivable future for mortals.

4. All of this giving of himself to his creatures in no way diminishes the powers reposed in Deity.

V. *REFERENCE*: Page 50, ¶4 - "To the mortals of time..."

COMMENT

1. We mortals have a future, but God inhabits eternity.

2. A Divine Counselor is finite—he does not fully comprehend Deity.

3. Only an infinite mind can comprehend infinity of existence and eternity of action.

VI. *REFERENCE*: Page 50, ¶5 - "Mortal man cannot..."

COMMENT

1. While man cannot know the infinitude of God, he can *feel*—experience—such a Father's infinite LOVE.

2. Quality of experience may be unlimited, but quantity is limited by capacity of spiritual receptivity.

VII. *REFERENCE*: Page 50, ¶6 - "Finite appreciation of..."

COMMENT

1. Finite comprehension of infinite qualities transcends the capacity of mortal logic because man is "made in the image of God"—God lives in man.

2. Cosmic sociology—Creator-creature relationship—augments the Father-child affection.

DISCUSSION

1. God is universal unity and unqualified reality. p. 645.

2. God's hand is on the mighty lever of circumstances. p. 52.

3. **Col. 1:17.** *"He is before all things, and in him all things hold together."*

5. THE FATHER'S SUPREME RULE

I. *REFERENCE*: Page 50, ¶7 - "In his contact..."

COMMENT

1. Outside of Havona, God rules through his Sons.

2. This delegation of power is in accordance with God's free will.

3. At any time God can act independently of all his subordinates.

4. Such acts of God would be in perfection and infinite wisdom.

II. *REFERENCE*: Page 51, ¶1 - "The Father rules..."

COMMENT

1. The Father rules through an unbroken line of Sons, ending with the Planetary Princes.

2. It is no mere poetic expression that "the earth is the Lord's," and that he "rules in the kingdoms of men."

   Ps. 24:1. *"The earth is the Lord's and the fulness thereof."*

   Dan. 2:21. *"He removes kings and sets up kings."*

   Dan. 4:17. *"That the living may know that the Most High rules in the kingdom of men."*

III. *REFERENCE*: Page 51, ¶2 - "In the affairs..."

COMMENT

1. God may not always have his way in the hearts of men, but in the cosmos his will prevails.

2. This triumphant eternal purpose is one of wisdom and love.

IV. *REFERENCE*: Page 51, ¶3 - "Said Jesus..."

COMMENT

1. This quote from Jesus is **John 10:28,29**. *"And I give them eternal life, and they shall never perish, and no one shall snatch them out of my hand. My Father, who has given them to me, is greater than all, and no one is able to snatch them out of the Father's hand."* **Note**: In the King James version it says "no *man*." Revised version is the same as *The Urantia Book*—"no *one*."

2. Even if we cannot grasp the whole of God's nature and acts, we can hold fast the concept of him—*here* and *there*. *Here*—in our hearts. *There*—on Paradise.

3. There is but one God—and in him all things consist.

   Eph. 4:6. *"One God and Father of us all, who is above all and through all and in all."*

   Col. 1:17. *"He is before all things, and in him all things hold together."*

V. *REFERENCE*: Page 51, ¶3 - "The uncertainties of life..."

COMMENT

The inevitabilities are self-explanatory.

VI. *REFERENCE*: Page 51, ¶1 - "Throughout the universe..."

COMMENT

1. Survival of the part is dependent on co-operation with the plan and purpose of the whole.

2. An evolutionary world without error (unwise judgment) would be one without free will.

3. Evolving man must be fallible if he is to be free.

4. Evil becomes sin only when it is knowingly embraced.

VII. *REFERENCE*: Page 52, ¶2 - "The full appreciation..."

COMMENT

1. Havona natives are able to live by truth, beauty, and goodness without contrastive and thought-compelling situations of evil.

2. These perfect beings are such by fact of existence; they earned none of it.

3. Mortal man earns even his faith-status.

4. All of man now and in the future is an experiential attainment.

VIII. *REFERENCE*: Page 52, ¶3 - "The creatures of Havona..."

COMMENT

Havona natives and mortals contrasted.

6. THE FATHER'S PRIMACY

I. *REFERENCE*: Page 52, ¶4 - "With divine selflessness..."

COMMENT

1. God relinquishes authority and delegates power with selflessness and generosity. **Note**: Effort to employ English terms to denote divine attitudes.

2. But God is always primal—his hand is on the mighty lever of circumstances.

3. God permits nothing—not even his delegated authority—to interfere with the progress of his *eternal purpose*.

4. Meaning of primal—first, primary, original, chief. First in importance.

II. *REFERENCE*: Page 52, ¶5 - "The sovereignty of God..."

COMMENT

1. In the last analysis God's sovereignty is unlimited.

2. In time and space divine sovereignty is limited:
   A. By God's free will.
   B. By man's relative free will.

3. The universe was not inevitable. It is not an accident—not self-existent.

4. All creation is subject to the will of the Creator.

5. The will of God is true and living love. Finite universes are characterized by:
   A. Goodness—nearness to divinity.
   B. Evil—remoteness from divinity.
      Note: 1. The will of God is not a mathematical fact—it is truth and love.
      2. Reality of evolutionary creation is only relative.
      3. This reality relativity produces differential relation to divinity:
         A. Goodness—nearness to God's will.
         B. Evil—remoteness from God's will.

III. *REFERENCE*: Page 53, ¶2 - "All religious philosophy..."

COMMENT

1. Philosophy, sooner or later, arrives at the concept of one God.

2. Universe causes cannot be lower than effects. Cosmic mind must be above its lower manifestations.

3. Human mind cannot be explained in terms of lower orders of existence.

4. Man's mind can be comprehended only by recognition of higher orders of thought and purposive will.

5. Man as a moral being is inexplicable unless we acknowledge God.

DISCUSSION OF CHARACTERISTICS OF HUMAN MIND

1. **WORSHIP**. God-consciousness.

2. **WISDOM**. Experience consciousness.

3. **SELF-CONSCIOUSNESS**. Ego consciousness.

4. **ABSTRACTION**. Ability to get new truth from old.

5. **TRUTH CONSCIOUSNESS**. Ability to recognize truth by its flavor.

6. **ALTRUISM**. Unselfish service for one's fellows. Ethical brotherhood.

7. **IMITATION**. Ability to observe and repeat an act. Spontaneous learning.

8. **IDEALISM**. Consciousness of the superior.

9. **MORALITY**. Consciousness of the contrast of good and evil.

10. **CIVILIZATION**. Ability to execute the dreams of creative imagination.

11. **HUMOR**. Only man can laugh at a joke.

Note: Man's nearest of kin among animals very closely approaches some of these attainments, but never actually and in the human sense.

IV. *REFERENCE*: Page 53, ¶3 - "The mechanistic philosopher..."

COMMENT

1.   Mechanistic philosophers reject the very sovereign will which created the very universe laws they so deeply reverence.

2.   What homage the mechanist pays God when he conceives natural law to be self-acting.

V. *REFERENCE*: Page 53, ¶4 - "It is a great blunder..."

COMMENT

It is a great blunder to humanize God—but not so stupid as to mechanize him.

VI. *REFERENCE*: Page 53, ¶5 - "Does the Paradise Father..."

COMMENT

1.   Does God suffer? We do not know. The Creator Sons can and do.

2.   Perhaps God does through the Adjusters. **See Isa. 63:9**. *"In all their afflictions he was afflicted."*

3.   God has a fatherly sympathy, and may possibly suffer—even though we cannot understand *how*.

VII. *REFERENCE*: Page 53, ¶6 – "The infinite and..."

COMMENT

1. The infinite Ruler of the universe of universes is:

    Power—Form—Energy—Process—Pattern—Principle—Presence—Reality.

2. But God is more than all these:
    A. He is personal.
    B. He exercises a sovereign will.
    C. He experiences self-consciousness of divinity.
    D. He executes the mandates of a creative mind.
    E. He pursues the realization of an eternal purpose.
    F. He manifests a Father's love for his universe children.
3. And all of these personal traits can be best understood by observing the bestowal life of Michael on Urantia.

VIII. *REFERENCE*: Page 53, ¶7 – "God the Father..."

COMMENT

This has been adopted as the Urantia benediction.

PAPER 4
God's Relation to the Universe

PAPER 4
God's Relation to the Universe

1. THE UNIVERSE ATTITUDE OF THE FATHER
2. GOD AND NATURE
3. GOD'S UNCHANGING CHARACTER
4. THE REALIZATION OF GOD
5. ERRONEOUS IDEAS OF GOD

INTRODUCTION

I. *REFERENCE*: Page 54, ¶1 – "The Universal Father..."

COMMENT

1. God is executing an eternal purpose for the universe throughout all time.

2. A wise Creator created the universe in order to realize this eternal purpose.

3. Aside from Paradise Deities, probably no person or being in all creation really knows the nature of this eternal purpose.

4. Beings of post-eternity existence are not cognizant of future eternity.

5. Even perfect beings differ in opinions. We should be unafraid to hold diverse opinions respecting cosmic philosophy.

DISCUSSION OF GOD'S ETERNAL PURPOSE

1. The finite exists because of the eternal purpose. p. 1260.

2. Vast scope of the eternal purpose. p. 34.

3. Eternal purpose is a glorious plan. p. 364.

4. All things unfold according to the eternal purpose. p. 46.

5. The eternal purpose will triumph. p. 51.

6. Bible Texts.

   Eph. 3:11. *"This was according to the eternal purpose which he has realized in Christ Jesus our Lord."*

   Isa. 14:24. *"'As I have planned, so shall it be, and as I have purposed, so shall it stand.'"*

   Isa. 14:26. *"'This is the purpose that is purposed concerning the whole earth.'"*

Isa. 46:11. *"'I have purposed, and I will do it.'"*

Jer. 4:28. *"I have purposed: I have not relented nor will I turn back."*

II. *REFERENCE*: Page 54, ¶2 - "It is easy..."

COMMENT

1. The perfect universe of Havona could serve a multiple purpose:
    A. The satisfaction of Deity nature.
    B. The finishing school for the pilgrims of time on their way to Paradise.
    C. A pattern creation for the universes of time and space.

2. There is nothing wrong with experiencing pleasure—enjoying satisfaction.

3. God is neither puritanical nor epicurian.

III. *REFERENCE*: Page 54, ¶3 - "The amazing plan..."

COMMENT

1. The chief concern of the finite universes at present seems to be:
    A. Perfection of evolutionary mortals for Paradise ascension.
    B. Admission of these ascenders to the Corps of the Finality.
    C. Post-graduate training for some undisclosed future service.

2. But this scheme for educating and spiritualizing mortals is by no means the exclusive business of the universe intelligences.

3. There are many other fascinating pursuits which enlist the energies of the celestial hosts.

1. THE UNIVERSE ATTITUDE OF THE FATHER

IV. *REFERENCE*: Page 54, ¶4 - "For ages the inhabitants..."

COMMENT

1. There is such a thing as divine providence.

2. But providence is misunderstood. It is not childish and arbitrary.

3. God's providence consists in the interlocking activities of celestial beings working in harmony with cosmic laws.

4. Providence works for the honor of God and the good of man. **Note**: The honor of God and man's spiritual welfare are the same thing.

II. *REFERENCE*: Page 54, ¶5 – "Can you not advance..."

COMMENT

1. *Progress* is the watchword of the universe.
2. Throughout the ages providence has been working out the plan of progressive evolution.
3. Providence and evolution are not opposing forces.
4. Providence never opposes human progress, either temporal or spiritual.
5. Providence is always consistent with the divine nature of the Lawmaker.

DISCUSSION OF PROVIDENCE

1. Providence is the domain of the Conjoint Actor and the Supreme Being. p. 99.
2. Providence is a function. p. 1304.
3. Providence functions with regard to totals. p. 1304.
4. Wrong ideas about providence. p. 1305.
5. Spiritual insight may detect providence. p. 1306.
6. What providence really means. p. 1307.
7. Providence in the Bible.

    The word does not occur in the Old Testament.

    Gen. 50:20. *"You meant evil against me; but God meant it for good."*

    Hag. 2:9. *"'And in this place I will give prosperity, says the Lord of Hosts.'"*

    Note: In the New Testament the word providence occurs once in the **King James Version – Acts 24:2.** but not in the Revised Version.

    John 5:17. *"But Jesus answered them, 'My Father is working still, and I am working.'"*

    Rom. 8:28. *"We know that in everything God works for good with those who love him, who are called according to his purpose."*

III. *REFERENCE:* Page 55, ¶1 - "'God is faithful...'"

COMMENT

These texts are found:

1 Cor. 10:13. *"God is faithful, and he will not let you be tempted beyond your strength."* This same thought is also found in **Isa. 49:7; 1 Cor. 1:9; Heb. 10:23.**

Rom. 7:12. *"So the law is holy, and the commandment is holy and just and good."*

Ps. 119:172. *"My tongue will sing of thy word, for all thy commandments are right."*

Ps. 36.5. *"Thy steadfast love, O Lord, extends to the heavens, thy faithfulness to the clouds."*

Ps. 119:89,90. *"Forever, O Lord, thy word is firmly fixed in the heavens. Thy faithfulness endures to all generations; thou hast established the earth, and it stands fast."*

1 Peter 4:19. *"Therefore let those who suffer...entrust their souls to a faithful creator."*

IV. *REFERENCE:* Page 55, ¶2 - "There is no limitation..."

COMMENT

1   There is no limitation to the forces which God will employ to uphold his purpose.

2.   Again we have a group of scriptures.

   Deut. 33:27. *"The eternal God is your dwelling place, and underneath are the everlasting arms."*

   Ps. 91:1. *"He who dwells in the shelter of the Most High, who abides in the shadow of the Almighty."*

   Ps. 121:4. *"Behold, he who keeps Israel will neither slumber nor sleep."*

   Rom. 8:28. *"We know that in everything God works for good with those who love him, who are called according to his purpose."*

   Ps. 34:15. *"The eyes of the Lord are toward the righteous, and his ears toward their cry."*

V. *REFERENCE*: Page 55, ¶3 - "God upholds..."

COMMENT

1. God upholds all things—material and spiritual.

   Heb. 1:3. *"He reflects the glory of God...upholding the universe by his word of power."*

   Ps. 104:30. *"When thou sendest forth thy Spirit, they are created."*

   Ps. 145:20. *"The Lord preserves all who love him."*

   Ps. 121:7. *"The Lord will keep you from all evil; he will keep your life."*

2. The universe is stable—even in apparent instability. There is security in the presence of cataclysmic upheavals.

VI. *REFERENCE*: Page 55, ¶4 - "The Universal Father..."

COMMENT

1. God is not an absentee landlord. His presence prevents cosmic collapse.

2. God is reality. The divine reach extends around the circle of eternity.

3. The universe is not wound up like a clock—destined to run down.

4. The Father unceasingly pours forth energy, light, and life.

5. God is real—not figurative.

   Job. 26:7. *"He stretches out the north over the void, and hangs the earth upon nothing."*

VII. *REFERENCE*: "Page 55, ¶5 - "A being of my order..."

COMMENT

1. Much in the cosmos that appears haphazard to man appears constructive to higher beings.

2. To a Divine Counselor the cosmos may appear *ultimate*—to man at best only *supreme*.

3. But even a Divine Counselor does not understand everything that is going on in the cosmos.

VIII. *REFERENCE*: Page 55, ¶6 - "I am entirely competent..."

COMMENT

1.   The Divine Counselor fairly well understands the functioning of the Paradise Deities, but he has trouble with the performances of the Absolutes.

2.   While the universe is not infinite, it seems to be permeated by infinity.

3.   The Absolutes seem to:

    A.   Supersede matter.
    B.   Transcend mind.
    C.   Supervene spirit.

4.   While English words can only partially convey cosmic meanings, let us examine these terms:

    A.   **SUPERSEDE**. To make void by superior power; to cause to be set aside. To replace. To displace. To supplant. To defer action.

    B.   **TRANSCEND**. To rise above or beyond the limits or powers of— to overpass. To excel; to outstrip. To go beyond the limits of knowledge or experience.

    C.   **SUPERVENE**. To happen as something additional—unlooked for. To occur without reference or relation to something else. To be added to. To occur otherwise than as an additive. To occur in a manner not antecedently predictable.

IX. *REFERENCE*: Page 56, ¶1 - "These Absolutes must be..."

COMMENT

1.   Why primordials of force, concept, or spirit are unpredictable.

2.   Presence of space potency and other super-ultimates explains why neither physicists nor philosophers can explain the cosmos.

X. *REFERENCE*: Page 56, ¶2 - "There is also..."

COMMENT

1.   There is an organic unity in the cosmos—the living presence of the evolving Supreme.

2.   This Immanence of the Projected Incomplete is Providence—the realm of the Supreme Being and the Conjoint Actor.

XI. *REFERENCE*: Page 56, ¶3 - "I am inclined..."

COMMENT

The variegated and confused medley of cosmic phenomena is so co-ordinated as to work for the glory of God and the good of men and angels.

XII. *REFERENCE*: Page 56, ¶4 - "But in the larger..."

COMMENT

The apparent "accidents" of the cosmos suggest the Infinite manipulating the Absolutes.

2. GOD AND NATURE

I. *REFERENCE*: Page 56, ¶5 - "Nature is..."

COMMENT

1. In a sense, nature is the physical habit of God.
2. God's action in the material realms is qualified by the evolutionary patterns of local creations.
3. Thus are the plans of the Infinite limited by the plans of the finite.
4. God is a wise Father—he allows each Creator Son to work out—unfold—his own universe plans.

II. *REFERENCE*: Page 56, ¶6 - "Therefore, nature..."

COMMENT

1. The changeless background of nature is modified by the fluctuations of finite evolution.
2. God's laws for our local universe are modified by the plans, defaults, and other prevailing circumstances.

III. *REFERENCE*: Page 56, ¶7 - "Nature is a..."

COMMENT

1. Nature is a time-space resultant of two cosmic factors:
   A. The perfect rectitude of Paradise Deity.
   B. The finitude of local universe creations:
      (1) Experimental plans.
      (2) Executive blunders.

  (3) Insurrectionary errors.

  (4) Incompleteness of development.

  (5) Finite wisdom.

2. The majestic and perfect background of nature is qualified—even marred—by the mistakes and disloyalties of the finite creations.

3. Therefore is nature whimsical—stable underneath, but otherwise variegated and changeable.

IV. *REFERENCE*: Page 57, ¶2 - "Nature is the perfection..."

COMMENT

1. Nature is the perfection of Paradise divided by the evil and sin of unfinished universes. The quotient embraces both the perfect and the partial.

2. Progressive evolution augments the good and lessens the evil in nature.

V. *REFERENCE*: Page 57, ¶3 - "God is not..."

COMMENT

1. God is not personally present in nature.

2. Nature is a combination of evolutionary imperfections and Paradise laws of perfection.

3. Nature can never be a portrayal of the infinite God.

VI. *REFERENCE*: Page 57, ¶4 - "Nature, on your world..."

COMMENT

1. Nature is a qualification of the laws of perfection by the plans of evolutionary creation.

2. What a mistake to worship nature because it is in a limited sense pervaded by God.

3. Nature represents the present status of finite cosmic evolution.

VII. *REFERENCE*: Page 57, ¶5 - "The apparent defects..."

COMMENT

1. Cosmic defects are not indicative of corresponding defects in the character of God.

2. These defect-interruptions in the perfection-continuity enable finite man to glimpse divinity reality.

3. Finite mind can only discern perfection in nature by means of morontia mota or revelation.

VIII. *REFERENCE*: Page 57, ¶6 - "And nature is marred..."

COMMENT

1. The face of nature is marred and scarred by misthinking and rebellion.

2. Nature is not God—not an object of worship.

3. GOD'S UNCHANGING CHARACTER

I. *REFERENCE*: Page 57, ¶7 - "All too long..."

COMMENT

1. God is not manlike—he is never jealous of anyone.

2. But the Old Testament presents the picture of a jealous God. See the second commandment—**Ex. 20:5**. *"You shall not bow down to them or serve them; for I the Lord your God am a jealous God."* **See also Ex. 34:14**. *"For you shall worship no other god, for the Lord, whose name is Jealous, is a jealous God."*

3. This concept of a jealous God was later exalted to a higher level. **See Zec. 1:14**. *"'Thus says the Lord of hosts: I am exceedingly jealous for Jerusalem and for Zion.'"*

4. Intending man to be the masterpiece of creation, God is jealous *for* him when he in any manner belittles himself.

II. *REFERENCE*: Page 57, ¶8 - "The eternal God..."

COMMENT

God is incapable of despicable wrath and anger. Such attitudes are foreign to the nature of God.

III. *REFERENCE*: Page 58, ¶1 - "Much, very much..."

COMMENT

Much of our misunderstanding of God is due to the distortions and perversions of the Lucifer rebellion.

IV. *REFERENCE*: Page 58, ¶2 - "God repents of nothing..."

COMMENT

1. God is all-wise; he never repents of anything. Divine foreknowledge directs his free will.

2. Man gains wisdom by trial and error—experience.

V. *REFERENCE*: Page 58, ¶3 - "The Universal Father..."

COMMENT

1. God does nothing that would cause sorrow or regret. But the wrong-doing of his creatures may cause divine sorrow.

2. When the Father fully provides for our spiritual attainment, our failure to grow in grace grieves the divine heart.

VI. *REFERENCE*: Page 58, ¶4 - "The infinite goodness..."

COMMENT

1. The finite mind can comprehend the infinite goodness of God only by contrastive comparison with evil (not sin).

2. Hence, the necessity for these comparisons of cosmic realities in the motions of space.

VII. *REFERENCE*: Page 58, ¶5 - "The character of God..."

COMMENT

God is so infinitely superhuman that his character can only be grasped as personalized in his divine Sons.

DISCUSSION OF GOD'S CHANGELESSNESS

1. The fact of God, the divine law, is changeless. p. 1126.

2. God and the universe are not identical—one is cause, the other effect. p. 1126.

3. Bible texts.

   Mal. 3:6. *"'For I the Lord do not change.'"*

   James 1:17. *"Every perfect gift is from above, coming down from the Father of lights with whom there is no variation or shadow due to change."*

   Ps. 33:4. *"All his work is done in faithfulness."*

   Ps. 119:90. *"Thy faithfulness endures to all generations."*

4. THE REALIZATION OF GOD

I. *REFERENCE*: Page 58, ¶6 - "God is the only..."

COMMENT

A word portrait of God.

II. *REFERENCE*: Page 58, ¶7 - "Since God is self-existent..."

COMMENT

1. God is self-existent, independent, and changeless. **Mal. 3:6**. *"For I the Lord do not change."*

2. Only on Paradise will we understand how God can encompass infinity and finitude at the same time.

3. God can thus modify his universe relationships because of his free will.

III. *REFERENCE*: Page 58, ¶8 - "God is the being..."

COMMENT

1. God is a being of unqualified self-determination.

2. God's free will is conditioned by the prerogatives of his divine nature.

3. God's free will is directed by infinite wisdom and divine fore-knowledge.

4. God is related to the cosmos as a being of final goodness plus a free will of creative infinity.

IV. *REFERENCE*: Page 58, ¶9 - "The Father-Absolute is..."

COMMENT

1. The Father-Absolute is the creator of the central universe and all other Creators.
   A. Father of Universes. Universal Father.
   B. Father of Trinities.
   C. Father of Creators.
   D. Father of Paradise Sons.
   E. Father of Fathers.
   F. Father of Absolutes.

2. God shares much of his nature with others—but not his infinity of will.

3. Even Creator Sons do not possess all of God's infinity.

4. To deny God the possibility of self-limitation would be to deny his absoluteness.

V. *REFERENCE*: Page 59, ¶2 - "God's absoluteness pervades..."

COMMENT

1. God's absoluteness pervades all seven levels of universe reality.

2. God as a father transcends God as a judge. (A person may be a citizen and a physician, but being a father and grandfather can transcend all these.)

3. First and last—eternally—God is a Father.

VI. *REFERENCE*: Page 59, ¶3 - "In God the Father..."

COMMENT

1. Love rather than power characterizes God's relation to his universes.

2. God is a Father in the highest meaning of that term.

3. God is eternally motivated by the perfect idealism of divine love.

VII. *REFERENCE*: Page 59, ¶4 - "In science, God is..."

COMMENT

1. God is:
   A. In science—the First Cause.
   B. In religion—a loving Father.
   C. In philosophy—the self-existent one.

2. It requires revelation to show to know God as a Father—God can be thus experienced.

3. But it does not require revelation to know God as a Father—God can be thus experienced.

VIII. *REFERENCE*: Page 59, ¶5 - "We crave the concept..."

COMMENT

We crave the concept of the Infinite, but we worship the God of experience—a personal Father.

IX. *REFERENCE*: Page 59, ¶6 - "The consciousness of..."

COMMENT

1. "Even if I cannot do this, there lives in me one who can." The battle cry of human salvation.

2. And this is the victory—even our *faith*. **1 John 5:4**. *"And this is the victory that overcomes the world, our faith."*

5. ERRONEOUS IDEAS OF GOD

I. *REFERENCE*: Page 59, ¶7 - "Religious tradition is..."

COMMENT

Religious tradition fails in revealing God because primitive man was a mythmaker.

II. *REFERENCE*: Page 60, ¶2 - "One of the greatest..."

COMMENT

1. The great cause of confusion about God is the failure of the world's sacred books to distinguish between the diverse personalities of Deity.

2. Many messages of subordinate personalities have been presented as coming from God.

3. Urantia religions still confuse the personalities of Deity.

III. *REFERENCE*: Page 60, ¶3 - "The people of Urantia..."

COMMENT

1. Many Urantians still entertain primitive concepts of God.

2. These whimsical and temperamental gods are not the rulers of the universe.

3. Modern man is beginning to recognize a universe of law and order.

IV. *REFERENCE*: Page 60, ¶4 - "The barbarous idea..."

COMMENT

1. The idea of winning God's favor by sacrifices is puerile and primitive—unworthy of a scientific and enlightened age.

2. These ideas are repulsive to the celestial beings of our universe.

3. It is an affront to God to believe the atonement doctrine.

V. *REFERENCE*: Page 60, ¶5 - "The Hebrews believed..."

COMMENT

1. The Hebrews believed that "without the shedding of blood there could be no remission of sin." **Heb. 9:22**. *"Under the law almost everything is purified with blood, and without the shedding of blood there is no forgiveness of sins."*

2. Man holds onto the pagan concept of blood atonement. But Moses at least made an end of human sacrifice.

VI. *REFERENCE*: Page 60, ¶6 - "The bestowal of..."

COMMENT

1. The bestowal of Jesus was not for the purpose of winning the favor of God.

2. Michael's bestowal was the final act in earning the sovereignty of his universe.

3. What a travesty—to believe that God could only be appeased by the sight of his Son dying on the cross.

VII. *REFERENCE*: Page 60, ¶7 - "But the inhabitants..."

COMMENT

1. Urantians are finding deliverance from these superstitions about God.

2. These revelations portray God as revealed in the earth life of Jesus.

PAPER 5
God's Relation to the Individual

PAPER 5
God's Relation to the Individual

1. **THE APPROACH TO GOD**
2. **THE PRESENCE OF GOD**
3. **TRUE WORSHIP**
4. **GOD IN RELIGION**
5. **THE CONSCIOUSNESS OF GOD**
6. **THE GOD OF PERSONALITY**

INTRODUCTION

I. *REFERENCE*: Page 62, ¶1 – "If the infinite mind..."

COMMENT

1. In the Adjusters God fraternizes with man. A fragment of God resides in man.

   A. *Fraternize*: "To associate or hold fellowship with as brothers or upon comradely terms; to have brotherly feelings."

   B. *Reside*: "To have an abiding place; to be present as an element; inhere as a quality; to be vested as a right—chiefly within."

2. Every normal-minded and morally conscious mortal has just such a God fragment.

II. *REFERENCE*: Page 62, ¶2 – "God has distributed..."

COMMENT

1. The infinity of God exists in his six absolutes—but he makes personal contact with us by means of his prepersonal spirit.

2. He also bestows personality upon us.

3. And then all of this is maintained by means of his personality circuit.

4. The six absolute co-ordinates:

   A. The Eternal Son.
   B. The Infinite Spirit.
   C. The Isle of Paradise.
   D. The Deity Absolute.
   E. The Universal Absolute.
   F. The Unqualified Absolute.

1. THE APPROACH TO GOD

I. *REFERENCE*: Page 62, ¶3 - "The inability of..."

COMMENT

1. God is not aloof—it is hard to approach him because of our limitations.

2. There is a great gulf between the highest and the lowest personalities in the universe.

3. If we were standing on Paradise today we would not see God.

4. Great changes must be made in us before we can see God.

II. *REFERENCE*: Page 62, ¶4 - "Our Father is not..."

COMMENT

1. The Father is not in hiding. He desires to reveal himself.

2. In the grandeur of his love God yearns to associate with his creatures.

3. Only our limitations keep us away from Deity.

III. *REFERENCE*: Page 63, ¶2 - "Although the approach..."

COMMENT

1. Our seeing the Father must await our attainment of the highest finite spiritualization.

2. But even now we can commune with his indwelling spirit.

IV. *REFERENCE*: Page 63, ¶3 - "The mortals of the realms..."

COMMENT

Mental, moral, or social status does not interfere with man's spiritual progress on the evolutionary worlds.

V. *REFERENCE*: Page 63, ¶4 - "However Urantia mortals..."

COMMENT

1. Regardless of human opportunities, man's spiritual endowment is uniform and equal.

2. Every mortal can accept the leading of the Mystery Monitors.

VI. *REFERENCE*: Page 63, ¶5 - "If mortal man..."

COMMENT

The indwelling Adjuster insures that every mortal can know God and strive to be more and more like him.

VII. *REFERENCE*: Page 63, ¶6 - "Man is spiritually indwelt..."

COMMENT

1. Our Adjusters are certain of survival.
2. If the soul is dedicated to doing the Father's will, there is no power in the cosmos that can prevent such a soul from ascending to Paradise.

VIII. *REFERENCE*: Page 63, ¶7 - "The Father desires..."

COMMENT

1. God craves personal contact with all his creatures.
2. There is a place on Paradise for all who have surviving qualities.
3. Settle it: God is attainable—the way is open.
4. Everything essential to Paradise ascension has been provided by the divine love.

IX. *REFERENCE*: Page 63, ¶8 - "The fact that..."

COMMENT

1. God's presence is real, notwithstanding that it takes a long time to find him in personality.
2. We can be sure of the progress from level to level on our Paradise journey to God.
3. The Thought Adjuster will return with us to the high spiritual level of its origin.

X. *REFERENCE*: Page 64, ¶2 - "The Father is not..."

COMMENT

God is not in hiding; we hide away from him in the mists of our own selfishness, perversity, and intolerance.

XI. *REFERENCE*: Page 64, ¶3 – "Mortal man may draw..."

COMMENT

1. Mortal man may forsake God many times and return as long as the power of choice remains.

    A. Difference between acute and chronic diseases.

    B. Habit formation.

    C. Time of irrevocable choice. Thought Adjuster fusion.

    D. The case of Lucifer.

2. Man's doom is sealed only when he has lost the power to choose.

3. God never closes his heart. It is man who closes his heart to all divine influences.

4. Man is lost only when he refuses to do the will of God.

    A. God-consciousness—to know God.

    B. God-oneness—righteousness.

        (1) Divinity of character.

        (2) Bearing fruits of the spirit.

        (3) Oneness with the Adjuster.

5. Adjuster fusion assures man's eternal destiny. The decision is irrevocable.

Note: The status of "irrevocable choice" pertains to the status of salvation as well as to that of destruction. That is:

    A. Lucifer can't (won't) repent.

    B. An Adjuster-fused mortal can't (won't) sin.

    C. The vital difference: In the one case free will ceases to function. In the other, it still operates, but has become eternally spiritualized.

XII. *REFERENCE*: Page 64, ¶4 – "The great God..."

COMMENT

1. God gives a part of his infinite self to live in man.

Note: The difference between selfhood and personality. The Thought Adjuster is not a part of the Father's personality, but *is* a part of his self. The Adjuster has individuality—selfhood—but not personality.

2. God has embarked on the eternal adventure with us.

3. If we yield to our spirit helpers we cannot fail to attain our Paradise destiny.

4. The secret of salvation is "yielding to spirit leadings."

A. The spirit *leads*—does not drive or compel—free will choosing.
B. Having yielded—you cannot fail.
C. Survival—if you want it—is sure, certain, and *simple*.
D. It would be easy if it were not for the doubts born of fear.

2. THE PRESENCE OF GOD

I. *REFERENCE*: Page 64, ¶5 - "The physical presence..."

COMMENT

1. The physical presence of God is the reality of the material cosmos. **Note**: God has a physical presence as well as a mind, spirit, personality, and selfhood (Adjuster) presence.

2. Deity mind presence is determined by depth of mentality and the personality level.

3. Spiritual presence is determined by spiritual capacity of receptivity and dedication to the Father's will.

4. Spirituality depends on two conditions:

   A. Actual capacity of spirit receptivity. Factual and literal. Dependence on antecedents.
   B. Consecration of creature will—free will on the spiritual level—to doing the Father's will. Definitions:
      (1) *CONSECRATE*: To dedicate—to devote to some purpose.
      (2) *DEDICATE*: To devote exclusively to the service of worship of a divine being.

II. *REFERENCE*: Page 64, ¶6 - "God lives in..."

COMMENT

1. God lives in everyone of his spirit-born sons.

2. The Paradise Sons always have access to the "right hand of the Father."

3. Let us make a study of the "right hand of God" in the Bible:

   Moses in his farewell address said: **Deut. 33:2**. *"'The Lord came from Sinai...with flaming fire at his right hand.'"*

   Symbol of Authority. Ps. 20:6. *"I know that the Lord will help his anointed...with mighty victories by his right hand."*

***Symbol of Power*. Ps. 63:8**. *"My soul clings to thee; thy right hand upholds me."*

***Symbol of Security*. Isa. 62:8**. *"The Lord has sworn by his right hand and by his mighty arm."*

***Symbol of Dependable Force*. Matt. 26:64**. *"'Hereafter you shall see the Son of man seated at the right hand of Power."* **Note:** This is the associated power of God the Father and God the Creator Son.

***Symbol of Sovereignty*. Mark 16:19**. *"So then the Lord Jesus, after he had spoken to them, was taken up into heaven, and sat down at the right hand of God."*

Peter, in discoursing on this elevation of Jesus, said: *Acts 2:33*. *"Being therefore exalted at the right hand of God."*

Paul envisaged Jesus as remaining at the Father's right hand—probably until his second coming. **See Rom. 8:34**. *"It is Christ Jesus…who is at the right hand of God, who indeed intercedes for us."*

That Paul conceived the "right hand of God" as symbolic of universe sovereignty is shown in **Eph. 1:20-22**. *"When he raised him from the dead and made him sit at his right hand in the heavenly places, far above all rule and authority and power and dominion, and above every name that is named, not only in this age but also in that which is to come; and he has put all things under his feet and has made him the head over all things."*

After all, Paul understood the *real* purpose of the bestowal. The theological twisting of the atonement doctrine was a compromise attempt to convert the Jews.

Other texts which show the belief that Jesus is *now* sitting at the "right hand of God" are:

Col. 3:1. *"If then you have been raised with Christ, seek the things that are above, where Christ is, seated at the right hand of God."*

Heb. 12:2. *"Looking to Jesus the pioneer and perfecter of our faith, who for the joy that was set before him endured the cross, despising the shame, and is seated at the right hand of the throne of God."*

Note: In Pauline philosophy the right hand of God is Salvington, headquarters of the local universe of Nebadon.

Note: It is the practice to raise the right hand in taking an oath.

4. "The bosom of the Father" refers to the personality circuit of God— no matter where communion may take place.

III. *REFERENCE*: Page 64, ¶7 – "The divine presence..."

COMMENT

1. The divine presence is best realized in communion with the Adjuster.

2. Dream not of God far off in the skies when he lives within you.

IV. *REFERENCE*: Page 64, ¶8 – "It is because..."

COMMENT

1. Adjusters assist us in making use of all spiritual influences which surround us.

2. Being more or less unconscious of the presence of the Adjuster does not disprove his reality.

3. Exceptional spiritual experience may occur at such a high level in the superconscious as to be wholly beyond conscious awareness, just as many human experiences transpire so deep in the subconscious as to elude all conscious recognition by the thinking levels of the mind.

4. Proof of fraternity with the Adjuster consists in "the fruits of the spirit." **Matt. 7:20.** *"Thus you will know them by their fruits."*

DISCUSSION OF FRUITS OF THE SPIRIT

1. **Luke 6:44.** *"Each tree is known by its own fruit."*

2. "The fruits of the spirit are the substance of the Supreme as he is realizable in human experience." p. 1290.

3. "The fruits of the spirit, your sincere and loving service, are the mighty social lever to uplift the races of darkness, and this Spirit of Truth will become your power-multiplying fulcrum." p. 1930.

4. Fruits of the spirit in the King James Version—**Gal. 5:22.**

    Love
    Joy
    Peace
    Long-suffering
    Gentleness
    Goodness
    Faith
    Meekness
    Temperance

5. Fruits of the spirit in the Revised Version.

    Love
    Joy

Peace
Patience
Kindness
Goodness
Faithfulness
Gentleness
Self-control

6. In *The Urantia Book* - p. 381. Exactly the same as in the King James Version—**Gal. 5:22**.

7. In *The Urantia Book* - p. 2054.

Loving service
Unselfish devotion
Courageous loyalty
Sincere fairness
Enlightened honesty
Undying hope
Confiding trust
Merciful ministry
Unfailing goodness
Forgiving tolerance
Enduring peace

8. As summarized on p. 648 of *The Urantia Book*.

Intellectual peace
Social progress
Moral satisfaction
Spiritual joy
Cosmic wisdom

Note: Goodness is found in four lists; peace is in all five.

9. **SUMMATION**

1. Love
2. Joy
3. Peace
4. Long-suffering
5. Patience
6. Gentleness
7. Kindness
8. Goodness
9. Faith
10. Faithfulness
11. Meekness
12. Temperance
13. Self-control
14. Service

15. Devotion
16. Loyalty
17. Fairness
18. Honesty
19. Hope
20. Trust
21. Ministry
22. Tolerance
23. Intellectual peace
24. Social progress
25. Moral satisfaction
26. Spiritual joy
27. Cosmic wisdom

V. *REFERENCE*: Page 65, ¶2 - "It is exceedingly difficult..."

COMMENT

1. It is difficult for the material mind to become conscious of the activities of divine entities like the Adjusters.

2. Increased spirituality enhances the recognition of the spiritual activities of the indwelling Monitors.

VI. *REFERENCE*: Page 65, ¶3 - "The entire experience..."

COMMENT

1. The experience of Adjuster communion involves:

    A. Mortal status.
    B. Motivation.
    C. Spiritual experience.

2. Such an attitude is not merely:

    A. Mild moral inclination.
    B. Intellectual wishfulness.
    C. Spiritual ecstasy.

3. The realization of the Adjuster is largely a matter of soul consciousness.

4. The proofs of all this inner experience are "the fruits of the spirit."

3. TRUE WORSHIP

I. *REFERENCE*: Page 65, ¶4 - "Though the Paradise Deities..."

COMMENT

1. There is a difference between the Deities in such matters as prayer, communion, and worship.

2. In the last analysis, we worship the Universal Father—and him only.

3. True, we do also worship the Father as revealed in his Creator Sons.

II. *REFERENCE*: Page 65, ¶5 - "Supplications of all kinds..."

COMMENT

1. Supplications belong to the realm of the Eternal Son.

2. Prayers (not adoration and worship) belong to the local universe—to the realm of the Creator Son.

3. What is the difference between supplication and prayer?

   A. *Supplication*. Act of humble and earnest entreaty. Prayer for mercy, aid, or some blessing. To implore God, Beseech, petition, importune, solicit, crave, beg.

   B. *Prayer*. An earnest request to someone for something. An entreaty. The act of addressing Divinity. A petition to God.

4. There seem to be three levels concerned in this discussion.

   A. *Supplication*: The lower levels of conscious and formal communion with Deity. The less articulate and more spontaneous expression of creature dependence upon the Creator. The more *emotional* type of Deity address.

   B. *Prayer*: The higher level of Deity communication. The more *intellectual* and better formulated appeal of man to God. A group could hardly supplicate, but they could agree on a prayer.

   C. *Worship*: The highest type of Deity communion. The more *spiritual* type of address to God. May have both emotional and intellectual content, but is predominately spiritual. Worship seeks and asks nothing specific for the worshipper.

5. Worship is recognized by the Adjuster and dispatched to the Father over his personality circuit.

   Question: How does a prepersonal entity function on a personality circuit? The Adjuster must be acting as vicegerent of the human personality.

6. Other word meanings:

   A. *Homage*. Solemn public ceremony by which a man acknowledges that he is the man of a lord, and promises faith and support in return for his lord's protection.

   B. *Worship*. Act of paying divine honors to Deity. The adoration or reverence paid to God. To adore, to venerate, to revere.

7. So all types of Father fragments are able to register the adoration of their subjects in the presence of the Universal Father.

8. Adjusters may also make use of prepersonal channels and the spirit gravity circuit of the Eternal Son.

Question: What are prepersonal channels of communication? Probably the omnipresence of God.

III. *REFERENCE*: Page 65, ¶6 - "Worship is for..."

COMMENT

1. Worship is for its own sake; prayer embodies a self- or creature-interest.

2. We worship God for what we comprehend him to be.

3. Worship asks nothing and expects nothing for the worshipper.

4. We freely worship God because of his lovable nature and adorable attributes.

IV. *REFERENCE*: Page 65, ¶7 - "The moment the element..."

COMMENT

1. When self-interest intrudes—that moment worship translates to prayer.

2. But it is proper to address prayer to the Father as a part of true worship.

V. *REFERENCE*: Page 66, ¶2 - "When you deal..."

COMMENT

1. In our daily living we are dealing with the personalities of the Infinite Spirit.

2. Worship the Father. Pray to the Sons. Work out the details of living with the children of the Infinite Spirit.

VI. *REFERENCE*: Page 66, ¶3 - "The Creator or Sovereign Sons..."

COMMENT

1. The Creator Son of the local universe stands in the place of both the Universal Father and the Eternal Son.

2. These Creator Sons give ear to both the worship of the Father and the supplications of their universe children.

3. To local universe citizens, the Creator Son is, to all practical purposes, God.

4. The Infinite Spirit keeps in touch with the children of a local universe through the Creative Mother Spirit.

VII. *REFERENCE*: Page 66, ¶4 - "Sincere worship connotes..."

COMMENT

1. Worship connotes all powers of personality functioning under the dominance of the soul and directionized by the Adjuster.

2. Mortal mind can never become highly conscious of the reality of worship.

3. It is the evolving soul that is able to realize the reality of worship.

4. Soul growth occurs independently of self-consciousness.

VIII. *REFERENCE*: Page 66, ¶5 - "The worship experience..."

COMMENT

1. In worship, the Adjuster is attempting to express the aspirations of the human soul.

2. There must be two phases of worship:
   A. The conscious—the spiritual upreach of man's mind.
   B. The superconscious—the attempt of the Adjuster to tell God about the status and attitude of the evolving soul.

3. There are three phases of the relation of man to his Maker:
   A. Supplication—his emotional expression.
   B. Prayer—the intellectual life.
   C. Worship—expression of the soul. Spiritual. (Morontial?)

4. Considering all, no wonder worship is largely unconscious.

5. Note that the evolving soul experiences "inexpressible longings and unutterable aspirations." (See Rom. 8:26.)

6. The Adjuster may not always succeed in his efforts—but he does *attempt*.

7. Worship is the act of the mind assenting to the attempt of the soul under the guidance of the Adjuster to communicate with the Universal Father as a faith son.

8. Note the steps in worship:
   A. The material conscious mind *acts*.

    B.   This *act* of mind—not thought, wish, or longing—consists in *assenting* to something.

    C.   This something is: The attempt of the *soul* (its spiritualizing self) to communicate with God.

    D.   This soul thus communicates as "a faith son" of the Universal Father.

    E.   The mind assents to this adventure with the understanding that the whole transaction will be carried out "under the guidance" of the Adjuster—the "associated spirit."

9.   Thus the technique of worship is performed by means of the following:

    A.   The mortal mind consents to worship.

    B.   The immortal soul craves worship.

    C.   The divine Adjuster conducts this worship.

    D.   All this is in behalf of the mortal mind and the evolving immortal soul.

10. True worship, in the last analysis, becomes an experience realized on four cosmic levels:

    A.   The intellectual.

    B.   The morontial.

    C.   The spiritual.

    D.   The personal.

11. And all of this embraces the consciousness of mind, soul, and spirit—and their unification in and as *personality*.

DISCUSSION OF WORSHIP

1.   Worship is the sincere pursuit of divine values. p. 195.

2.   Personal communion with reality. p. 2095.

3.   Primitive worship insurance against misfortune. p. 962.

4.   Worship deals directly with God. p. 66.

5.   Worship is spiritual communion. p. 1133.

6.   Prayer can lead to worship. p. 1621.

7.   Source of the worship urge. p. 950.

8.   Worship yields spiritual strength. p. 1777.

9.   Adjuster's part in worship. p. 66.

10. Jesus' teaching about worship. p. 1616.

11. Worship on Paradise. p. 304.

12. Worship as related to mysticism. p. 1100.

13. Worship in the Bible.

    A. **Private worship**.

        Ps. 111:1. *"I will give thanks to the Lord with my whole heart."*
        Phil. 3:3. *"Who worship God in spirit."*(**John 4:23.**)
        Ps. 7:17. *"I will give to the Lord the thanks due to his righteousness."*
        Ps. 29:2. *"Worship the Lord in holy array."*
        Note: The psalms of praise are: **100, 104, 113-118, 136, 145, 150.**

    B. **Public worship**.

        Ps. 22:22. *"In the midst of the congregation I will praise thee."*
        Ps. 89:5. *"Let the heavens praise thy wonders, O Lord, thy faithfulness in the assembly of the holy ones."*
        Ps. 5:7. *"I...will enter thy house, I will worship toward thy holy temple."*
        Luke 18:10. *"'Two men went up into the temple to pray.'"*
        Heb. 10:25. *"Not neglecting to meet together."*
        Ps. 107:32. *"Let them extol him in the congregation of the people, and praise him in the assembly."*
        Note: Praise and adoration are a part of worship, but the word "adoration" does not appear in the King James Version. Praise is an attitude ranging somewhere between prayer and worship, and is related to thanks-giving.

4. GOD IN RELIGION

I. *REFERENCE*: Page 66, ¶6 - "The morality of the religions..."

COMMENT

1. Evolutionary religion *drives* men to seek God because of fear.

2. Religions of revelation *allure* men to seek God because they crave to become like him.

3. Religion is not just a feeling of passive security—it is a dynamic experience of divinity attainment predicated on humanity service.

II. *REFERENCE*: Page 66, ¶7 - "The great and immediate service..."

COMMENT

1. The mission of true religion is:

    A. Unity in human experience.
    B. Lasting peace.
    C. Profound assurance.

2. Man comes to regard God as:

    A. Reality of values.
    B. Substance of meanings.
    C. Life of truth.

3. This means: God is the reality, substance, and life of value, meanings, and truth.

III. *REFERENCE*: Page 67, ¶2 - "God is not only..."

COMMENT

1. God is the determiner of destiny—he is man's destiny.

2. Without religion, man seeks to bend the universe to his service; with religion man bends himself to the service of the universe.

IV. *REFERENCE*: Page 67, ¶3 - "The domains of philosophy..."

COMMENT

Art and philosophy function in the realm between science and religion—pointing man toward spiritual realities and eternal meanings.

V. *REFERENCE*: Page 67, ¶4 - "All religions teach..."

COMMENT

1. All religions teach the worship of Deity and some scheme of human salvation.

2. What the religious promise:

    A. **Buddhist**—Peace, salvation from suffering.
    B. **Jewish**—Prosperity, salvation from difficulties.
    C. **Greek**—Beauty, salvation from disharmony.

    D.   **Christian**—Sanctity, salvation from sin.

    E.   **Islam**—Deliverance from the rigorous moral standards of Judaism and Christianity.

3.   The religion of Jesus is:

    A.   Salvation from self.

    B.   Deliverance from the isolation of individuality in time and eternity.

4.   The religion of Jesus is not merely the promise of something—it *is* something.

5.   The greatest evil of time and eternity is the isolation of the self.

VI. REFERENCE: Page 67, ¶5 - "The Hebrews based.:."

COMMENT

What religion is based on:

    1.   **Hebrews**—goodness.

    2.   **Greeks**—beauty.

    3.   **Christians**—truth.

    4.   **Jesus**—revelation of a God of love.

   Note: Love is all-embracing of truth, beauty, and goodness.

VII. REFERENCE: Page 67, ¶6 - "The Zoroastrians had..."

COMMENT

1.   Basis of still other religions:

    A.   **Zoroastrians**—morals.

    B.   **Hindus**—metaphysics.

    C.   **Confucianists**—ethics.

2.   Jesus lived a religion of *service*.

3.   The value of any religion consists in its validity of approach to Jesus.

4.   Religion unifies the good, true, and beautiful in human experience.

VIII. REFERENCE: Page 67, ¶7 - "The Greek religion..."

COMMENT

1.   The slogans of religion:

    A.   **Greeks**—Know yourself.

    B.   **Hebrews**—Know your God.

    C.   **Christians**—Know the Lord Jesus Christ.

    D.   **Jesus**—Know God and yourself as a son of God.

2. These differing attitudes determine the nature and depth of our habits of worship.

3. The spiritual status of any religion is determined by the nature of its prayers.

IX. *REFERENCE*: Page 67, ¶8 - "The concept of a..."

COMMENT

1. Anthropomorphism represents the transition from polytheism to monotheism.

2. Christianity presents the highest anthropomorphism—elevation of the ideal of the human to the concept of the glorified Christ.

X. *REFERENCE*: Page 67, ¶9 - "The Christian concept of God..."

COMMENT

Christians try to combine three concepts:

A. A righteous God—Hebrew.

B. A God of wisdom—Greek.

C. A loving Father—Jesus.

XI. *REFERENCE*: Page 68, ¶2 - "It must therefore..."

COMMENT

1. Composite Christianity encounters difficulty in attaining consistency.

2. The doctrines of early Christianity were based upon the personal experience of three persons:

   A. Philo of Alexandria.
   B. Jesus of Nazareth.
   C. Paul of Tarsus.

XII. *REFERENCE*: Page 68, ¶3 - "In the study..."

COMMENT

1. View the life of Jesus positively—think not so much of his sinlessness as his righteousness—his life of loving service.

2. Jesus upstepped the passive love of the Hebrew God to the higher and *active* love of the heavenly Father for *every* creature.

5. THE CONSCIOUSNESS OF GOD

I. *REFERENCE*: Page 68, ¶4 - "Morality has its origin..."

COMMENT

1. While morality is superanimal, it is wholly evolutionary in origin.

   Note: Morality is not merely a sex attitude.

2. Human evolution enjoys the ministry of all endowments antecedent to the bestowal of the Adjusters and the Spirit of Truth.
   Note: The Life Carriers *folded up* the evolutionary patterns—we observe them unfolding.

3. The struggles of mortal existence:

   A. Resisting the physical environment.
   B. Ethical adjustments of social surroundings.
   C. Reason choices of the moral situation.
   D. The demands of spiritual experience.

II. *REFERENCE*: Page 68, ¶5 - "Religion is not..."

COMMENT

1. Religion appears in all stages of postmoral evolution.

2. Religion is not grounded on:

   A. The facts of science.
   B. Social obligations.
   C. Philosophic assumptions.
   D. Duties of morality.

3. Religion may permeate all four levels of cosmic values:

   A. Physical level of self-preservation.
   B. Emotional social level of fellowship.
   C. Moral level of reason.
   D. Spiritual level of worship.

III. *REFERENCE*: Page 68, ¶6 - "The fact-seeking scientist..."

COMMENT

How God is regarded:

1. Scientist—First Cause, God of force.

2. Artist—God of beauty, aesthetics.

3. Philosopher—God of unity.

4. Religionist—Father, God of love.

IV. REFERENCE: Page 68, ¶7 - "Moral conduct is..."

COMMENT

1. Moral conduct is always antecedent to religion, but it is not the whole of religious experience.

2. Social service depends on moral thinking and religious living.

3. Adoration of beauty and reverence for nature or unity are not worship.

V. REFERENCE: Page 68, ¶8 - "Evolutionary religion is..."

COMMENT

1. Evolutionary religion is the mother of science, art, and philosophy.

2. Evolutionary religion prepared man for revelation and the Spirit of Truth.

3. Human experience begins with evolutionary religion and ends with revelatory religion.

4. Religion is normal and natural, but it is optional—man does not have to be religious.

VI. REFERENCE: Page 69, ¶2 - "Religious experience..."

COMMENT

1. Religious experience, being spiritual, is not fully understood by the material mind—hence theology—the psychology of religion.

2. The paradox of religion is God's immanence and transcendence.

3. Definitions:

    IMMANENCE: *Urantia Book*. God within and a part of every individual.

    > *Webster*. The indwelling presence of God in the world--including man.
    > Note differing concepts of idealists, realists, and pantheists. Theists hold that God is present more with the personal than the impersonal.

    TRANSCENDENCE: *Urantia Book*. The divine domination of the universe of universes.

    > *Webster*. Relation of God to the universe of physical things and finite spirits, as being, in his essential nature, prior to it. Exalted above it, and having real being apart from it.

4. These concepts of Deity—immanence and transcendence—are unified by faith, through worship and the hope of survival.

5. The paradoxes of religion derive from the fact that such realities are beyond mortal comprehension.

VII. *REFERENCE*: Page 69, ¶3 - "Mortal man secures..."

COMMENT

Even on earth man gets intellectual, philosophical, and spiritual satisfaction from his religious experience.

VIII. *REFERENCE*: Page 69, ¶4 - "God-consciousness..."

COMMENT

1. God-consciousness consists of three levels of reality realization:

   A. Mind consciousness—the *idea* of God.

   B. Soul consciousness—the *ideal* of God.

   C. Spirit consciousness—the realization of the spirit *reality* of God.

2. The unification of these concepts in the mind of a finaliter may eventuate in the realization of the *ultimacy* of God.

IX. *REFERENCE*: Page 69, ¶5 - "The experience of..."

COMMENT

1. Time does not change God-consciousness—but it should change philosophical concepts and theologic definitions.

2. Religious experience is real—but it should not be apart from the totality of human experience.

X. *REFERENCE*: Page 69, ¶6 - "Eternal survival of personality..."

COMMENT

1. When the mind believes God and the soul knows God, and with the Adjuster they all *desire* God—then survival is assured.

2. The Adjuster is the potential of a surviving immortal soul.

3. The presence of the divine spirit cannot be invalidated by:

   A. Limitation of intellect.

   B. Curtailment of education.

    C.   Deprivation of culture.

    D.   Impoverishment of social status.

    E.   Inferiority of moral standards.

XI. *REFERENCE*: Page 70, ¶2 - "The ability of mortal parents..."

COMMENT

1. The ability of parents to procreate is not dependent on educational, social, or economic status.

2. A moral human mind and the Adjuster can foster a surviving soul.

3. The secret of it all is the desire to do the will of the Father in heaven.

6. THE GOD OF PERSONALITY

I. *REFERENCE*: Page 70, ¶3 - "The Universal Father..."

COMMENT

1. The Universal Father is the God of personality.

2. All personality has its center and circumference in God.

    A.   Center—Paradise Father.

    B.   Circumference—personality circuit.

3. God is the origin, conservation, and destiny of God-craving personalities.

II. *REFERENCE*: Page 70, ¶4 - "Personality is one..."

COMMENT

1. Personality is one of the unsolved mysteries of the universe.

2. We can form concepts of many factors composing personality: physical, chemical, mental, social, moral, and spiritual.

III. *REFERENCE*: Page 70, ¶5 - "Personality is potential..."

COMMENT

1. Personality is potential in all creatures with a mind endowment ranging from self-consciousness to God-consciousness.

2. Personality is exclusively bestowed by God upon living energy systems.

3. The other-than-personal never attains the personal except by direct act of God.

IV. *REFERENCE*: Page 70, ¶6 - "The bestowal of personality..."

COMMENT

1. Personalization of living energy systems endows them with relative creative consciousness and free will.

2. There is no personality apart from God and all personality exists for God.

V. *REFERENCE*: Page 70, ¶7 - "The Adjusters of prepersonal..."

COMMENT

1. The Adjuster is the potential of morontia survival and ultimate spirit attainment.

2. Such a survivor can aspire to the destiny of the Ultimate—even the Absolute.

VI. *REFERENCE*: Page 71, ¶1 - "Capacity for Divine..."

COMMENT

1. Capacity for personality is inherent in the Adjuster and potential in cosmic mind endowment.

2. Experiential personality is associated with self-consciousness and self-determination.

3. The material self is unqualifiedly personal.

VII. *REFERENCE*: Page 71, ¶2 - "The material self..."

COMMENT

1. The material self has personality and temporal identity.

2. The Adjuster has eternal identity, but only potential personality.

3. The union of these two can create the surviving soul.

VIII.*REFERENCE*: Page 71, ¶3 - "The material self..."

COMMENT

1. God has so liberated man from all material fetters that he can will the creation of his immortal soul.

2. When man so wills, no power in the universe can interfere with the evolution of the soul.

3. As pertains to survival, man's will is sovereign by the absolute decree of God.

IX. *REFERENCE*: Page 71, ¶4 – "The bestowal of..."

COMMENT

1. All personalities are ever drawn toward the personality of the Paradise Father.

2. There is a kinship of divine spontaneity in all personality.

X. *REFERENCE*: Page 71, ¶5 – "The personality circuit..."

COMMENT

The personalities of the universe are a part of God's self-consciousness, apart from the mission of the Thought Adjusters.

XI. *REFERENCE*: Page 71, ¶6 – "As all gravity..."

Just as the gravity and mind circuits operate, the personality circuit functions to transmit our worship.

XII. *REFERENCE*: Page 71, ¶7 – "Concerning those personalities..."

COMMENT

1. Even creatures who do not have Adjusters are embraced in the Father's personality circuit.

2. God provides for the sovereign choice of all true personalities.

3. The portal of eternity opens to the freewill choice of the free will sons of the God of free will.

XIII. *REFERENCE*: Page 72, ¶1 – "And this represents..."

COMMENT

The conclusion of the whole matter is: God is our Father—we are all his planetary children.

DISCUSSION OF PERSONALITY AND INDIVIDUALITY

1. Personality is an endowment of will creatures and other types of superfinite beings.

2. Animals do not have personality, but they do possess *individuality*.

3. There are a host of beings in the universe who are not personal. There are also superpersonal and subpersonal beings.

4. Thought Adjusters do not have personality.

PAPER 6
The Eternal Son

PAPER 6
The Eternal Son

1. **IDENTITY OF THE ETERNAL SON**
2. **NATURE OF THE ETERNAL SON**
3. **MINISTRY OF THE FATHER'S LOVE**
4. **ATTRIBUTES OF THE ETERNAL SON**
5. **LIMITATIONS OF THE ETERNAL SON**
6. **THE SPIRIT MIND**
7. **PERSONALITY OF THE ETERNAL SON**
8. **REALIZATION OF THE ETERNAL SON**

INTRODUCTION

I. *REFERENCE*: Page 73, ¶1 - "The Eternal Son..."

COMMENT

1. The Eternal Son is the perfect expression of the Father's "first" personal and infinite concept.

   Definition of concept: "Original idea; purpose; design."

2. Note that "first" is in quotes. What does that signify? The dictionary gives six uses of quotes in this manner:

   A. Technical or slang terms.
   B. Nicknames.
   C. Expressions of doubtful propriety.
   D. Expressions for which the writer apologizes.
   E. That for which he disavows responsibility.
   F. Words which have special *meanings*.

3. The Son is a *perfect* expression of something which is both personal and infinite—an infinite personality.

4. He is also the *final* expression—not the beginning or the end, but the *completed*. One of the definitions of final is: "Conclusive; decisive; definitive."

5. **Note:** This was not the first concept of the I AM or the First Source and Center—but of the Universal Father.

6. **Query:** The First Source and Center could not be a Father until he had a Son. Since he has always had a Son he has always been a Father. This explains the use of quotes with the term "first" personal and infinite concept.

7. Again, we encounter the attempt of the authors to make eternal conceptions "graspable" by time-bound mortal mind.

8. Note the term "expression"—the introduction of the thought-word concept. The Father personally expresses himself through the Eternal Son—the divine WORD.

    See John 1:1-4. *"In the beginning was the Word, and the Word was with God, and the Word was God. He was in the beginning with God; all things were made through him, and without him was not anything made that was made. In him was life, and the life was the light of men."*

    This WORD concept is shown in other Scriptures. **See 1 John 5:7.** (King James) *"For there are three that bear record in heaven, the Father, the Word, and the Holy Ghost: and these three are one."*

9. The Eternal Son is residential on Paradise, enshrouding the personal presence of the Universal Father.

II. *REFERENCE*: Page 73, ¶2 - "We speak of..."

COMMENT

1. Talking about God's "first" thought is a contact-compromise with the time-bound mortal mind.

2. In fact, God never could have had a first thought—the Eternal Son could never have had a beginning.

3. Only in philosophy can we conceive of a beginning. Neither can we conceive of future eternity without an *end*.

4. The author was told to portray the eternity doings of Deity so as to reach the finite mortal mind. **Question:** Who instructed him? Probably the Revelatory Commission.

III. *REFERENCE*: Page 73, ¶3 - "The Eternal Son..."

COMMENT

1. The Eternal Son is the Father's spiritual personalization of:
    A. Divine reality.
    B. Unqualified spirit.
    C. Absolute personality.
2. The Father's Concept is:
    A. Universal--scope.
    B. Infinite--value.
3. This concept of the Father has three meanings:
    A. Divine reality--universal and infinite.

    B.   Unqualified spirit—universal and infinite.

    C.   Absolute personality—universal and infinite.

4.   The Son is the revelation of the creator identity of the Universal Father.

5.   The Son's personality discloses that the Father is the source of all meanings and values of the:

    A.   Spiritual.

    B.   Volitional.

    C.   Purposeful.

    D.   Personal.

6.   The Father is the *source*:

    A.   Eternal—time value.

    B.   Universal—space value.

7.   **Definitions**:

MEANING: "That which is intended; purpose; aim; object; that which one intends to convey by an act, significance, understanding, purport."

VALUE: "Non-material meaning. The quality or fact of being worthwhile. Excellent, useful, desirable. Principle, quality, importance, intrinsic worth."

8.   Meanings and values of what?

    A.   The spiritual.

        (1) Meaning: Eternal and universal.

        (2) Value: Eternal and universal.

    B.   The volitional.

        (1) Meaning: Eternal and universal.

        (2) Value: Eternal and universal.

    C.   The purposeful.

        (1) Meaning: Eternal and universal.

        (2) Value: Eternal and universal.

    D.   The personal.

        (1) Meaning: Eternal and universal.

        (2) Value: Eternal and universal.

9.   All of this is what the perfect personality of the Son tells us about the Father as the source of all such meanings and values.

IV. *REFERENCE*: Page 73, ¶4 - "In an effort..."

COMMENT

1. We refer to the Father's *first* thoughts and acts in order to help the finite mind to form some conception of the performances of infinity.

2. Since man cannot understand the eternity relations of Deity, we try to portray Deity relations in the eras of times.

3. We are taught that the Son sprang from the Father, but that both, are unqualifiedly eternal.

4. But no time-creature can ever fully comprehend such a mystery.

1. IDENTITY OF THE ETERNAL SON

I. *REFERENCE*: Page 73, ¶5 - "The Eternal Son..."

COMMENT

1. The Eternal Son is the original and only-begotten Son of God.

    Discussion: A number of texts are involved in this statement.
    John 1:18. *"No one has ever seen God; the only Son, who is in the bosom of the Father, he has made him known."*

    How true: The Eternal Son enshrouds the Father. This is a direct attempt to separate the concepts of Michael and the Eternal Son.

    John 3:16. *"For God so loved the world that he gave his only Son, that whoever believes in him should not perish but have eternal life."*
    Note: This passage does not appear in *The Urantia Book*.

    1 John 4:9. *"God sent his only Son into the world, so that we might live through him."*
    Note: This is not a *fact*—but how *true*.

2. The office of the Eternal Son:

    A. God the Son.
    B. Second Person of Deity.
    C. Associate creator of all things.
    D. The Second Great Source and Center.

II. *REFERENCE*: Page 74, ¶1 - "The Eternal Son..."

COMMENT

1. The Eternal Son is the spirit center and divine administrator of the universal spiritual government.
    Note: While the Son is cocreator, he is spiritual administrator in his own right.

2. God is spirit and the Son is a personal revelation of that spirit.
    Note: There are many revelations of God's spirit which are not personal—the Thought Adjusters.

3. The First Source and Center is the Volitional Absolute; the Second Source and Center is the Personality Absolute.
    Note: And yet he alone does not create personalities as we understand.

III. *REFERENCE*: Page 74, Par. 2 - "The Universal Father..."

COMMENT

1. God does not function as a personal creator without the Son.
    Question: Does God function other than as a personal creator? Perhaps in the Absolutes.

2. The Bible reference is **John 1:1-3**. *"In the beginning was the Word, and the Word was with God, and the Word was God. All things were made through him, and without him was not anything made that was made."*

IV. *REFERENCE*: Page 74, Par. 3 - "When a Son..."

COMMENT

1. The Bible reference is **1 John 1:1**. *"That which was from the beginning, which we have heard, which we have seen with our eyes, which we have looked upon and touched with our hands, concerning the word of life."*

2. One of the prayers of this Son implies he came from the Father as did the Original Son.
    John 17:5. *"And now, Father, glorify thou me in thy own presence with the glory which I had with thee before the world was made."*

V. *REFERENCE*: Page 74, Par. 4 - "The Eternal Son..."

COMMENT

1. Different names of the Eternal Son are listed.

2. In our universe he is called the Second Eternal Source and Center.

3. Note confusion of the Eternal Son with Michael of Nebadon, only on our planet.

VI. *REFERENCE*: Page 74, Par. 5 - "Although any of the..."

COMMENT

Only the Original Son is called the Eternal Son.

2. NATURE OF THE ETERNAL SON

I. *REFERENCE*: Page 74, Par. 6 - "The Eternal Son is just..."

Comment

1. The Son, like the Father, is changeless, and is just as truly an unlimited spirit.
2. To mortals the Son might appear to be even more personal than the Father.

II. *REFERENCE*: Page 74, Par. 7 - "The Eternal Son is the..."

Comment

1. The Eternal Son is the Word of God--God personally manifest to the universes.
   Note: The Word of God is living, personal, infinite—even absolute—not human verbiage mandated by some human council.
2. The Bible reference is **John 14:9**. *"Jesus said to him, 'Have I been with you so long, and yet you do not know me, Philip? He who has seen me has seen the Father.'"*

III. *REFERENCE*: Page 74, Par. 8 - "In nature the Son..."

Comment

God the Son is just as divinely real and eternal in nature as God the Father.

IV. *REFERENCE*: Page 75, Par. 1 - "The Son not only possesses..."

Comment

1. The Son shares the Father's righteousness and holiness.
2. The Son, like the Father, assists all creatures seeking perfection.

V. *REFERENCE*: Page 75, Par. 2 - "The Eternal Son possesses..."

Comment

The Son shares the Father's attributes and is the embodiment of his absolute personality.

VI. *REFERENCE*: Page 75, Par. 3 - "God is, indeed..."

Comment

1. The spirit nature of the Father is personalized in the Deity of the Eternal Son.

2. All spiritual qualities appear to be enhanced in the Son.

3. As the Father shares his nature with the Son, in turn, the Son just as fully shares the divine spirit with the Conjoint Actor.

VII. *REFERENCE*: Page 75, ¶4 - "In the love of truth..."

COMMENT

The Son is devoted to the realization of the spirit beauty of universe values.

VIII. *REFERENCE*: Page 75, ¶5 - "In divine goodness..."

COMMENT

God loves his creatures as a father. The Son loves us as a father and as a brother.

3. MINISTRY OF THE FATHER'S LOVE

I. *REFERENCE*: Page 75, ¶6 - "The Son shares..."

COMMENT

1. The Son shares the justice of the Trinity, but overshadows it with the Father's love and mercy.

2. Administration of justice is a group function—illustration:
   A. The Trinity.
   B. Three Ancients of Days.
   C. Conciliating Commissions.

3. *Overshadow*: Definition. "To cover protectingly with a superior influence. To tower above; to dominate; to be more important than."

4. All of the Paradise Sons are a divine personalization of the Father's love, but not an *infinite* personalization.

5. Christ Michael, who personally reveals the Father's love to our universe, reveals it just as fully as would the Eternal Son.

6. As God is love, so the Son is mercy.

7. The Son cannot love more than the Father. But he can show mercy in one additional way—he is not only a creator, but also a son.

II. *REFERENCE*: Page 75, ¶7 - "The Eternal Son..."

COMMENT

1. The Eternal Son is the mercy minister to all creation.

2.   The Son is not merely merciful—he is a *mercy minister*.

3.   Mercy is the essence of the Son's character.

     ESSENCE: Definition. "Substance as distinguished from all support-
     ing attributes. Prime character. Ultimate or intrinsic nature."

4.   Mandates of the Eternal Son are keyed in tones of mercy.

     KEY: Definition. "A system of family tones based on their relation to
     a keynote. The total harmonic or melodic relations of such a system."

III. *REFERENCE*: Page 75, ¶8 - "To comprehend the love..."

COMMENT

The love which the son receives from the Father, who *is* love, he bestows
by means of a host of ministering personalities.

IV. *REFERENCE*: Page 75, ¶9 - "The ministry of the..."

COMMENT

1.   The Son is devoted to revealing a God of love to the universes.

2.   The Son does not function as a mediator—he is a revealer.

3.   The Father's love is the real and eternal source of the Son's mercy.

V. *REFERENCE*: Page 75, ¶10 - "God is love..."

COMMENT

1.   God is love, the Son is mercy. Mercy is applied love.

2.   God's love might be compared to a Father's affection—the Son's love
     to that of a mother.

4. ATTRIBUTES OF THE ETERNAL SON

I. *REFERENCE*: Page 76, ¶2 - "The Eternal Son..."

COMMENT

1.   The Eternal Son motivates the spirit level of cosmic reality. ·

2.   His spiritual power is *absolute* concerning *actuals*.

3.   The Son's grasp of spirit gravity is also absolute.

4.   This gives the Son control over all spirit energy and actualized spirit
     reality.

5. All pure unfragmented spirit and all spirit beings and values are responsive to the Son.

6. **Question**: These three realities are responsive, but is the degree of control different?

7. Adjusters may also be responsive, but not controlled.

8. The Son's spirit gravity and spirit power are adequate for the administration of an infinite universe.

9. Note that spirit gravity and spirit power are not identical.

II. *REFERENCE*: Page 76, ¶3 - "The Son is..."

COMMENT

1. The Son is omnipotent only in the spiritual realm.

2. The Deities are not given to useless duplication of universe ministry.

III. *REFERENCE*: Page 76, ¶4 - "The omnipresence of..."

COMMENT

1. The omnipresence of the Original Son constitutes the spiritual unity of the universe.

2. It is difficult to differentiate the presence of the spirit of the Father and the Son.

3. The Father's spirit lives in the Son's spirit.

IV. *REFERENCE*: Page 76, ¶5 - "The Father must be..."

COMMENT

When the spirit of the Father and the spirit of the Son are both present, they are co-ordinate.

V. *REFERENCE*: Page 76, ¶6 - "In his contact..."

COMMENT

1. The Father contacts personality by means of the personality circuit and the Father spirit fragments.

2. Always does the spirit of the Son function with the spirit of the Father.

3. Father fragments have a special and exclusive function—solitary and unique.

Definitions:

SOLITARY: "Being, living, or going alone—without companions. Characterized by seclusion—solitude."

UNIQUE: "Single, sole. Being without a like or equal. Single inkind or excellence. Unequaled. Unusual; notable."

EXCLUSIVE: "Single, sole, an exclusive agent. Singly, devoted. Undivided—giving exclusive attention to a matter."

VI. REFERENCE: Page 76, ¶7 - "Spiritually the Eternal Son..."

COMMENT

1. Spiritually the Eternal Son is omnipresent.
2. The Son's spirit is around us, but not within us.
3. The Adjusters help us to be more responsive to the Son's spirit-gravity circuit.

VII. REFERENCE: Page 76, ¶8 - "The Original Son..."

COMMENT

1. The Original Son is spiritually and universally self-conscious.
2. What is self-consciousness?
    A. *CONSCIOUSNESS*: "Awareness, especially of something within oneself. Mind in the broadest possible sense. That form of existence which is able to distinguish itself from other existences. The totality of conscious status."
    B. *SELF-CONSCIOUSNESS*: "Consciousness of one's acts or states as belonging to, or originating in oneself. Consciousness of oneself as an object of observation by others. Awareness of oneself as an individual who experiences, desires, and acts."
    C. Note: The papers say animals are conscious—but not self-conscious.
3. In wisdom, the Son equals the Father.
4. The Son is equal with the Father in omniscience--he knows all.

VIII. REFERENCE: Page 77, ¶1 - "The Father and..."

COMMENT

1. Both the Father and the Son know the whereabouts of all spirits and spiritualized beings in the universe.
2. The Son is also cognizant of all that passes over the reflectivity service.

3. The Son has an omnipresent spirit.
   Question: Is this separate from the spirit gravity circuit? It appears to be.

4. It may be that the spirit gravity circuit is a specialized phenomenon occurring *within*, and as a part of, the Son's universally manifested spirit, just as the Gulf Stream functions in, and is a part of, the Atlantic Ocean.

5. **Another Question:** If infinite beings have such perfect techniques for knowing all things, why should they make use of such partial information as is supplied by the reflectivity system?

   Answer: All of finity is a part of the *experience* of infinity. The Infinite God is no wiser because he indwells mortal man, but the Universal Father has a new experience in the life of each one of us.

6. And there are other ways in which the Paradise Son is omniscient.
   A. Universal mind of the Infinite Spirit.
   B. Infinity of the First Source and Center.

IX. *REFERENCE*: Page 77, ¶2 - "The Eternal Son..."

COMMENT

The Eternal Son is just as affectionate as the Universal Father and just as kind and patient as the Paradise Sons who bestow themselves upon the evolutionary worlds.

X. *REFERENCE*: Page 77, ¶3 - "It is needless..."

COMMENT

If you study the attributes of God the Father, you will know the attributes of God the Son.

5. LIMITATIONS OF THE ETERNAL SON

I. *REFERENCE*: Page 77, ¶4 - "The Eternal Son..."

COMMENT

1. The Eternal Son does not function in the physical domain, nor in the mind realms.

2. The Son does function in the domains of spiritual omniscience, omnipotence, and omnipresence.

II. *REFERENCE*: Page 77, ¶5 – "The Eternal Son does not personally pervade..."

COMMENT

1. The Eternal Son does not pervade the potentials of the Deity Absolute, but when these spirit potentials become *actuals*, the spirit gravity acts.

2. What is the difference between potentials and actuals?
    Illustration: Potential energy is subject to Paradise gravity, but not to *linear gravity*.

III. *REFERENCE*: Page 77, ¶6 – "Personality is the..."

COMMENT

1. Personality derives from the Father—the Son does not bestow personality.

2. We know of no personalities derived from the Son. There may be some unknown type of Son-created beings living on the Son's Paradise spheres.

3. The Son creates a host of spirits. If they become personalities, it is by act of the Father or the Infinite Spirit.

4. The Son is thus a cocreator of personality. He is creator of many types of other than personal reality.

IV. *REFERENCE*: Page 77, ¶7 – "The Eternal Son is limited..."

COMMENT

1. The Eternal Son is limited in transmittal of a creator prerogatives.

    PREROGATIVE: "The right is to exercise a power in priority to, or to the exclusion of, others. The right attached to an office or rank. To exercise a special function, an official and hereditary right which may be asserted without question."

2. The Father and the Son join in producing Sons with creative attributes.

3. But with these co-ordinate Sons, the prerogatives of creatorship are not transmissable.

4. Thus Creator Sons receive the prerogatives of creatorship, but they do not transmit the same to their sons.

5. **Note**: The Father Melchizedek does participate in the creation of his order.

V. *REFERENCE*: Page 78, ¶1 - "The Eternal Son..."

COMMENT

1. The Eternal Son cannot fragmentize his nature, as does the Father and the Infinite Spirit.

2. The Gods bestow themselves upon entities as well as beings.

    ENTITY: "Being; existence; essence. That of which predictions can be made. An existence—whether an actuality or an ideal conception."

3. *The Urantia Book* uses entity to denote a being who is not a personality—Thought Adjuster, for example.

4. The Son bathes all creation in his spirit and draws all spirit realities to himself.

VI. *REFERENCE*: Page 78, ¶2 - "Ever remember..."

COMMENT

1. The Son is the personal portrayer of the Father to all creation.

2. In the Deity sense, the Son is personal and nothing but personal.

3. Such an absolute personality cannot be fragmentized.

4. God the Father and God the Spirit are truly personal, but they are also everything else in addition to being personal.

VII. *REFERENCE*: Page 78, ¶3 - "Though the Eternal Son..."

COMMENT

1. The Son does not participate in the bestowal of Adjusters, but he co-operates.

2. When God proposed: "Let us make mortal man in our own image," the Son pledged endless co-operation in the Father's plan.

3. As the Father's spirit dwells within you, the spirit presence of the Son envelops you.

6. THE SPIRIT MIND

I. *REFERENCE*: Page 78, ¶4 - "The Eternal Son is spirit..."

COMMENT

1. The spirit and mind of the Eternal Son are beyond human comprehension.

2. Man can perceive mind on the finite level—from animal to angel—but not on the infinite level.

3. Spirit mind differs from the mind which co-ordinates spirit and matter—the cosmic mind, human type.

4. Also there is mind which is allied only with matter.

II. *REFERENCE*: Page 78, ¶5 - "Spirit is ever conscious..."

COMMENT

1. Spirit is always conscious—in some manner minded.

2. Deity is never mindless. Always can Deity communicate with all entities, beings, and personalities.

III. *REFERENCE*: Page 78, ¶6 - "The mind of the Eternal Son..."

COMMENT

1. The mind of the Son is like that of the Father and with the Father ancestor to the absolute mind of the Infinite Spirit.

2. Even the Adjusters have some sort of premind, for they know as they are known.

IV. *REFERENCE*: Page 78, ¶7 - "The Eternal Son is wholly..."

COMMENT

1. Man's material mind is not able to comprehend the infinite spirit mind of the Eternal Son.

2. As we ascend Paradiseward, we will be increasingly able to grasp the "mind of the spirit" because of our augmenting spiritual insight.

7. PERSONALITY OF THE ETERNAL SON

I. *REFERENCE*: Page 79, ¶2 - "The Eternal Son is that infinite..."

COMMENT

1. The Eternal Son is that unqualified personality from which the Father escaped by the technique of trinitization.

2. The Son is absolute personality; God is father personality—the bestower of personality.

II. *REFERENCE*: Page 79, ¶3 - "The personality of..."

COMMENT

The absolute personality of the Son is the pattern personality, first, of the personality of the Conjoint Actor, then of all other personalities.

III. *REFERENCE*: Page 79, ¶4 - "The Eternal Son is truly..."

COMMENT

1. The Eternal Son is:

    A. A merciful minister.
    B. A divine spirit.
    C. A spiritual power.
    D. A real personality.
    E. The personal and spiritual nature of God manifest to the universes.

2. The Son is the sum of the First Source and Center divested of all that which is:

    A. Nonpersonal.
    B. Extradivine.
    C. Nonspiritual.
    D. Pure potential.

3. But it is impossible for mortal mind to conceive of such a supernal personality.

8. REALIZATION OF THE ETERNAL SON

I. *REFERENCE*: Page 79, ¶5 - "Concerning identity, nature..."

COMMENT

1. In nature and attributes, the Eternal Son is the full equal of the Universal Father.

    COMPLEMENT: "That which fills up or completes. To complete a symmetrical whole; one of two mutually complementing parts. Implies two things which mutually complete each other and together constitute a whole."

    COUNTERPART: "That which seems to complete or complement something else. A person closely resembles another." Syn.: Double, like, twin, complement.

2. As God is the Universal Father, the Son is the Universal Mother.

II. *REFERENCE*: Page 79, ¶6 - "To appreciate the character..."

COMMENT

1. To understand the Son—study the Father. They are inseparably one.

2. Higher beings can better distinguish their separate domains of universe administration.

III. *REFERENCE*: Page 79, ¶7 - "As persons you may..."

COMMENT

1. As persons, you can distinguish the Father and the Son, but in universe administration they are so intertwined that it is not always possible to distinguish them.

   INTERTWINE: "To wind about, to embrace, to encircle. To unite or become mutually involved by twining one with another; to entangle; to interlace; intertwist."

2. When you cannot distinguish Father and Son, remember that God is the initiating thought and the Son is the expressionful word.

3. In the local universe this inseparability is personalized in the Creator Son.

IV. *REFERENCE*: Page 80, ¶2 - "The Eternal Son is infinite..."

COMMENT

1. The infinite Eternal Son is approachable through his Paradise Sons and the Infinite Spirit.

2. Through these celestial agencies mortal man ascends to Paradise and stands in the presence of the majestic Son.

V. *REFERENCE*: Page 80, ¶3 - "Even though the..."

COMMENT

1. Since our personality comes from the Father and our mind from the Spirit, we grasp their reality more readily than we do that of the Son.

2. But as we ascend we increasingly discern the infinitely spiritual mind of the Eternal Son.

VI. *REFERENCE*: Page 80, ¶4 - "Never can the concept..."

COMMENT

Not until we become spirits will the concept of the Eternal Son equal our appreciation of the Creator Son of our native universe.

VII. *REFERENCE*: Page 80, ¶5 - "Throughout your local..."

COMMENT

During the morontia life the Creator Son compensates our failure to understand the Eternal Son. In Orvonton and Havona we will begin to comprehend the Original Son.

VIII. *REFERENCE*: Page 80, ¶6 - "The Eternal Son..."

COMMENT

The Eternal Son is a glorious personality. The Divine Counselor testifies to the reality of this Original Son.

PAPER 7

Relation of the Eternal Son to the Universe

PAPER 7
Relation of the Eternal Son to the Universe

1. THE SPIRIT-GRAVITY CIRCUIT
2. THE ADMINISTRATION OF THE ETERNAL SON
3. RELATION OF THE ETERNAL SON TO THE INDIVIDUAL
4. THE DIVINE PERFECTION PLANS
5. THE SPIRIT OF BESTOWAL
6. THE PARADISE SONS OF GOD
7. THE SUPREME REVELATION OF THE FATHER

INTRODUCTION

I. REFERENCE: Page 81, ¶1 - "The Original Son..."

COMMENT

1. The Original Son is always concerned with execution of the spiritual aspects of the Father's eternal purpose.

2. We do not fully understand it, but the Son undoubtedly does.

II. REFERENCE: Page 81, ¶2 - "The Son is like..."

COMMENT

1. Like the Father, the Son seeks to bestow everything possible upon his co-ordinate Sons.

2. **Question**: Does the Eternal Son of himself create any Sons? If so, they would not be personal beings. The Sons we know are created by the Son and other Deities.

3. Like the Father, he also bestows of himself upon the Spirit, their conjoint executive.

III. REFERENCE: Page 81, ¶3 - "As the upholder..."

COMMENT

1. As the upholder of spirit realities, the Son is the counterpoise of the Isle of Paradise.

   COUNTERPOISE: "To counterbalance. To act against with equal effect, with equal power. To equalize; to compensate; to offset; to counteract."

2. As Paradise reveals the material beauty of the Father, his spiritual values are revealed by the Son.

IV. *REFERENCE*: Page 81, ¶4 - "The Eternal Son is..."

COMMENT

1. The Eternal Son upholds all spirit realities and spiritual beings.
2. **Note**: All spirit reality is not personal. What is on the Son's Paradise worlds?
3. The spirit world is the habit of the Eternal Son.
4. All spirit reality is responsive to the will of the Original Son.

IV. *REFERENCE*: Page 81, ¶5 - "The Son is not..."

COMMENT

1. The Son is not responsible for the conduct of all freewill spirit personalities.
2. Even as nature may not be representative of the Father, sometimes the spirit world may not be representative of the Son.
3. Regardless—the universal gravity control of all spirit reality remains absolute.

1. THE SPIRIT-GRAVITY CIRCUIT

I. *REFERENCE*: Page 81, ¶6 - "Everything taught concerning..."

COMMENT

1. All that is true of the immanence of God is also true of the Son in the spiritual world.
2. The control of the spirit-gravity circuit constitutes absolute spiritual sovereignty.
3. The Son holds all spirit realities and values in the "hollow of his hand."
4. **Note**: The spirit-gravity circuit is not a personality circuit—it is a spirit value (reality) circuit.

II. *REFERENCE*: Page 82, ¶1 - "This gravity control..."

COMMENT

1. Spirit gravity control operates independently of time and space—no energy is lost in transmission.

2. Spirit never suffers time delay, nor does it undergo space diminution.

3. Spirit energy is not retarded by material mass—it does not decrease in accordance with the square of the distance.

4. All of this is inherent in the absoluteness of the Son—it is not due to the interposition of the antigravity forces of the Infinite Spirit.

III. *REFERENCE*: Page 82, ¶2 – "Spirit realities respond..."

COMMENT

1. Spirit realities respond to the Son's drawing power in accordance with qualitative value.

2. Spirit substance (quality) is just as responsive to spirit gravity as physical matter (quantity) is responsive to physical gravity.

3. Spirit values and forces are real.

IV. *REFERENCE*: Page 82, ¶3 – "The reactions and..."

COMMENT

1. The reactions of spirit gravity are always true to the content of spiritual values.

2. Spirit drawing power instantly responds to both inter- and intraspirit values.

3. **Discussion**:

    A. *Inter*spirit values. Definition: "As carried on between mutuals. Reciprocal."
    B. *Intra*spiritual. Definition: "Within; interior."

4. **Note**: Spirit gravity not only brings kindred spirits together and propels them Son-ward, but it also draws the spirit values of a person together. It unifies spirit presences of diverse nature and sources, such as:

    A. The Thought Adjuster.
    B. The Spirit of Truth.
    C. The Holy Spirit.
    D. The omnipresent spirits of: (1) Father, (2) Son, (3) Spirit.
    E. Spirit values of the evolving morontia soul.
    F. Spirit realities of the spiritualizing human mind.
    G. Any and all other spirit realities impinging upon us.

5. Every time a spirit reality actualizes, spirit gravity experiences immediate readjustment.

6. Such a new spirit value is an actual part of the Second Source and Center.

V. *REFERENCE*: Page 82, ¶4 - "The Son's spiritual..."

COMMENT

1. This spirit drawing power of the Son is, in lesser degree, inherent in many orders of Paradise Sons.

2. The Michaels have this "drawing power." **See John 12:32.** *"And I, when I am lifted up from the earth, will draw all men to myself."*

3. Subgravity circuits exist within the absolute circuit. One is found in a local universe—just as in the individual. Illustration:

    A. Inter- and intraphysical gravity.
    B. Brain waves: General and local areas.

4. There is a relation between these subabsolute spirit-gravity systems and the emerging overcontrol of the Supreme Being.

5. As central control of Paradise personalities diminishes out in time and space—the overcontrol (co-ordination) of the emerging Supreme Being increases.

VI. *REFERENCE*: Page 82, ¶5 - "Spirit-gravity pull..."

COMMENT

1. Spirit gravity operates not only on the universe, but also as between individuals and groups of individuals.

2. All things are accentuated when presented to a group. Story. Sermon.

3. There is attractiveness between persons of like tastes and longings.

4. The term *kindred spirits* is not wholly a figure of speech.

VII. *REFERENCE*: Page 82, ¶6 - "Like the material gravity..."

COMMENT

1. The spirit-gravity circuit of the Eternal Son is absolute; nothing can interfere with it.

2. Spiritual quarantine of Urantia in no way affects the spirit presence or the gravity circuit of the Eternal Son.

VIII. *REFERENCE*: Page 82, ¶7 - "All reactions of..."

COMMENT

1. The reactions of spirit gravity are dependable and predictable.

2. Spirit gravity can be measured just as man attempts to compute finite physical gravity.

3. The Son's spirit response to all beings is in accordance with the actuality of qualitative spiritual values.

IX. *REFERENCE*: Page 83, ¶2 - "But alongside this..."

Comment

1. We are confronted with unpredictable spiritual phenomena— probably due to the action of the Deity Absolute.

2. The actions of the Deity Absolute are not of a personal nature.

X. *REFERENCE*: Page 83, ¶3 - "Viewed from the..."

Comment

1. The Eternal Son dominates the realm of *actual* spiritual values. The Deity Absolute pervades the domain of *potential* spirit values.

2. Only *actual* spirit values are responsive to the Son's spirit-gravity circuit.

XI. *REFERENCE*: Page 83, ¶4 - "Spirit seems to emerge..."

Comment

1. Spirit emerges from the Deity Absolute; evolving spirit is correlated in the Supreme and Ultimate, and finds destiny in the grasp of the Son's spirit-gravity circuit.

2. This is the cycle of experiential spirit. Existential spirit is inherent in the infinity of the Second Source and Center.

2. THE ADMINISTRATION OF THE ETERNAL SON

I. *REFERENCE*: Page 83, ¶5 - "On Paradise the presence..."

Comment

1. The Eternal Son is spiritually absolute on Paradise—as you move outward, you detect less of the Son's personal activity.

2. As you penetrate the post-Havona universes the presence of the Eternal Son is:

   A. Personalized in the Paradise Sons.
   B. Experientially conditioned by the Supreme and Ultimate.
   C. Co-ordinated with the Deity Absolute.

II. *REFERENCE*: **Page 83, ¶6 - "In the central universe..."**

COMMENT

In the central universe, spirit energy states are in perfect balance.

III. *REFERENCE*: **Page 83, ¶7 - "In the superuniverses..."**

COMMENT

1. The Eternal Son is not personally present in the superuniverses. His representations are not in the Father's personality circuit.

2. The Son's representatives are:

    A. Superpersonalities.
    B. Finite beings.
    C. Neither absonite nor absolute.

IV. *REFERENCE*: **Page 83, ¶8 - "The administration of..."**

COMMENT

1. The Son's presence in the superuniverses is superpersonal and therefore not discerned by creature personalities.

2. In the local universes, the Eternal Son manifests himself in the co-ordinate Creator Sons.

3. RELATION OF THE ETERNAL SON TO THE INDIVIDUAL

I. *REFERENCE*: **Page 84, ¶1 - "In the local universe..."**

COMMENT

1. As pilgrims ascend, they are increasingly energized by the spirit of the Eternal Son.

2. But at no stage of ascension does the spirit of the Son indwell the ascender.

II. *REFERENCE*: **Page 84, ¶2 - "The spiritual-gravity pull..."**

COMMENT

1. The spirit-gravity grasp of the Son securely holds all survivors.

2. The ascender's mortal mind becomes less and less subject to material gravity and more and more responsive to spirit gravity.

III. *REFERENCE*: Page 84, ¶3 - "The spirit-gravity circuit..."

COMMENT

1. The spirit-gravity circuit is the basic channel for transmitting prayer from man to God.

2. This circuit differentially sorts out the unspiritual from the true spiritual values.

3. Regardless of how we address our prayers, they reach the proper destination.

IV. *REFERENCE*: Page 84, ¶4 - "The discriminative operation..."

COMMENT

This discriminative operation of the spirit-gravity circuit may be compared to the differential functioning of the various levels of the human nervous system.

V. *REFERENCE*: Page 84, ¶5 - "But how much more..."

COMMENT

All petitions of true spirit value are sure to reach the Absolute Personality on Paradise.

VI. *REFERENCE*: Page 84, ¶6 - "Conversely, if your..."

COMMENT

1. Purely self-centered prayers can find no lodgment in the Son's spirit circuit.

2. All material petitions fall dead on the spirit circuits. **See 1 Cor. 13:1.** *"If I speak in the tongues of men and of angels, but have not love, I am a noisy gong or a clanging cymbal."*

VI. *REFERENCE*: Page 85, ¶1 - "It is the motivating..."

COMMENT

Prayer is validated by its motivating content—words are valueless.

4. THE DIVINE PERFECTION PLANS

I. *REFERENCE*: Page 85, ¶2 - "The Eternal Son..."

COMMENT

The Eternal Son is in liaison with the Father's "plan of progress"—the ascension and perfection of evolutionary will creatures.

II. *REFERENCE*: Page 85, ¶3 - "The Father and his Son..."

COMMENT

The Father, Son, and Spirit are in partnership to advance this gigantic attainment plan.

III. REFERENCE: Page 85, ¶4, 5, 6, 7 and Page 86, ¶1 - "This divine plan..." to end of section.

COMMENT

1. The Eternal Son is the Father's trustee for the plan of creature ascension.

2. The Father's mandate is: "Be you perfect, even as I am perfect." This is found in **Matt. 5:48**. *"You, therefore, must be perfect, as your heavenly Father is perfect."*

3. **See also: John 17:23**. *"I in them and thou in me, that they may become perfectly one, that the world may know that thou hast sent me."*

4. Thus do the Deities co-operate in the work of:

    A. Creation.
    B. Control.
    C. Evolution.
    D. Revelation.
    E. Ministration.
    F. Restoration.
    G. Rehabilitation.

5. THE SPIRIT OF BESTOWAL

I. *REFERENCE*: Page 86, ¶2 - "The Eternal Son without..."

COMMENT

1. The Eternal Son and his associated Sons work with the Father in executing the survival plan.

2. The bestowal plan is a part of the perfection scheme.

3. The bestowal Sons are the way, the truth, and the life. **See John 14:6.** *"Jesus said to him, 'I am the way, and the truth, and the life; no one comes to the Father, but by me.'"*

II. REFERENCE: Page 86, ¶3 - "The Eternal Son cannot..."

COMMENT

The Son cannot contact man as does the Father, but his Sons can become as man himself.

III. *REFERENCE*: Page 86, ¶4 - "The purely personal nature..."

COMMENT

1. The Son cannot fragmentize—he ministers only as a person.

2. The Son cannot become a part of creature experience, as does the Adjuster. But through the incarnation of his Paradise Sons, he can become the creature.

3. The Father fragments—the Sons incarnate.

IV. *REFERENCE*: Page 86, ¶5 - "The Eternal Son comes not..."

COMMENT

1. When a Creator Son incarnates, the Eternal Son has come.

2. By incarnation, the Son escapes the fetters of personality absolutism.

V. *REFERENCE*: Page 86, ¶6 - "Long, long ago..."

COMMENT

1. The Eternal Son bestowed himself seven times on the circuits of Havona.

2. This took place during the times of Grandfanda. (See p. 1308.)

VI. *REFERENCE*: Page 86, ¶7 - "Neither did he pass..."

COMMENT

1. The Son's bestowals were unique for he could not suspend consciousness of personality.

2. Central lodgment of spirit luminosity and gravity continued unchanged.

VII. *REFERENCE*: Page 87, ¶1 - "The bestowals of..."

COMMENT

What the Eternal Son acquired on his bestowals is not known—but whatever it was, he has retained it.

VIII. *REFERENCE*: Page 87, ¶2 - "Whatever our difficulty..."

COMMENT

1. Much is understood respecting the bestowal of the Original Michael Son.

2. This Michael traveled with mortal ascenders from circuit to circuit in Havona and in the times of Grandfanda.

IX. *REFERENCE*: Page 87, ¶3 - "Whatever else this..."

COMMENT

This bestowal of the original Michael made the transcendent bestowal of the Eternal Son forever real to all Havona natives and ascending pilgrims.

X. *REFERENCE*: Page 87, ¶4 - "The Eternal Son..."

COMMENT

1. The bestowal of the Eternal Son is an example for all other bestowal Sons.

2. All of the Paradise Sons partake of this spirit of bestowal.

3. In the bestowal of every Paradise Son, the Eternal Son has bestowed himself.

XI. *REFERENCE*: Page 87, ¶5 - "In spirit and nature..."

COMMENT

The Paradise Sons are a portraiture of the Original Son. He who has seen a Paradise Son has seen the Eternal Son of God.

6. THE PARADISE SONS OF GOD

I. *REFERENCE*: Page 87, ¶6 - "The lack of a knowledge..."

COMMENT

1. Ignorance of the multiple Sons of God has created great confusion on Urantia.

2. Every millennium the divine Sons foregather for their periodic conclaves.

   Job 38:7. *"When the morning stars sang together, and all the sons of God shouted for joy."*

   Job 1:6. *"Now there was a day when the Sons of God came to present themselves before the Lord, and Satan also came among them."*

II. *REFERENCE*: Page 87, ¶7 - "The Eternal Son is..."

COMMENT

1. The Eternal Son is the source of all the spirit of ministry characterizing all of the descending Sons.

2. The Eternal Son transmits his divine nature to all of the Paradise Sons who go out to the universes.

III. *REFERENCE*: Page 88, ¶1 - "The Original and Eternal..."

COMMENT

1. The Original Son is the offspring-person of the Father's "first" infinite thought.

2. Every time the Father and the Son jointly project a thought which is: new—original—identical—unique—personal—absolute—THEN a new and original Creator Son is personalized.

IV. *REFERENCE*: Page 88, ¶2 - "The Creator Sons..."

COMMENT

1. The Creator Sons, with the help of the agencies of the Infinite Spirit, go out in space to organize the local universes of progressive evolution.

2. The Creator Sons are limited by the primacy of the First Source and Center and the Absolutes.

3. The Creator Sons administer only that which they create.

V. *REFERENCE*: Page 88, ¶3 - "Much as the..."

COMMENT

1. As the Creator Sons are personalized by the Father and the Son, the Magisterial Sons are personalized by the Eternal Son and the Infinite Spirit.

2. Because of creature incarnation, the Magisterial Sons earn the right to serve as survival judges on the worlds of time and space.

VI. *REFERENCE*: Page 88, ¶4 - "The Father, Son, and Spirit..."

COMMENT

The Father, Son, and Spirit unite to personalize the Trinity Teacher Sons who range the universes as teachers of all persons, human and divine.

VII. *REFERENCE*: Page 88, ¶5 - "Between the Original Mother Son..."

COMMENT

1. Between the Original Mother Son and all of these Paradise Sons there is a channel of direct communication.

2. This communication is instantaneous and independent of the spirit gravity and all other circuits.

3. These communications are independent of time though sometimes conditioned by space.

VIII. REFERENCE: Page 88, ¶6 – "The Eternal Son not only..."

COMMENT

The Eternal Son is aware of all that concerns all Paradise Sons and also knows everything of spiritual value in the hearts of all creatures in Havona and the superuniverse.

7. THE SUPREME REVELATION OF THE FATHER

I. REFERENCE: Page 88, ¶7 – "The Eternal Son is..."

COMMENT

1. The Eternal Son is a complete, final, and universal revelation of the spirit and personality of the Universal Father.

2. As concerns the relation of the Father and the Son, they are:
   A. As one with each other.
   B. In personality, co-ordinate.
   C. In spiritual nature, equal.
   D. In divinity, identical.

II. REFERENCE: Page 89, ¶1 – "The character of God..."

COMMENT

1. The character of God could not be improved upon in the Son, but it is amplified by divestment of the nonpersonal and the nonspiritual.

2. While the First Source and Center is more than personality, the personality qualities are manifested in the absolute personality of the Eternal Son.

III. REFERENCE: Page 89, ¶2 – "The primal Son..."

COMMENT

1. The primal Son and his Sons are making a personal revelation of the Father to all creation.

2. These same Paradise Sons are the avenue of approach to the Father for men and angels.

IV. *REFERENCE*: Page 89, ¶3 - "The Father comes down..."

COMMENT

Through the ministry of the Paradise Sons the Father comes to us, and by their guidance we ascend to the Father.

V. *REFERENCE*: Page 89, ¶4 - "In all these..."

COMMENT

As a person, you will find the Son before you attain the Father.

VI. *REFERENCE*: Page 89, ¶5 - "More of the character..."

COMMENT

To know more of the nature of the Eternal Son, we should study his revelation in the life of our own Creator Son in the Urantia bestowal.

PAPER 8
The Infinite Spirit

PAPER 8
The Infinite Spirit

INTRODUCTION

I. *REFERENCE*: Page 90, ¶1 - "Back in eternity..."

COMMENT

Back in eternity the Thought-God and the Word-God desire a universal and infinite agent for (1) mutual expression and (2) combined action.

II. *REFERENCE*: Page 90, ¶2 - "In the dawn of eternity..."

COMMENT

1. The Father and the Son, recognizing their absolute oneness, form an everlasting partnership.

2. The purpose of this partnership is the execution of their united concepts throughout the circle of eternity.

   Note: This is all related just as if "it happened"—but it never could have happened in time because it is an "eternity event." This statement is a linguistic paradox, since event is a time designation.

III. *REFERENCE*: Page 90, ¶3 - "We are now..."

COMMENT

1. We now confront the origin of the Infinite Spirit. Note that we again have this eternity-time paradox.

2. When the Father and the Son conceive infinite and identical *action*— the Infinite Spirit exists.

   Note: *Moment* is a term of *time*. An eternal being does not "spring" into existence—except in our philosophic concept. Note the use of the present tense. There is no past or future on the circle of eternity.

IV. *REFERENCE*: Page 90, ¶4 - "In thus reciting..."

COMMENT

God the Father, God the Son, and God the Spirit are:

1. Three eternally associated persons.
2. Existential—without beginning or ending.
3. Co-ordinate.
4. Supreme.
5. Ultimate.
6. Absolute.
7. Infinite.

1. THE GOD OF ACTION

I. *REFERENCE*: Page 90, ¶5 - "In the eternity..."

COMMENT

1. The Infinite Spirit completes the personality cycle—the God of Action is existent.
2. The space stage is set for the stupendous drama of creation.
3. **Question.** What is "personality cycle"? It must require three beings. (Recall Rodan's objections to regarding God as a person. *The Urantia Book*, p. 1783.)
4. Space is a stage—creation is a drama:
   A. A universal adventure—not a mechanistic action or reaction.
   B. A divine panorama. A panorama has no beginning or end. In concept it always has a beginning.

II. *REFERENCE*: Page 90, ¶6 - "The first act..."

COMMENT

1. The "first" acts of the Infinite Spirit.

   Note: There never could have been a "first act" of a being who never had a beginning. (Continued use of the present tense.)

2. The Conjoint Actor:
   A. Pledges loyalty to God the Father.
   B. Acknowledges dependence on God the Son.
3. Even among beings of infinite *equality*, there exists co-ordination—even apparent subordination for purposes of administration.

III. *REFERENCE*: Page 90, ¶7 - "Inherent in the nature..."

COMMENT

1. Inherent in the Deity union:

    A. The cycle of eternity is established.
    B. The Trinity is existent.

2. The Trinity does not establish eternity—but it has something to do with the "cycle of eternity."

3. The stage of universal space is now set for the unfolding of the purpose of the Universal Father.

4. The Father works through the Son by the execution of the God of Action.

IV. *REFERENCE*: Page 91, ¶2 - "The God of Action..."

COMMENT

1. The God of Action functions and the dead vaults of space are astir.

2. Hitherto space energies were potential, now they are actual—but all this is hypothetical. In reality all this is eternal.

3. From the "beginning," gravity has been adequate to control the universes.

V. *REFERENCE*: Page 91, ¶3 - "There now flashes..."

COMMENT

1. Now becomes operative the spirit gravity of the Eternal Son. Just as physical gravity becomes operative only after material energy has been created in the form of the material universe, so does spirit gravity become operative only after spiritual energy is present for it to operate upon.

2. The gravity-embraced universe is:

    A. Touched with the energy of infinity.
    B. Immersed in the spirit of divinity.

3. In this way was the cosmos prepared for the bestowal of mind by the Infinite Spirit.

VI. *REFERENCE*: Page 91, ¶4 - "Upon these seeds..."

COMMENT

1. Now the Father acts and creature personality appears.

2. The Deities dominate all space and draw all things toward Paradise.

VII. *REFERENCE*: Page 91, ¶5 - "The Infinite Spirit..."

COMMENT

1. The Infinite Spirit eternalizes concurrently with the birth of Havona.

2. Havona is "created" by the Infinite Spirit, obeying the combined concepts and united wills of the Father and the Son.

    Note: You combine concepts, but you *unite* wills. *Eternalize* is used synonomously with *create*.

3. The Third Person deitizes by this very act of conjoint creation.

VIII. *REFERENCE*: Page 91, ¶6 - "These are the grand...

COMMENT

1. These are the grand and awful times of the creative expansion of Deity.

2. There are no records of these eternity transactions.

IX. *REFERENCE*: Page 91, ¶7 - "In brief..."

COMMENT

1. Both the Infinite Spirit and Havona are eternal.

2. Before Havona lie the unsearchable transactions of eternity and the depths of infinity—absolute mystery.

X. *REFERENCE*: Page 91, ¶8 - "And we thus portray..."

COMMENT

1. The sequential origin of the Conjoint Actor is a condescension to the time-bound and space-conditioned mortal mind.

2. There is such a thing as "consciousness of sequence" which is not time related. It is present on Paradise.

3. This presentation is made to enable man to have a starting point for universe history.

4. But, in reality, the Son and the Spirit are coeternal with the Father.

5. This is done without being disregardful of the eternity of Paradise and the three Absolutes.

XI. *REFERENCE*: Page 92, ¶2 - "It is enough..."

Comment

1. As a child of the cosmos, it is best first to grasp the child-parent relationship—the Universal Father.

2. Then let the mind reach out to the community, the race, the world, and the universe.

2. NATURE OF THE INFINITE SPIRIT

I. *REFERENCE*: Page 92, ¶3 - "The Conjoint Creator..."

Comment

The Conjoint Creator is from eternity and reflects the perfection of both the Father and the Son.

II. *REFERENCE*: Page 92, ¶4 - "The Third Source and Center..."

Comment

This paragraph lists the numerous titles of the Infinite Spirit.

III. *REFERENCE*: Page 92, ¶5 - "It is altogether proper..."

Comment

The Infinite Spirit may properly be called the Infinite Reality, the Universal Organizer, or the Personality Co-ordinator.

IV. *REFERENCE*: Page 92, ¶6 - "The Infinite Spirit..."

Comment

To sense the absoluteness of the Spirit, you should contemplate the infinity of the Father and the eternity of the Son.

V. *REFERENCE*: Page 92, ¶7 - "There is mystery..."

Comment

Even if the master universe expands to infinity, the potential of the Infinite Spirit will be adequate.

VI. *REFERENCE*: Page 92, ¶8 - "Though in every way..."

Comment

1. While sharing the perfect attributes of the Father, the Spirit inclines toward the mercy nature of the Son. "It is enough..."

2. Always is the Spirit a mercy minister. The Spirit depicts the mercy of God.

VII. *REFERENCE*: Page 93, ¶1 - "It is not possible..."

COMMENT

1. The goodness of God is better comprehended in the acts of the Spirit.

2. The ceaseless service of the Spirit reveals the Father's faithfulness and the Son's constancy.

VIII. *REFERENCE*: Page 93, ¶2 - "The Conjoint Creator..."

COMMENT

The Father's beauty of thought and character of truth are co-ordinated and revealed in the subordinate cosmic manifestation of the limitless mind of the Infinite Spirit.

3. RELATION OF THE SPIRIT TO THE FATHER AND THE SON

I. *REFERENCE*: Page 93, ¶3 - "As the Eternal Son..."

COMMENT

1. The Conjoint Actor is the result of the "first" creative concept of the Father-Son partnership. **Note**: "First" is in quotes.

2. The Conjoint Actor eternalized concurrently with the Havona creation.

II. *REFERENCE*: Page 93, ¶4 - "Since the personalization..."

COMMENT

The Son, receiving all things from the Father, bestows all possible power upon the Conjoint Actor.

III. *REFERENCE*: Page 93, ¶5 - "The Eternal Son..."

COMMENT

1. The Son and the Spirit have fashioned all post-Havona creations.

2. In later creations, the Spirit sustains the same relation to the Son that the Son sustained to the Father in the Havona creation.

IV. *REFERENCE*: Page 93, ¶6 - "A Creator Son..."

COMMENT

Our local universe was created by a Son of the Eternal Son and a Spirit Daughter of the Infinite Spirit.

V. *REFERENCE*: Page 93, ¶7 - "The Infinite Spirit is the effective..."

COMMENT

1. The Spirit is the effective drawing agent for the Father and the Son.

2. The Infinite Spirit is the trustee of the Father-Son project of mortal ascension.

3. The Spirit is dedicated to the plan of exalting will creatures to Paradise perfection.

VI. *REFERENCE*: Page 93, ¶8 - "The Infinite Spirit is a complete..."

COMMENT

The Infinite Spirit is the exclusive revelation of the Father and the Son to the universes.

VII. *REFERENCE*: Page 93, ¶9 - "The Eternal Son..."

COMMENT

Only by the ministry of the Infinite Spirit can the ascending pilgrim discover the Eternal Son.

VIII.*REFERENCE*: Page 94, ¶2 - "At the center..."

COMMENT

The Infinite Spirit is the first Deity to be attained by all ascending pilgrims.

IX. *REFERENCE*: Page 94, ¶3 - "And in many other..."

COMMENT

The Spirit represents the Father and the Son in many ways besides ministering to mortal ascenders.

4. THE SPIRIT OF DIVINE MINISTRY

I. *REFERENCE*: Page 94, ¶4 - "Paralleling the physical universe..."

COMMENT

1. The word of the Son interprets the thought of the Father and when "made flesh" demonstrates the loving mercy of the combined Deities.

2. All creation is a stage whereon the Spirit shows forth the affection of the divine parents for their children.

3. The Conjoint Actor is a mind minister and all his children share his service urge.

II. *REFERENCE*: Page 94, ¶5 - "God is love..."

COMMENT

1. God is love, the Son mercy, the Spirit ministry. The Spirit is the personification of the Father's love and the Son's mercy.

2. The Spirit is *love applied*—the combined love of the Father and the Son.

III. *REFERENCE*: Page 94, ¶6 - "On Urantia the Infinite Spirit..."

COMMENT

1. On Urantia the Infinite Spirit is a universal presence; in Nebadon, an example for the Creative Mother Spirit.

2. The Spirit participated in the Havona bestowals of the Eternal Son and the original Michael Son.

IV. *REFERENCE*: Page 94, ¶7 - "When a Creator Son..."

COMMENT

1. Personalities of the Spirit co-operate with the Creator Sons in their creative adventures.

2. The Creative Daughters—the local universe Mother Spirits— foster the Paradise creature ascension plan.

V. *REFERENCE*: Page 94, ¶8 - "As the Sons of God..."

COMMENT

1. As the Sons reveal the Father, the Spirit reveals the combined love of the Father and the Son.

2. The Spirit does not incarnate like the Sons, but he does draw near the creature as a guardian angel.

VI. *REFERENCE*: Page 95, ¶2 - "By this very diminishing..."

COMMENT

This drawing close to animal-origin beings does not in the least affect the Spirit as the Third Person of Deity.

VII. *REFERENCE*: Page 95, ¶3 – "The Conjoint Creator..."

COMMENT

The Spirit is the universal mercy minister—both for the Father-Son plan and in his own behalf.

VIII. *REFERENCE*: Page 95, ¶4 – "As man learns more..."

COMMENT

1. The more we learn of the tireless ministry of the children of the Infinite Spirit, the more we will adore the combined Action of the Father and Son in the Conjoint Actor.

2. Indeed, the Spirit is the protecting "eyes of the Lord" and the divine prayer-hearing ears. **1 Peter 3:12**. *"For the eyes of the Lord are upon the righteous, and his ears are open to their prayer."*

5. THE PRESENCE OF GOD

I. *REFERENCE*: Page 95, ¶5 – "The outstanding attribute..."

COMMENT

The outstanding attribute of the Infinite Spirit is his omnipresence.

II. *REFERENCE*: Page 95, ¶6 – "The Father is *infinite*..."

COMMENT

1. The infinite Father is limited only by volition.

2. The Father acts alone in the bestowal of Adjusters and in the personality circuit.

3. The Father is also present *with* the Son and in the Spirit.

III. *REFERENCE*: Page 95, ¶7 – "In your sacred writings..."

COMMENT

This clears up confusion in terms: Spirit of God and the Holy Spirit.

IV. *REFERENCE*: Page 95, ¶8 – "There are many..."

COMMENT

1. There are many spirit influences, but they function as *one*.

2. These united spirits function as the influence of the Supreme—who is "able to keep you from falling and to present you blameless before your Father on high."

3. This is **Jude 24**. *"Now to him who is able to keep you from falling and to present you without blemish before the presence of his glory with rejoicing."*

V. *REFERENCE*: Page 96, ¶2 - "Ever remember that..."

COMMENT

Since the Spirit represents both the Father and the Son, as well as himself, the Infinite Spirit is often called "the spirit of God."

VI. *REFERENCE*: Page 96, ¶3 - "It would also be..."

COMMENT

The Spirit also may represent God the Sevenfold as well as God the Supreme.

6. PERSONALITY OF THE INFINITE SPIRIT

I. *REFERENCE*: Page 96, ¶4 - "Do not allow..."

COMMENT

The Infinite Spirit is a person, notwithstanding that he is also:

1. A universe presence.
2. An eternal action.
3. A cosmic power.
4. A holy influence.
5. A universal mind.

II. *REFERENCE*: Page 96, ¶5 - "The Infinite Spirit is..."

COMMENT

The Spirit is just as much a person as the Father and the Son—and even easier to visualize.

III. *REFERENCE*: Page 96, ¶6 - "The Infinite Spirit, the Third Person..."

COMMENT

1. The Spirit possesses all attributes of personality—mind and will.

2. See these two texts: **1 Cor. 2:10**. *"For the Spirit searches everything, even the depths of God."* **1 Cor. 12:11**. *"All these are inspired by one and the same Spirit, who apportions to each one individually as he wills."*

IV. *REFERENCE*: Page 96, ¶7 - "'The love of the Spirit'..."

COMMENT

1. "The love of the Spirit" is real, as also are his sorrows. **Rom. 15:30.** *"I appeal to you, brethren, by our Lord Jesus Christ and by the love of the Spirit."* **Eph. 4:30.** *"And do not grieve the Holy Spirit of God, in whom you were sealed for the day of redemption."*

2. The Spirit speaks to us. **Rev. 2:7.** *"He who has an ear, let him hear what the Spirit says."* This occurs three more times in this same chapter and three times in Chapter 3. **See also Rev. 13:9.** *"If any one has an ear, let him hear."*

3. The Spirit makes intercession for us. **Rom. 8:26.** *"Likewise the Spirit helps us in our weakness; for we do not know how to pray as we ought, but the Spirit himself intercedes for us with sighs too deep for words."*

4. Led by the Spirit of God. **Rom. 8:14.** *"For all who are led by the Spirit of God are the sons of God."*

V. *REFERENCE*: Page 96, ¶8 - "Even though we behold..."

COMMENT

The Spirit is a person—notwithstanding his far-flung ministry and omnipresence.

VI. *REFERENCE*: Page 96, ¶9 - "In the administration..."

COMMENT

All three Deities work as *one* in the service and control of all creation.

VII. *REFERENCE*: Page 97, ¶2 - "In the person..."

COMMENT

The Spirit is like the Father and the Son and also like the Father-Son.

PAPER 9

The Relation of the Infinite Spirit to the Universe

PAPER 9

The Relation of the Infinite Spirit to the Universe

INTRODUCTION

I. *REFERENCE*: Page 98, ¶1 - "A strange thing..."

COMMENT

1. The Conjoint Actor personalizes as an unlimited spirituality, co-ordinated with absolute mind, and with prerogatives of energy manipulation.

2. The Conjoint Actor delivers the Father from:

   A. Bonds of centralized perfection.
   B. Fetters of personality absolutism.

3. All this is disclosed by the power of the Conjoint Actor to create such a host of ministering spirits.

II. *REFERENCE*: Page 98, ¶2 - "The Father is infinite..."

COMMENT

1. The Father is the universal upholder.

2. The Son is the universal revealer.

3. Paradise is the universal stabilizer.

4. The Conjoint Actor is versatile. He has:

   A. Unique powers of synthesis.
   B. Capacity to co-ordinate all energies, minds, and spirits.

5. He is a unifier of manifold energies.

III. *REFERENCE*: Page 98, ¶3 - "The Infinite Spirit..."

COMMENT

1. The Spirit ministers the Father's love and the Son's mercy in harmony with the justice of the Trinity.

2. His influence is ever near you, and his personalities really understand you.

IV. *REFERENCE*: Page 98, ¶4 - "Throughout the universes..."

COMMENT

1. The agencies of the Conjoint Actor manipulate the energies of all space.

2. The Spirit is responsive to both the spiritual and the material.

3. The Conjoint Actor reveals the unity of God in:

Things.	Meanings.	Values.
Energies.	Minds.	Spirits.

V. *REFERENCE*: Page 98, ¶5 - "The Infinite Spirit pervades..."

COMMENT

The Spirit is absolute. He pervades all space and indwells the circle of eternity.

1. ATTRIBUTES OF THE THIRD SOURCE AND CENTER

I. *REFERENCE*: Page 98, ¶6 - "The Third Source and Center..."

COMMENT

1. God the Spirit is the personality co-ordinate and divine equal of God the Father and God the Son.

2. The Infinite Spirit is also:

   A. Omnipresent spiritual influence.
   B. The universal manipulator.
   C. Representative of the Father-Son partnership.
   D. The Absolute Mind.
   E. Ancestor of change and relationship.

II. *REFERENCE*: Page 99, ¶2 - "Some of the attributes..."

COMMENT

1. The attributes of the Third Source and Center are variously derived— even from Paradise absoluteness.

2. The Conjoint Actor embodies the fullness of the combined concepts of the Father and the Son.

III. *REFERENCE*: Page 99, ¶3 - "While you envisage..."

COMMENT

1. The Conjoint Actor is a universal co-ordinator—minister of co-operation.
2. The Spirit is the correlator of all actual reality—Father, Son, and Paradise.
3. Providence is the domain of the Conjoint Actor and the Supreme Being.
4. All actual or actualizing reality is related to the Third Source and Center.

IV. *REFERENCE*: Page 99, ¶4 - "The Universal Father..."

COMMENT

1. The Conjoint Actor not only represents the spiritual activities of the Son, but also the energies of Paradise.
2. Thus does the Spirit produce the universal and absolute mind.
3. The Spirit functions throughout the grand universe as a personality in the higher spheres of:
    A. Spiritual values.
    B. Physical-energy relationships.
    C. True mind meanings.
4. He functions wherever energy and spirit are associated. He:
    A. Dominates all reactions of mind.
    B. Wields great spiritual power.
    C. Exerts influence over energy and matter.

V. *REFERENCE*: Page 99, ¶5 - "The Third Source and Center..."

COMMENT

1. The Third Person shares the omnipresence, omnipotence, and omniscience of the Deities.
2. The Third Person is master of the mind realms—here he is absolute.

VI. *REFERENCE*: Page 99, ¶6 - "The Conjoint Actor..."

COMMENT

While representing the Father-Son association, the Conjoint Actor also compensates for the incompleteness of God the Supreme and God the Ultimate.

VII. *REFERENCE*: Page 100, ¶2 - "And herein is..."

COMMENT

The Conjoint Actor reveals the Father and the Son and also activates Paradise pattern. Of all Deity, he seems the most versatile in *action*.

VIII. *REFERENCE*: Page 100, ¶3 - "In addition to this..."

COMMENT

1. The Conjoint Actor is:

    A. Superb in patience, mercy, and love.
    B. Endowed with supercontrol of energy.
    C. Able to minister love and overshadow justice with mercy.

2. Our universe is being forged out between the anvil of justice and the hammer of suffering, but the children of mercy wield the hammer.

2. THE OMNIPRESENT SPIRIT

I. *REFERENCE*: Page 100, ¶4 - "God is spirit..."

COMMENT

1. God is spirit in multiple ways:

    A. God is spirit.
    B. In the Son, he is spirit without qualification.
    C. In the Conjoint Actor, he is spirit allied with mind.

2. There may also be experiential levels—the spirits of the Supreme Being, Ultimate Deity, and Deity Absolute.

II. *REFERENCE*: Page 100, ¶5 - "The Infinite Spirit..."

COMMENT

The Infinite Spirit is a personalized spiritualization of the Son and the Father.

III. *REFERENCE*: Page 100, ¶6 – "There are many..."

COMMENT

Linking the people of Urantia with Deity there are:

1. Thought Adjusters and the Father.
2. Spiritual gravity and the Son.
3. Spiritual presence of the Infinite Spirit.

IV. *REFERENCE*: Page 100, ¶7 – "In addition to..."

COMMENT

In addition to these direct Deity influences, there are numerous ministering personalities who lead us upward.

V. *REFERENCE*: Page 100, ¶8 – "The presence of..."

COMMENT

1. We can realize the presence of spirit influences as:
    A. The Father's Thought Adjuster.
    B. The spirit of the Eternal Son.
    C. The Infinite Spirit as the Holy Spirit.
2. And these all act as *one* spirit influence in creature life.

3. THE UNIVERSAL MANIPULATOR

I. *REFERENCE*: Page 101, ¶2 – "The Isle of Paradise..."

COMMENT

1. Paradise is the source of dependable gravity—a universe reality.
2. Gravity can be annulled only by forces resident in the Conjoint Actor.

II. *REFERENCE*: Page 101, ¶3 – "The Infinite Spirit..."

COMMENT

1. The Infinite Spirit possesses antigravity, not observably present in the Father or the Son.
2. Heredity can produce qualities in the offspring which are not discernible in the parents.
3. This force (antigravity) is transmissable to some of the higher personalities of the Infinite Spirit.

III. *REFERENCE*: Page 101, ¶9 – "Paradise is the pattern..."

COMMENT

1. Paradise is the pattern of infinity; the God of Action is the activator of that pattern.

2. Paradise is the fulcrum of infinity—the agents of the Conjoint Actor are the levers of control for this universe mechanism.

4. THE ABSOLUTE MIND

I. *REFERENCE*: Page 102, ¶1 – "There is an..."

COMMENT

1. The Third Source and Center has a mind apart from his physical and spiritual attributes.

2. But we do not contact this mind apart from physical or spiritual manifestations.

II. *REFERENCE*: Page 102, ¶2 – "The absolute mind..."

COMMENT

1. The mind of God the Spirit is absolute.

2. Mind is not inherent in energy. It can be superimposed upon energy.

3. Pure spirit is innately conscious—minded in some way.

4. Spirit insight knows. It transcends and antedates consciousness of mind.

III. *REFERENCE*: Page 102, ¶3 – "The Conjoint Creator..."

COMMENT

1. The Conjoint Actor is absolute only in mind. His mind is the infinite source of all mind.

2. Superuniverse mind—cosmic mind—comes from the Seven Master Spirits.

3. The local universes have a type of this cosmic mind.

IV. *REFERENCE*: Page 102, ¶4 – "Infinite mind ignores time..."

COMMENT

1. Infinite mind ignores time, ultimate mind transcends time, cosmic mind is conditioned thereby.

2. Infinite mind is independent of space, but as mind descends to the adjutant level it increasingly is limited by space.

V. *REFERENCE*: Page 102, ¶5 - "Cosmic force responds..."

COMMENT

1. Cosmic force responds to mind even as mind responds to spirit.

2. Energy is thing, mind is meaning, spirit is value.

VI. *REFERENCE*: Page 102, ¶6 - "Mind transmutes..."

COMMENT

1. Mind can change spirit values into mind meanings. Volition can translate these into action.

2. Personality is the unifier of mind, spirit, and energy.

5. THE MINISTRY OF MIND

I. *REFERENCE*: Page 102, ¶7 - "The Third Source..."

COMMENT

The mind potential of the Infinite Spirit is adequate for an infinite universe.

II. *REFERENCE*: Page 102, ¶8 - "In the Domain..."

COMMENT

1. The Third Source and Center bestows creature mind and rules therein supreme.

2. Adjusters cannot indwell man's mind until it has been spiritually prepared.

III. *REFERENCE*: Page 103, ¶2 - "The unique feature..."

COMMENT

1. Mind can range from the mechanical type to highest spiritual levels.

2. Always is the direction of mind entrusted to mind-spirit or mind-energy personalities.

IV. *REFERENCE*: Page 103, ¶3 - "Since the Third person..."

COMMENT

1. Since man gets his mind from the Spirit, he finds it easier to comprehend the Spirit God as compared to the other Deities.

2. Man's mind is a part of the local universe type of the cosmic mind.

V. *REFERENCE*: Page 103, ¶4 - "Because the Third Person..."

COMMENT

1. All phenomena of mind are not divine.

2. The Conjoint Creator is the source of mind, but mind is not the Conjoint Creator.

VI. *REFERENCE*: Page 103, ¶5 - "Mind, on Urantia..."

COMMENT

1. The plan for human mind is one of perfection, but mortal mind falls far short of that goal.

2. Mind has a divine origin and a divine destiny, but mortal mind is not yet of divine dignity.

VII. *REFERENCE*: Page 103, ¶6 - "Too often..."

COMMENT

1. Human mind is marred by insincerity, animal fear, and useless anxiety.

2. Mind cannot become an object of admiration, much less of worship.

3. To contemplate the mortal mind can lead only to reactions of humility.

6. THE MIND-GRAVITY CIRCUIT

I. *REFERENCE*: Page 103, ¶7 - "The Third Source..."

COMMENT

1. The universal intelligence of the Infinite Spirit is conscious of every mind in all creation.

2. All mind activity is grasped by the absolute mind-gravity circuit of the Infinite Spirit.

II. *REFERENCE*: Page 103, ¶8 - "Much as the Father..."

COMMENT

1. As the Father draws all personality and the Son all spirits, so does the Conjoint Actor draw all minds to himself.

2. All genuine mind values are drawn into the absolute mind circuit.

III. *REFERENCE*: Page 104, ¶2 – "Mind gravity can operate..."

COMMENT

1. Mind gravity acts independently of material and spiritual gravity.

2. When all three are associated—personality gravity *may* embrace the creature—physical or morontial.

3. Mind endowment provokes thought even in the absence of personality.

IV. *REFERENCE*: Page 104, ¶3 – "Selfhood of personality dignity..."

COMMENT

1. Personality—human or divine—is the bestowal of the Universal Father.

2. Personality gravity acts independently of mind, matter, or spirit.

3. Personality gravity may embrace wholly spiritual or wholly nonspiritual beings.

4. Operation of personality gravity is always a volitional act of the Father.

V. *REFERENCE*: Page 104, ¶4 – "While mind is..."

COMMENT

1. Mind is associated with purely material and purely spirit personalities.

2. In man, mind is associated with both energy and spirit.

3. Hence, the human mind responds to the pull of both physical and spirit gravity.

VI. *REFERENCE*: Page 104, ¶5 – "Cosmic mind..."

COMMENT

1. Pure cosmic mind is subject only to the mind gravity of the Conjoint Actor.

2. Pure mind is kin to infinite mind—a co-ordinate of absolute spirit and energy.

VII. *REFERENCE*: Page 104, ¶6 – "The greater the spirit-energy..."

COMMENT

1. The greater the spirit-energy divergence, the greater the function of mind.

2. Mind functions between energy and spirit, but on Paradise energy and spirit are one.

VIII. *REFERENCE*: Page 104, ¶7 - "The mind-gravity circuit..."

COMMENT

1. The mind-gravity circuit is dependable—predictable. But always does mind present a non-predictable phase.

2. The unpredictability of mind is probably due to the Universal Absolute, but very little is known about it.

IX. *REFERENCE*: Page 104, ¶8 - "Certain phases of the..."

COMMENT

1. Certain phases of mind unpredictability may be due to the incompleteness of the Supreme Being.

2. Two things about mind are certain:
   A. The Infinite Spirit is the perfect expression of the mind of the Creator to the creature.
   B. The Supreme Being is the expression of the mind of the creature to the Creator.

7. UNIVERSE REFLECTIVITY

I. *REFERENCE*: Page 105, ¶1 - "The Conjoint Actor..."

COMMENT

1. The Conjoint Actor can simultaneously focus all actuality—material, mental, and spiritual.

2. This is universe reflectivity—the ability to see, hear, sense, and know all that transpires in a superuniverse.

3. All reflectivity is finally focalized on Paradise.

II. *REFERENCE*: Page 105, ¶2 - "The phenomenon of reflectivity..."

COMMENT

1. Reflectivity is a most amazing interassociation of all phases of existence.

2. This interassociation embraces all phases of material, mindal, and spiritual phenomena.

III. *REFERENCE*: Page 105, ¶3 - "Much of the technique..."

COMMENT

1. Reflectivity is not fully understood. It may concern the dominance of absolute mind.

2. The cosmic mind circuits focus in the Seven Master Spirits and converge on Paradise.

IV. *REFERENCE*: Page 105, ¶4 - "The relationship between..."

COMMENT

1. Relations between the finite cosmic mind and infinite absolute mind are evolving in the experiential mind of the Supreme.

2. Certain phases of reflectivity can be understood only by postulating activity of the Supreme Mind.

3. Reflectivity is the consciousness of the cosmos.

V. *REFERENCE*: Page 105, ¶5 - "Reflectivity appears to be..."

COMMENT

1. Reflectivity appears omniscient within the experiential finite—it may be the emerging consciousness of the Supreme.

2. It is possible that reflectivity represents partial contact with the consciousness of the Supreme.

8. PERSONALITIES OF THE INFINITE SPIRIT

I. *REFERENCE*: Page 105, ¶6 - "The Infinite Spirit..."

COMMENT

The Infinite Spirit transmits many of his powers to his varied agencies.

II. *REFERENCE*: Page 105, ¶7 - "The first Deity-creating..."

COMMENT

The first creative act of the Infinite Spirit in association with the Father and the Son was the personalization of the Seven Master Spirits.

III. *REFERENCE*: Page 106, ¶2 - "There is no direct..."

COMMENT

On superuniverse headquarters the Infinite Spirit is represented by the Reflective Spirits of the Master Spirits.

IV. *REFERENCE*: Page 106, ¶3 - "The next and continuing..."

COMMENT

The next creative act of the Infinite Spirit was the production of the Creative Mother Spirits for the local universes, and this continues each time a Creator Son is personalized by the Father and the Son.

V. *REFERENCE*: Page 106, ¶4 - "Just as it is necessary..."

COMMENT

What the Infinite Spirit is to the total creation, the Creative Spirit is to a local universe, and it is necessary to distinguish between the two.

VI. *REFERENCE*: Page 106, ¶5 - "The Third Source and Center..."

COMMENT

1. The Conjoint Actor is represented in the grand universe by a vast array of helpers, not all of which are personalities.
2. Finite personality is characterized by:
   A. Subjective self-consciousness.
   B. Objective response to the personality circuit.

VII. *REFERENCE*: Page 106, ¶6 - "There are creator personalities..."

COMMENT

1. In the cosmos there are three types of personality:
   A. Creator personalities.
   B. Creature personalities.
   C. Personalities of the Conjoint Actor.
2. Third Source personalities are not a part of the Father's personality circuit, but are contactable.

VIII. *REFERENCE*: Page 106, ¶7 - "The Father bestows..."

COMMENT

The three bestowals of personality:

1. Father personality—by his free will.
2. Third Source personality—non-Father.
3. The Infinite Spirit can also act for the Father in the bestowal of Father personality.

IX. *REFERENCE*: Page 106, ¶8 - "There are numerous types..."

COMMENT

1. Many personalities of the Infinite Spirit are not in the Father's personality circuit—certain of the power directors.

2. There are other groups not in the Father's circuit—such as the creative Spirits of a local universe.

X. REFERENCE: Page 106, ¶9 - "Both First Source and Third Source..."

COMMENT

1. All types of personality are endowed with all and more than man associates with personality.

2. Among other things, personality embraces memory, reason, judgment, creative imagination, idea association, decision, and choice.

XI. *REFERENCE*: Page 107, ¶1 - "Even you will be..."

COMMENT

Many spiritual beings are visible to morontians.

XII. *REFERENCE*: Page 107, ¶2 - "The functional family..."

COMMENT

This is a listing of the three main groups functioning under the Infinite Spirit.

XIII. *REFERENCE*: Page 107, ¶3 - "These groups serve..."

COMMENT

These groups function all over the grand universe.

XIV. *REFERENCE*: Page 107, ¶4 - "The spirit personalities..."

COMMENT

1. The personalities of the Infinite Spirit minister the Father's love and the Son's mercy to all the worlds of time and space.

2. They are the living ladder whereby man climbs from chaos to glory.

PAPER 10
The Paradise Trinity

PAPER 10
The Paradise Trinity

INTRODUCTION

I. *REFERENCE*: Page 108, ¶1 - "The Paradise Trinity..."

COMMENT

1. The Trinity facilitates the Father's escape from personality absolutism.

2. The Trinity associates God's infinite will with the absoluteness of Deity.

3. The Son and the Spirit provide for the Father's liberation from the limitations of primacy, perfection, changelessness, eternity, universality, absoluteness, infinity.

II. *REFERENCE*: Page 108, ¶2 - "The Paradise Trinity effectively..."

COMMENT

1. The Trinity provides for the full revelation of Deity.

2. The Stationary Sons of the Trinity provide for the full revelation of justice.

3. The Stationary Sons are:

Trinitized Secrets of Supremacy.
Eternals of Days.
Ancients of Days.
Perfections of Days.
Recents of Days.
Unions of Days.
Faithfuls of Days.
Perfectors of Wisdom.

Divine Counselors.

Universal Censors.

4.   The Trinity is Deity unity.

III. *REFERENCE*: Page 108, ¶3 - "From the present situation..."

COMMENT

1.   Looking back on the circle of eternity, the Trinity is deemed to have been inevitable.

2.   Without the Trinity, that which is could not have been.

3.   No concept of creation is equal to the absoluteness of Deity unity associated with the volitional liberation of personalization.

1. SELF-DISTRIBUTION OF THE FIRST SOURCE AND CENTER

I. *REFERENCE*: Page 108, ¶4 - "It would seem..."

COMMENT

1.   In the Father's policy of self-distribution, he reserves only those powers which are impossible of delegation or bestowal.

2.   The unselfish Father provides for the fullest possible experience for all his associates and creatures.

II. *REFERENCE*: Page 108, ¶5 - "The Universal Father..."

COMMENT

1.   The Father bestows upon his Sons all power and authority.

2.   He makes each Creator Son just as authoritative as would be the Eternal Son.

3.   Upon all persons, everywhere, God has bestowed everything of himself that is bestowable.

III. *REFERENCE*: Page 109, ¶2 - "Divine personality..."

COMMENT

Deity is not self-centered. The Father shares reality of being, equality of self, with the Son and the Spirit.

IV. *REFERENCE*: Page 109, ¶3 - "For knowledge concerning..."

COMMENT

1.   For knowledge of the Father we must depend on the Son. The Father has ceased to exist as an unqualified personality.

2. God bestowed absolute personality upon the Son—they both gave their conjoint personality to the Spirit.

V. *REFERENCE*: Page 109, ¶4 - "For these and other reasons..."

COMMENT

So it becomes difficult to know God except as revealed by the Son and ministered by the Spirit.

VI. *REFERENCE*: Page 109, ¶5 - "Since the Paradise Sons..."

COMMENT

Man's best understanding of Deity is derived from the incarnations of the Paradise bestowal Sons.

2. DEITY PERSONALIZATION

I. *REFERENCE*: Page 109, ¶6 - "By the technique..."

COMMENT

1. God, by divesting himself of absolute personality, becomes the potential Father of all other universe personalities—the Universal Father.

2. As absolute personality, the Father can function only with the Son.

3. As personal Father he is not limited in the bestowal of personality upon the creatures of the far-flung cosmos.

II. *REFERENCE*: Page 109, ¶7 - "After the Father..."

COMMENT

The joint bestowal, by the Father and the Son, of conjoint personality upon the Infinite Spirit completes the existential personalization of Deity.

III. *REFERENCE*: Page 110, ¶2 - "The Son is..."

COMMENT

The Son was indispensable to fatherhood. For a social group the Spirit was inevitable.

IV. *REFERENCE*: Page 110, ¶3 - "The First Source..."

COMMENT

1. The First Person of Deity is the infinite father-personality.

2. The Eternal Son is the unqualified personality—absolute.

3. The Spirit is the unique conjoint personality.

V. *REFERENCE*: Page 110, ¶4 – "The personality of..."

COMMENT

1. The personality of the Father is the personality of infinity minus the absolute personality of the Eternal Son.

2. The personality of the Infinite Spirit is the superadditive bestowal of:

    A. The liberated Father-personality.
    B. The absolute Son-personality.

VI. *REFERENCE*: Page 110, ¶5 – "The Universal Father..."

COMMENT

The Father, Son, and Spirit are each unique, individual, and original.

VII. *REFERENCE*: Page 110, ¶6 – "The Eternal Son alone..."

COMMENT

1. Only the Eternal Son experiences the fullest possible personality relationship:

    A. Sonship with the Father.
    B. With the Father, joint paternity of the Spirit.
    C. Equality with both Father and Spirit.

2. The Father knows the experience of having a Son—but he knows no ancestral antecedents.

3. The Eternal Son enjoys a dual experience:

    A. The experience of having a Father.
    B. The experience of being co-parent to the Infinite Spirit.

4. The Spirit enjoys the experience of twofold personality ancestry.

VIII. *REFERENCE*: Page 110, ¶7 – "I am of origin..."

COMMENT

The Universal Censor depicts various Trinity associations and explains why universe reality appears in seven variations of values, meanings, and personality.

3. THE THREE PERSONS OF DEITY

I. *REFERENCE*: Page 110, ¶8 - "Notwithstanding there is..."

COMMENT

1. There is only one Deity—but three personalizations.

2. In endowing man with the Adjuster, God said: "Let us make man in our own image." This is **Gen. 1:26**. *"Then God said, 'Let us make man in our image, after our likeness.'"*

3. **Note**: Plural Deity. The Creator addresses an equal—"us." Thus, the first chapter of our Bible recognizes the Trinity.

II. *REFERENCE*: Page 110, ¶9 - "We are taught..."

COMMENT

As viewed in the finite cosmos, the persons of the Trinity disclose diverse relationships with the universes.

III. *REFERENCE*: Page 111, ¶2 - "The Divine Sons..."

COMMENT

1. The divine Sons are the "Word of God," the children of the Spirit are the "Act of God."

2. The Son and Spirit work as two equal brothers for the honor of a common Father.

IV. *REFERENCE*: Page 111, ¶3 - "The Father, Son, and Spirit..."

COMMENT

Deities differ in their universe performances. When acting alone they seem to be limited in absoluteness.

V. *REFERENCE*: Page 111, ¶4 - "The Universal Father..."

COMMENT

1. Before divesting himself of that which constitutes the Son and the Spirit, the Father was a Deity: unqualified, absolute, infinite.

2. God could never be a Father without a Son.

3. God could never have existed alone—this relation has always existed. The Deities are all eternal.

VI. *REFERENCE*: Page 111, ¶5 - "We observe that..."

COMMENT

1. The Father divested himself of all absoluteness except:

    A. Absolute fatherhood.
    B. Absolute volition.
2. The Father has infinity of WILL.

VII. *REFERENCE*: Page 111, ¶6 - "In bestowing absoluteness..."

COMMENT

1. In bestowing absolute personality on the Son, the Father makes it impossible for himself to act alone as the personality-absolute.

2. By eternalizing the Conjoint Actor, there ensues the trinitarian interdependence of all three of the Deities.

VIII.*REFERENCE*: Page 111, ¶7 - "God is the..."

COMMENT

God is the Father-Absolute of all universe personalities, but in the universes of time and space he is absolute only in the Paradise Trinity.

IX. *REFERENCE*: Page 111, ¶7 - "The First Source..."

COMMENT

God functions in the superuniverses in seven ways and mostly through other personalities or agencies.

X. *REFERENCE*: Page 112, ¶1 - "All these relinquishments..."

COMMENT

Remember: All of the Father's limitations of universe authority are self-imposed.

XI. *REFERENCE*: Page 112, ¶2 - "The Eternal Son..."

COMMENT

The Son functions as one with his Deity associates, except in:

1. The Father's bestowal of Adjusters.

2. The Spirit's control of:

    A. Mind ministry.
    B. Energy manipulation.

XII. *REFERENCE*: Page 112, ¶3 - "The Infinite Spirit..."

COMMENT

1.   The Conjoint Actor is amazingly versatile—performing in spheres of mind, matter, and spirit.

2.   The Spirit acts for the Father-Son partnership and also for himself.

3.   The Conjoint Actor does not work directly with:
     A.   The physical gravity circuit.
     B.   The spirit gravity circuit.
     C.   The personality circuit.

4.   The Infinite Spirit exercises three supercontrols over even primary forces and energies—cosmic reality.

4. THE TRINITY UNION OF DEITY

I. *REFERENCE*: Page 112, ¶4 - "Of all absolute..."

COMMENT

1.   The Paradise Trinity is the first trinity. The members of a triunity are partners rather than corporative, but the triunity itself is an association. The Father, Son, and Spirit make up the first triunity.

2.   God functions as absolute Deity only in the Trinity and in relation to universe totality.

II. *REFERENCE*: Page 112, ¶5 - "Eternal Deity is..."

COMMENT

The Trinity makes possible, at the same time, the expression of all the diversity and unity of Deity.

III. *REFERENCE*: Page 112, ¶6 - "The Trinity is..."

COMMENT

1.   The Trinity is an association of infinite persons functioning in a nonpersonal capacity, but not in contravention of personality.

2.   The Trinity is like the forming of a corporation by father, son, and grandson.

IV. *REFERENCE*: Page 112, ¶7 - "The Paradise Trinity is..."

COMMENT

The Deities can function personally, as the Trinity, or as two, or as all three in collaboration.

V. *REFERENCE:* Page 112, ¶8 - "Ever remember that..."

COMMENT

The Trinity mystery cannot be explained: three as one and in one.

VI. *REFERENCE:* Page 112, ¶9 - "The Trinity is so related..."

COMMENT

1. The Trinity as related to universe totality must be recognized in contemplating any isolated cosmic event.

2. The Trinity functions on all levels of the cosmos. Man can have only a finite concept of the Trinity.

VII. *REFERENCE:* Page 113, ¶2 - "As a mortal..."

COMMENT

Just now we have only a finite view of the Trinity, but as we ascend we discover Trinity supremacy and ultimacy—if not absoluteness.

5. FUNCTIONS OF THE TRINITY

I. *REFERENCE:* Page 113, ¶3 - "The personal Deities..."

COMMENT

1. Deities have attributes, but the Trinity has functions such as totality attitudes and cosmic overcontrol.

2. These functions may pertain to the supreme, ultimate, and even the absolute.

II. *REFERENCE:* Page 113, ¶4 - "The functions of the..."

COMMENT

1. The Trinity is not just the sum of the Father's endowment plus the specialized attributes of the Son and the Spirit.

2. The Trinity results in deitization of new meanings, values, powers, and capacities.

3. Even creature associations are not augmented by mere arithmetical summation. Group potential exceeds the sum of the component parts.

III. *REFERENCE:* Page 113, ¶5-8 - "The Trinity maintains..."

COMMENT

Trinity attitudes may be presented in three groups:

1. *Attitude toward the Finite.* Trinity attitude toward the finite can best be understood by observation of the emerging Supreme Being. The Paradise Trinity in relation to the finite level is referred to as the Trinity of Supremacy.

2. *Attitude toward the Absonite.* This attitude may be comprehended by observation of the Ultimate. This relationship has been referred to as the Trinity of Ultimacy.

3. *The Absolute Attitude.* This represents the final action of total Deity.

IV. *REFERENCE*: Page 113, ¶9 - "The Trinity Infinite…"

COMMENT

The Trinity Infinite involves total relationships of the First Source and Center—deified and undeified. It is all but beyond human comprehension.

V. *REFERENCE*: Page 114, ¶1 - "But I do not…"

COMMENT

Language is inadequate to portray the nature and functions of the Trinity.

6. THE STATIONARY SONS OF THE TRINITY

I. *REFERENCE*: Page 114, ¶2 - "All law takes origin…"

COMMENT

1. Law *originates* in the First Source and Center.

2. Spiritual law *inheres* in the Second Source.

3. Law is *interpreted* by the Third Source.

4. Law is *applied* by the Trinity (justice) through certain Sons.

II. *REFERENCE*: Page 114, ¶3 - "*Justice* is inherent…"

COMMENT

1. Justice is inherent in the Trinity. Justice is the Trinity attitude of the personal Deities of love, mercy, and ministry.

2. No single person of Deity fosters justice. Justice is always a plural function.

III. *REFERENCE*: Page 114, ¶4 - *"Evidence, the basis of fairness..."*

COMMENT

The basis of *fairness* (justice associated with mercy) is *evidence* and is supplied by the personalities of the Third Source and Center.

IV. *REFERENCE*: Page 114, ¶5 - *"Judgment,* the final application..."

COMMENT

Judgment, the application of justice, is the work of the Stationary Sons of the Trinity.

V. *REFERENCE*: Page 114, ¶6 - "This group of Trinity Sons..."

COMMENT

This is a list of the 10 groups.

VI. *REFERENCE*: Page 114, ¶7 - "We are the children..."

COMMENT

These Trinity Sons represent the attitude of the Trinity only in the domains of executive judgment—justice. They were created for that purpose.

VII. *REFERENCE*: Page 115, ¶1 - "The Ancients of Days..."

COMMENT

The centers of final executive judgment are the headquarters of the seven superuniverses, where the Ancients of Days and their associates hold court.

VIII. *REFERENCE*: Page 115, ¶2 - "Justice is the..."

COMMENT

1. Mercy is the personal attitude of love; justice, the collective decision of law. Divine judgment is the soul of fairness.

2. Man cannot fully understand that the love of the Father and the justice of the Trinity are in reality co-ordinate.

7. THE OVERCONTROL OF SUPREMACY

I. *REFERENCE*: Page 115, ¶3 - "The First, Second..."

COMMENT

1. The three persons of Deity are equal to each other and they are one. "The Lord our God is one God." **See Deut. 6:4.** *"Hear, O Israel: The Lord our God is one Lord."*

2.   There is perfection of purpose and oneness of execution in the acts of the Trinity.

3.   The Father, Son, and Spirit are **one**. **See Isa. 44:6**. *"Thus says the Lord, the King of Israel...'I am the first and I am the last; besides me there is no god.'"*

II. *REFERENCE*: Page 115, ¶4 - "As things appear..."

COMMENT

The Trinity appears to be concerned only with totals—planets or universes. This totality attitude derives from the fact that the Trinity is total Deity.

III. *REFERENCE*: Page 115, ¶5 - "The Supreme Being..."

COMMENT

1.   While the Supreme Being is something other than the Trinity, in this age he does appear to reflect the Trinity attitude toward the finite level.

2.   The Deities do not personally function with the Supreme—only as the Trinity.

3.   The relation of the Trinity to the Supreme when he is finally evolved is not known.

IV. *REFERENCE*: Page 115, ¶6 - "We do not find..."

COMMENT

The overcontrol of Supremacy is not wholly predictable—the earmark of the partial finite reaction to the Trinity.

V. *REFERENCE*: Page 115, ¶7 - "The Mortal mind..."

COMMENT

1.   While many mysterious things work out for the welfare of the universe, there are events which are hard to understand, such as: physical catastrophes, appalling accidents, horrific disasters, painful illnesses, and world-wide scourges.

2.   Maybe these inexplicable vicissitudes of living are all meaningful in the overcontrol of the Supreme and the Trinity.

VI. *REFERENCE*: Page 116, ¶1 - "As a son of God..."

COMMENT

As sons of God, mortals can comprehend the love attitude of the Father, but they cannot always recognize the acts of the Trinity as being meaningful and considerate.

8. THE TRINITY BEYOND THE FINITE

I. *REFERENCE*: Page 116, ¶2 - "Many truths and facts..."

COMMENT

Mortals can only understand the Trinity by recognizing that many of its acts transcend the finite.

II. *REFERENCE*: Page 116, ¶3 - "It would be inadvisable..."

COMMENT

1.   The Trinity of Ultimacy is only partially understood by Transcendentalers.
2.   The Ultimate is a qualified representation of Trinity function on the absonite level of universe reality.

III. *REFERENCE*: Page 116, ¶4 - "The Universal Father..."

COMMENT

The total Deity function of the Trinity transcends both the finite and the absonite.

IV. *REFERENCE*: Page 116, ¶5 - "While no single person..."

COMMENT

It would seem that three Deities are required to activate the potential of total Deity—the Deity Absolute.

V. *REFERENCE*: Page 116, ¶6 - "We know the..."

COMMENT

The author knows the three Gods as persons and worships them. He does not personally know the Deity Absolute, whom he respects and honors.

VI. *REFERENCE*: Page 116, ¶7 - "I once sojourned..."

COMMENT

The theory of finaliters becoming the children of the Deity Absolute is presented.

VII. *REFERENCE*: Page 116, ¶8 – "The Corps of the Finality..."

COMMENT

1. Finaliters really know God—they have attained perfection in doing the will of God.

2. Having attained God on the finite level, we will seek him on the absonite level.

3. We may attain the Ultimate, but it is doubtful if we will ever really attain absolute Deity.

VIII. *REFERENCE*: Page 116, ¶9 – "It may be possible..."

COMMENT

1. Finaliters may partially attain the Deity Absolute.

2. But they can hardly attain the Universal Absolute, because the Universal will grow as the universes expand.

IX. *REFERENCE*: Page 117, ¶2 – "Only infinity can..."

COMMENT

Only infinity can disclose the Father-Infinite.

DISCUSSION OF THE TRINITY

1. The word "Trinity" is not found in the Bible.

2. The Trinity was essential to the Father's plan of self-distribution. p. 108.

3. The Trinity was inevitable. p. 15.

4. The Trinity is the only Deity reality embracing infinity. p. 15.

5. Divine justice is the function of the Paradise Trinity. p. 115.

6. Children of the Paradise Trinity:
    A. Trinitized Secrets of Supremacy.
    B. Eternals of Days.
    C. Ancients of Days.
    D. Perfections of Days.
    E. Recents of Days.
    F.. Unions of Days.
    G. Faithfuls of Days.

7. Other Trinity-origin beings.

   A.   Trinity Teacher Sons.
   B.   Perfectors of Wisdom.
   C.   Divine Counselors.
   D.   Universal Censors.
   E.   Inspired Trinity Spirits.

8. The triunities are the functional balance wheel of infinity. p. 1150.

9. See the description of the triunities—all seven. p. 1148-50.

10. The Universal Father is a member of all triunities.

11. The Father is not a member of the triodities. p. 1151.

12. Theory of the Trinity of Trinities. p. 1170.

13. The relation of the Trinity to the Supreme Being is discussed in several papers and numerous passages.

14. The word "Trinity" first appears in Greek in A.D. 181, used by Theophilus of Antioch. The Latin word from which we derive our English was first used by Tertullian in A.D. 200. There are other common theologic words not found in the Bible, for example, incarnation.

THE TRINITY IN THE OLD TESTAMENT

Gen. 1:26. *"Then God said, 'Let us make man in our image, after our likeness.'"*

Isa. 63:10. *"They rebelled and grieved his holy Spirit."*

Isa. 6:3. "Holy, Holy, Holy is the Lord of Hosts."

Num. 6:24-26. *"The Lord bless you and keep you:*
"The Lord make his face to shine upon you...
"The Lord lift up his countenance upon you..."

THE TRINITY IN THE NEW TESTAMENT

Eph. 2:18. *"Through him we both have access in one Spirit to the Father."*

Acts 2:33. *"Being therefore exalted at the right hand of God, and having received from the Father the promise of the Holy Spirit."*

OTHER REFERENCES IN *THE URANTIA BOOK*

1. *Absolute Unity.* "In the Paradise Trinity there is absolute unity despite the eternal identities of the co-ordinates of God." p. 41.

2. ***The Trinity as Creators.*** "The Paradise Trinity is existent. The stage of universal space is set for the manifold and never-ending panorama of the creative unfolding of the purpose of the Universal Father through the personality of the Eternal Son and by the execution of the God of Action, the executive agency for the reality performances of the Father-Son creator partnership." p. 91.

3. ***Trinity as Ancestor of Ancients of Days.*** "The Ancients of Days are all basically identical; they disclose the combined character and unified nature of the Trinity. They possess individuality and are in personality diverse, but they do not differ from each other as do the Seven Master Spirits. They provide the uniform directorship of the otherwise differing seven superuniverses, each of which is a distinct, segregated, and unique creation. The Seven Master Spirits are unlike in nature and attributes, but the Ancients of Days, the personal rulers of the superuniverses, are all uniform and superperfect offspring of the Paradise Trinity." p. 209.

4. ***The Trinity Emblem.*** "In personal appearance, Melchizedek resembled the then blended Nodite and Sumerian peoples, being almost six feet in height and possessing a commanding presence. He spoke Chaldean and a half dozen other languages. He dressed much as did the Canaanite priests except that on his breast he wore an emblem of three concentric circles, the Satania symbol of the Paradise Trinity. In the course of his ministry this insignia of three concentric circles became regarded as so sacred by his followers that they never dared to use it, and it was soon forgotten with the passing of a few generations." p. 1015.

5. The whole of **Paper 104** is devoted to the growth of the Trinity concept on Urantia.

6. ***Relation to the Supreme Being.*** "The source of the Supreme is in the Paradise Trinity—eternal, actual, and undivided Deity. The Supreme is first of all a spirit person, and this spirit person stems from the Trinity. But the Supreme is secondly a Deity of growth—evolutionary growth—and this growth derives from the two triodities, actual and potential." p. 1264.

7. ***The Trinity Was Inevitable.*** "The Paradise Trinity is considered to be the absolute inevitability; the Seven Master Spirits are apparently Trinity inevitabilities; the power-mind-spirit-personality actualization of the Supreme must be the evolutionary inevitability." p. 1266.

8. ***The Finaliter Oath Is to the Trinity***. "When mortal ascenders are finaliter admitted to the finaliter corps of Paradise, they take an oath to the Paradise Trinity, and in taking this oath of allegiance, they are thereby pledging eternal fidelity to God the Supreme, who is the Trinity as comprehended by all finite creature personalities. Subsequently, as the companies function throughout the evolving universes, they are solely amenable to the mandates of Paradise origin until the eventful times of the settling of local universes in light aznd life. As the new governmental organizations of these perfected creations begin to be reflective of the emerging sovereignty of the Supreme, we observe that the outlying finaliter companies then acknowledge the jurisdictional authority of such new governments. It appears that God the Supreme is evolving as the unifier of the evolutionary Corps of the Finality, but it is highly probable that the eternal destiny of these seven corps will be directed by the Supreme as a member of the Ultimate Trinity." p. 1292.

APPENDIX
The Oriental Scriptures

The sacred books of the Hindu peoples are the oldest and largest collection of scriptural writings extant. They were unknown to the Occident until they were brought to light in 1787 A.D. by an official of the East India Company. These voluminous writings are conventionally subdivided into six groups:

1. **The Vedas.**
2. **The Bramanas.**
3. **The Upanishads.**
4. **The Mahabharata.**
5. **Laws of Manu.**
6. **Puranas.**

It is not always possible to make this segregation, as, for example, the Forest Books (which close the Bramanas) in part form the introductory books of the Upanishads.

1. **The Vedas.** *(1000 B.C. or prior)* Devotional.

   The word Veda is derived from Sanskrit VID—to know. The four Vedas are fundamentally *devotional*.

   a. **The Rig Veda**—a collection of 1028 lyrical hymns, approximately five times the length of the Hebrew psalms.

   b. **The Sama Veda**—rendition of a majority of the Rig Veda hymns with musical notations. Chants.

   c. **The Yajur Veda**—liturgical writings. Ceremonies.

   d. **The Atharva Veda**—a collection of 730 incantations and other ritualistic formulas designed to work charms, etc.

2. **The Bramanas.** *(1000-600 B.C.)* Ceremonial.

   These prose treatises deal with the ritual of sacrifice and its philosophical implications. Much as the Talmud is a rabbinical exposition of the Pentateuch, so the Bramanas are a priestly exposition of the preceding Vedas.

   The **Aranyakas**—the Forest Books—close the Bramanas. Designed to be read in the solitude of the forest by religious isolationists, these books are meditational in character. They contain much priestly philosophy and are the transition link between the ceremonial Bramanas and the philosophical Upanishads.

3. **The Upanishads**. *(600-300 B.C.)* Philosophical.

In the course of the profound metaphysical speculations regarding the nature of reality, embraced in the 108 Upanishads, several concepts are developed:

> The Brahman—oversoul.
> The Atman—the individual soul.
> Karma—causality continuity.
> Nirvana—ultimate union with the oversoul.

The Upanishads conclude that reality is a monism. They negate the reality of all things excepting the indefinable all-encompassing and unknowable Absolute.

4. **The Mahabharata**. *(500 B.C.)* An epic poem.

This is an epic poem of great length containing much of the mythology of the Aryan invaders of India.

The **Bhagavad-Gita**, of origin perhaps in the first century B.C., was sometime thereafter inserted in the Mahabharata. It is one of the most appealing of all the Hindu scriptures being written in such a manner as to be comprehensible to the average man. It stresses religious activity and devotion. Some scholars have considered the possibility of its indebtedness to the earlier Christian writings, but this hypothesis has been generally rejected.

5. **Laws of Manu**. *(200 B.C.)* Legal—ethical.

This collection is legal and ethical in nature, dealing with the following problems.

a. Function of the four castes.
b. Supremacy of the priestly caste.
c. Perpetuation of the priestly caste.
d. Conduct of men in the secular life.
e. Conduct of men in the religious life.

6. **The Puranas**. *(100-1000 A.D.)*

This collection of poetry deals with cosmology, mythology, and imparts a vast miscellany of social and religious instruction.

THE TAOIST SCRIPTURES

1. **The Tao-Teh-King**. *6th Century B.C.*

Supposed to have been written by Lao Tze.

Part I – Tao: Deals with nature and functions of the "ultimate cause," the "cosmic essence," the "trend of the universe."

Part II – Teh: Portrays that kind of ethical living which allegiance to Tao brings forth.

2. **Works of Chuang Tze**. *3rd-4th Century B.C.*

Chuang Tze is the Paul of Taoism.

His works are directed primarily against the factualism and worldliness of Confucianism.

THE KORAN.

This is dated in the 7th Century A.D.

Written by Mohammed and purporting to be a transcription of the revelations of the Angel Gabriel.

Arrangement: 114 Chapters (Suras) about one-fourth the length of the Old Testament.

Content: Shows Christian, Jewish, and Zoroastrian influences.

A collection of myths, legends, narratives, legal statutes, ethical precepts, and ceremonial injunctions.

Not new, but a new adaptation of extant teachings to Arabia.

SCRIPTURES OF THE SIKHS

Sikhism, a blend of Islam and Hinduism, was founded in the 15th century A.D. by Nanak. In northwestern India he gathered followers from among both faiths and became their "guru" or master. An apostolic line of succession was maintained for some time. The fifth guru after Nanak collected his writings, added to them, and produced the Holy Bible of the Sikhs—the **Granth Sahib**.

Teachings of the Granth Sahib:

1. No caste—all are equal before God.
2. Monotheistic.
3. Transmigration and karma are accepted.
4. Ultimate destiny is "absorption into the Eternal Light."
5. Salvation is a matter of inner attitude rather than external observance.

6. Ascetic practices are valueless—only work done out of love for God has merit.

CONFUCIANISM

Total sacred writings consist of nine books—five canonical and four uncanonical.

1. ## The Canonical "Kings"

    The first four books were edited by Confucius; the fifth is largely his own work.

    a. **The YI King.** *(The "Canon of Changes")*
        To man's senses the universe seems to be a chaos. This is appearance, but not reality. There is an unceasing creative activity which is constantly arranging an apparent chaos into an orderly and comprehensive universe of *harmony*.

    b. **The SHU King.** *(The "Canon of History")*
        Historical-ethical work extolling the virtues of two semi-mythical rulers of antiquity.

    c. **The SHI King.** *(The "Canon of Odes")*
        Three hundred five odes traversing the whole range of Chinese lyric poetry.

    d. **The LI KI King.** *(The "Canon of Rites")*
        Portrays an inner law of control and balance as the source of the external harmony of an ideal society arising out of the restrained conduct of its virtuous citizens.

    e. **CHUNTSIN** *("Spring and Autumn")*
        These are the **"Annals of LU"** *(700-550 B.C.)*, the principality in which Confucius was born, and are, in the main, original with Confucius.
        His eight fundamental conceptions of peace are here portrayed as:

        (1) Heaven is the Lord of the universe and loves all creatures.

        (2) Universal love of mankind irrespective of racial differences.

        (3) Civilization vs. barbarism is a matter of property and justice.

        (4) Reciprocity is fundamental to successful international relations.

        (5) Truthfulness is the stability of international relations.

(6) War cannot be justified.

(7) There are divisions of territories, but not of people; all people belong to one family.

(8) The whole world is a great unity.

2. The Uncanonical "Four Books"

Though uncanonical, they have the same standing as the "Kings." They were written after the death of Confucius by his disciples— immediate and remote.

a. **LUN-YU.** *(Analects of Confucius)*
Twenty-five books setting forth Confucius' teaching, especially with reference to piety.

b. **TA-HIO.** *(The "Great Learning")*
Self-culture in relation to social ethics. Society is presented as an extension of the individual.

c. **CHUNG-YUNG.** *(The "Doctrine of the Mean")*
Confucius' dominant conception of the "mean"—the middle path between extremes set forth as a cosmic principle of equilibrium or balance.
THE GOLDEN RULE: "Keep the balance true between thyself and thy neighbor, practice the principle of equilibrium."

d. **MONGTZI.** *("Menicus")*
Lived 372-289 B.C. Greatest of disciples. Expounded Confucian teachings by use of dialogue form. Continues the exposition of the Doctrine of the Mean with especial emphasis on its relation to government.

3. Teachings of Confucianism

a. *The chief end of man* is to become a desirable member of society.

b. *Belief in God.* Confucius recognized a superhuman power that was related to man but said little on this subject.
NAME OF GOD: The term TIEN *(Heaven)* is used in preference to SHANG-TI *(Highest Lord)* which carried certain anthropomorphic connotations.

c. *Immortality*—He was an agnostic. Didn't accept or deny immortality.

PAPER 11
The Eternal Isle of Paradise

PAPER 11
The Eternal Isle of Paradise

1. **THE DIVINE RESIDENCE**
2. **NATURE OF THE ETERNAL ISLE**
3. **UPPER PARADISE**
4. **PERIPHERAL PARADISE**
5. **NETHER PARADISE**
6. **SPACE RESPIRATION**
7. **SPACE FUNCTIONS OF PARADISE**
8. **PARADISE GRAVITY**
9. **THE UNIQUENESS OF PARADISE**

INTRODUCTION

I. *REFERENCE:*Page 118, ¶1 – "Paradise is the..."

COMMENT

1. Paradise is the center of the master universe and the home of Deity.
2. Paradise is the largest organized body of reality in existence.
3. Paradise is material as well as spiritual. Spirit things and beings are *real*.

II. *REFERENCE:* Page 118, ¶2 – "The material beauty..."

COMMENT

1. Paradise beauty consists in its physical, intellectual, and spiritual endowments.
2. The glory and splendor of Paradise are beyond mortal comprehension.
3. Paradise is from eternity — there are no records of a beginning.

DISCUSSION OF THE WORD "PARADISE" IN THE BIBLE

The term Paradise is found only three times in the Bible, being used once each by Jesus, Paul, and John.

Luke 23:43. *"And he said to him, 'Truly, I say to you, today you will be with me in Paradise.'"*
Note: Here is a question of punctuation—comma

before or after "today." No punctuation in the original tongues. On page 2009 of *The Urantia Book*, Jesus says: "Verily, verily, I say to you today, you shall sometime be with me in Paradise."

2 Cor. 12:3. *"And I know that this man was caught up into Paradise— whether in the body or out of the body I do not know, God knows."*

Rev. 2:7. *"To him who conquers I will grant to eat of the tree of life, which is in the paradise of God."*

1. THE DIVINE RESIDENCE

I. *REFERENCE*: Page 118, ¶3 - "Paradise serves many purposes..."

COMMENT

1. The Universal Father resides at the center of this well-nigh circular, but not spherical Isle.

2. The Father is surrounded by the presence of the Son and they both are invested by the glory of the Infinite Spirit.

II. *REFERENCE*: Page 118, ¶4 - "God dwells..."

COMMENT

The Father is cosmically focalized, spiritually personalized, and geographically resident at this center of the cosmos.

III. *REFERENCE*: Page 118, ¶5 - "We all know..."

COMMENT

1. Celestial beings can find God's residence just as we can find geographic locations on our planet.

2. So, if properly equipped, we can go through universe upon universe until we attain Paradise.

3 Not having visited Paradise has nothing to do with the reality of God and his universe.

IV. *REFERENCE*: Page 119, ¶2 - "The Father is always..."

COMMENT

1. The stability of the master universe depends upon God's presence at the center of all things.

2. All four gravity circuits lead us directly to God on Paradise.

3. From God's presence on Paradise, there flow life, energy, and personality to the universe of universes.

2. NATURE OF THE ETERNAL ISLE

I. *REFERENCE*: Page 119, ¶3 - "Since you are..."

COMMENT

The discernible cosmos has a capital commensurate with the dignity and infinitude of its universal Ruler.

II. *REFERENCE*: Page 119, ¶4 - "In form..."

COMMENT

Paradise is ellipsoid, essentially flat, and is longer from north to south than from east to west.

III. *REFERENCE*: Page 119, ¶5 - "These differences in dimensions..."

COMMENT

Differential dimensions and pressure variations establish universe directions.

IV. *REFERENCE*: Page 119, ¶6,7 - "The central Isle..." and "We speak of..."

COMMENT

1. The Deities dominate upper Paradise—the personal plane.
2. The Unqualified Absolute dominates nether Paradise—the impersonal plane.
3. Peripheral Paradise provides for activities which are not strictly personal or nonpersonal.

V. *REFERENCE*: Page 120, ¶2 - "The eternal Isle..."

COMMENT

1. Paradise is composed of *absolutum*—stationary systems of reality.
2. Paradise material is neither dead nor alive. This material is not found elsewhere in all the cosmos.

VI. *REFERENCE*: Page 120, ¶3 - "It appears to us..."

COMMENT

The First Source and Center has concentrated all absolute potential for the cosmos in Paradise.

VII. *REFERENCE*: **Page 120, ¶4 - "Roughly, space seemingly originates..."**

COMMENT

1. Space seems to originate just below nether Paradise; time just above upper Paradise.

2. While time is nonexistent on Paradise, they do have a nontime sequence of events.

3. Motion is volitional, not inherent, on Paradise. Distance is relative.

4. Paradise is nonspatial.

3. UPPER PARADISE

I. *REFERENCE*: **Page 120, ¶5 - "On upper Paradise..."**

COMMENT

1. Upper Paradise has three grand zones:
    A. Deity presence.
    B. Most Holy Sphere.
    C. Holy Area.
2. Everything pertaining to the Most Holy Sphere is purely spiritual— nothing else could there exist.

II. *REFERENCE*: **Page 120, ¶6 - "While there are..."**

COMMENT

In the Holy Area and on the periphery there are abundant reminders of material existence.

III. *REFERENCE*: **Page 120, ¶7 - "The Holy Area..."**

COMMENT

1. The seven residential zones of the Holy Area are often called "the Father's Paradise mansions."

2. Havona natives dwelling on Paradise live in the first sons.

3. The seven divisions of the second zone are occupied by the ascenders from the seven superuniverses.

IV. *REFERENCE*: **Page 121, ¶2 - "Each of the seven sectors..."**

COMMENT

1. Each residential unit is suitable for one billion working groups.

2.   These units are organized as follows:

> 1,000 units are a division.
>
> 100,000 divisions are a congregation.
>
> 10,000,000 congregations are an assembly.
>
> 1,000,000,000 assemblies are a grand unit.
>
> And this continues on through to the seventh grand unit.
>
> 7 grand units make a master unit.
>
> 7 master units make a superior unit.
>
> And thus by sevens the series extends through the superior, super-superior, celestial, supercelestial, on to the supreme units.

3.   And all of these residential units occupy less than one per cent of the Holy Land.

4. PERIPHERAL PARADISE

I. *REFERENCE*: Page 121, ¶3 - "The central Isle..."

COMMENT

The landing and dispatching fields of Paradise are on the periphery.

II. *REFERENCE*: Page 121, ¶4 - "The Seven Master Spirits..."

COMMENT

1.   The Seven Master Spirits:

   A.   Have personal headquarters on the seven worlds of the Spirit.
   B.   Maintain force-focal headquarters on the Paradise periphery.

2.   From these Paradise centers, force goes to the seven superuniverses.

III. *REFERENCE*: Page 121, ¶5 - "Here on peripheral Paradise..."

COMMENT

1.   The historic exhibits of the Creator Sons are on the periphery, with space reserved for seven trillion.

2.   Since only four per cent of this space is assigned, there must be reservations for the domains of outer space.

IV. *REFERENCE*: Page 121, ¶6 - "That portion of Paradise..."

COMMENT

Less than four per cent of Paradise area which has been assigned for existing universes is now occupied. The area assigned is one million times what is needed.

V. *REFERENCE*: Page 121, ¶7 - "But a further attempt..."

COMMENT

We will not appreciate Paradise until we get there. "Eye has not seen nor ear heard," etc. This is **1 Cor. 2:9**. *"'What no eye has seen, nor ear heard, nor the heart of man conceived, what God has prepared for those who love him.'"*

5. NETHER PARADISE

I. *REFERENCE*: Page 122, ¶2 and following - "Concerning nether Paradise..."

COMMENT

1. Personalities and spirit beings have nothing to do with nether Paradise.

2. Cosmic-force circuits originate on nether Paradise.

3. Underneath the Deities is the Zone of Infinity.

4. The outer margins have to do with space potency and force-energy. The force-charge of space is here focused.

5. The three zones have differential functions.

II. *REFERENCE*: Page 122, ¶3 - "The inner zone..."

COMMENT

1. The inner zone is like a gigantic force-heart whose pulsations send energy to the borders of physical space.

2. Force seems to flow in at the south and out at the north.

3. These forces, while not responsive to physical gravity, always respond to Paradise gravity.

III. *REFERENCE*: Page 122, ¶4 - "The mid-zone..."

COMMENT

1. The mid-zone appears to be static, but experiences three sorts of pulsation.

2. This zone may be concerned with the control of the mid-space zones of relative quiet between universe divisions.

3. This mid-area is also related to the nonpervaded-space mechanism.

IV. *REFERENCE*: Page 122, ¶5 – "The outer zone..."

COMMENT

1. The space potential of the outer zone sends energy to the very borders of all outer space.

2. This may be the focal center of the space presence of the Unqualified Absolute.

V. *REFERENCE*: Page 123, ¶2 – "All forms of force..."

COMMENT

1. In this zone of the Unqualified Absolute, energy is either coming in or going out—never both at the same time.

2. The zone pulsations are agelong—one billion years outgoing—one billion years incoming.

3. These space-force manifestations extend throughout all pervadable space.

VI. *REFERENCE*: Page 123, ¶3 – "All physical force..."

COMMENT

1. All force-energy proceeds from nether Paradise and eventually returns thereto.

2. But all of present universe reality did not come, as such, from nether Paradise.

3. Space is the womb of several forms of matter and prematter.

4. Space does not originate on nether Paradise.

5. Space is not force, energy, or power.

6. These zone pulsations do not account for space respiration, but they are synchronized with it.

6. SPACE RESPIRATION

I. *REFERENCE*: Page 123, ¶4 – "We do not know..."

COMMENT

The vertical reservoirs of unpervaded space are similar to an hourglass.

II. *REFERENCE*: Page 123, ¶5 - "As the universes..."

COMMENT

1.   Pervaded space and unpervaded space behave reciprocally.
2.   There is a confluence of the two phases of space under nether Paradise.
3.   In this transmuting channel, the two forms of space are adapted for the space respiration cycles.

III. *REFERENCE*: Page 123, ¶6 - "'Unpervaded' space means..."

COMMENT

1.   "Unpervaded" space means unpervaded by those forces and presences found in pervaded space.
2.   Unpervaded space reservoirs seem to counterbalance pervaded space.
3.   It is not known whether there is a future function of these unpervaded space reservoirs.

IV. *REFERENCE*: Page 123, ¶7 - "The cycles of..."

COMMENT

1.   The cosmos expands and contracts in billion year cycles.
2.   Just now pervaded space is at the mid-point of expansion.
3.   The unpervaded space reservoirs are at the mid-point of contraction.

V. *REFERENCE*: Page 124, ¶2 - "For a billion years..."

COMMENT

The complete space respiration cycle requires a little more than two billion years for completion.

7. SPACE FUNCTIONS OF PARADISE

I. *REFERENCE*: Page 124, ¶3 - "Space does not exist..."

COMMENT

Space does not touch Paradise—only the midspace zones do.

II. *REFERENCE*: Page 124, ¶4 - "Paradise is the..."

COMMENT

1.   Paradise is the center of the quiescent midspace zones—they appear to be an extension of Paradise
2.   These midspace zones separate pervaded and unpervaded space.

III. *REFERENCE*: Page 124, ¶5 – "The vertical cross section..."

COMMENT

1. A vertical cross section of total space resembles a maltese cross.

2. These quiescent midspace zones between pervaded and unpervaded space:

   A. Grow larger at greater distances from Paradise.
   B. Eventually encompass the borders of all space.
   C. Incapsulate the unpervaded space reservoirs and all pervaded space.

IV. *REFERENCE*: Page 124, ¶6 – "Space is neither..."

COMMENT

1. Space is:

   A. A bestowal of Paradise.
   B. Pervaded by the ancestral space potency of the Unqualified Absolute.

2. Space is not:

   A. A subabsolute condition within the Unqualified Absolute.
   B. The presence of the Unqualified Absolute.
   C. A function of the Ultimate.

3. Space extends from near Paradise periphery to beyond the borders of the master universe.

V. *REFERENCE*: Page 124, ¶7 – "If you imagine..."

COMMENT

An outline of pervaded space.

VI. *REFERENCE*: Page 124, ¶8 – "There is an upper..."

COMMENT

1. There is an upper and lower limit to pervaded space.

2. As we go out from Paradise, pervaded space thickens—even faster than does the plane of the universes.

VII. *REFERENCE*: Page 125, ¶2 - "The relatively quiet zone..."

COMMENT

1. These space quiet zones separate the seven superuniverses from the vast galaxies in the first outer space level racing around Paradise.
2. The first outer space level is bounded above and below by quiescent midspace zones and on the inner and outer margins by relatively quiet zones.

VIII. *REFERENCE*: Page 125, ¶3 - "A space level thus functions..."

COMMENT

A description of a space level.

IX. *REFERENCE*: Page 125, ¶4 - "This alternate zoning..."

COMMENT

1. The alternate zoning of the master universe, together with alternate clockwise and counterclockwise flow of the galaxies, contributes to control and stabilization.
2. These arrangements exert antigravity influence and prevent dangerous velocities.

8. PARADISE GRAVITY

I. *REFERENCE*: Page 125, ¶5 - "The inescapable pull..."

COMMENT

1. Paradise gravity effectively grips all the worlds of all the universes.
2. Gravity is the omnipotent strand on which are strung the gleaming stars, blazing suns, and whirling spheres.
3. This is the physical adornment of the God in whom all things consist. (This is a combination of **Eph. 1:23** and **Col. 1:17**.)

    Eph. 1:23. *"The fulness of him who fills all in all."*

    Col. 1:17. *"And in him all things hold together."*

II. *REFERENCE*: Page 125, ¶6 - "The center and focal point..."

COMMENT

1. The center of absolute gravity is Paradise, complemented by the dark gravity bodies.

2.   All emanations of nether Paradise respond to Paradise gravity as they follow the space circuits of the master universe.

3.   Every known form of cosmic reality has:

A. The bend of the ages.
B. The trend of the circle.
C. The swing of the great ellipse.

III. *REFERENCE*: Page 125, ¶7 - "Space is nonresponsive..."

COMMENT

1.   Space is nonresponsive to gravity, but it acts as an equilibrant.

2.   Space can neutralize linear gravity, but it cannot delay it.

3.   Absolute gravity is Paradise gravity. Local (linear) gravity pertains to the electrical stage of matter.

IV. *REFERENCE*: Page 125, ¶8 and following - "The numerous forms..."

COMMENT

1.   Cosmic forces disclose three stages of response to Paradise gravity:

A.   *Segregata*—space potency turning into pre-energy.
B.   *Ultimata*—appearance of negative and positive qualities in energy systems.
C.   *Triata* (3-fold organization in Havona) and *Gravita* (2-fold organization in superuniverses) — the stage where response to linear gravity appears.

2.   The Havona dark gravity bodies exercise both linear and absolute gravity.

V. *REFERENCE*: Page 126, ¶4 - "Space potency is not..."

COMMENT

1.   Space potency is not subject to any form of gravitation.

2.   But space potency is ancestral to all forms of nonspiritual reality.

3.   Space potency is not ancestral to space.

4.   Space potency includes those absolute potentials which emanate from Paradise and constitute the space presence of the Unqualified Absolute.

VI. *REFERENCE*: Page 126, ¶5 - "Paradise is the..."

COMMENT

1. Paradise is the source of all energy-matter in the cosmos.

2. The Unqualified Absolute is the revealer, regulator, and repository of all that which has Paradise as its source.

3. The Unqualified Absolute's presence explains the potential infinity of Paradise gravity extension.

4. This explains why gravity acts in the plane perpendicular to the mass.

9. THE UNIQUENESS OF PARADISE

I. *REFERENCE*: Page 126, ¶6 - "Paradise is unique..."

COMMENT

Paradise is the origin and goal of all spirit personalities.

II. *REFERENCE*: Page 126, ¶7 - "Paradise is the geographic center..."

COMMENT

Paradise is the geographic center of infinity.

III. *REFERENCE*: Page 127, ¶1 - "In the eternity..."

COMMENT

1. Paradise seems to have been the inevitable repercussion of the Father's will which eternalized the Original Son.

2. The Father thus created two kinds of reality—the personal and the nonpersonal.

3. Spiritual and nonspiritual tension gave origin to the Conjoint Actor and the central universe.

IV. *REFERENCE*: Page 127, ¶2 - "When reality is..."

COMMENT

1. That which is nonpersonal is not Deity.

2. Paradise is not Deity—it is not conscious.

V. *REFERENCE*: Page 127, ¶3 - "Paradise is not ancestral..."

COMMENT

1. Paradise is not a creator. Personality and mind-spirit realities are transmissible, but patterns are not.

2. Paradise is the absolute of pattern. Patterns can be reproduced.

VI. *REFERENCE*: Page 127, ¶4 - "God's residence is central..."

COMMENT

God's residence is the pattern for all universe headquarters.

VII. *REFERENCE*: Page 127, ¶5 - "Paradise is the universal..."

COMMENT

1. Paradise is the headquarters of personality and source of all energy.
2. All that is, has been, or ever will be has origin in Paradise.
3. Paradise is the source of all energy and all personality.

VIII.*REFERENCE*: Page 127, ¶6 - "After all, to mortals..."

COMMENT

1. Paradise is the destiny of all mortal ascenders.
2. Every God-knowing mortal is on the perfection trail to Paradise.
3. Attainment of Paradise is a transformation bordering on the limits of supremacy.

DISCUSSION OF PARADISE

1. Space as we understand it is nonexistent on Paradise. p. 2.
2. Paradise is the geographic center of infinity. p. 1.
3. Paradise:
   A. Is the Absolute of material-gravity control.
   B. Is motionless.
   C. Has a universe location.
   D. Has no position in space. p.7.
4. God is spirit but Paradise is not. p. 139.
5. On Paradise there is always more worship impulse than has been provided for. p. 304.

THE BIBLE ON HEAVEN AND HELL

I. **HEAVEN**

1. Hebrew concept of heaven.

    A. The earth is flat.
    B. Heaven is above the earth.
    C. Hell is under the earth.

2. God and the angels are in heaven. The dead are in hell—the pit.

3. Heaven rests on pillars—foundation.

    2 Sam. 22:8. *"Then the earth reeled and rocked; the foundations of the heavens trembled."*

    Prov. 8:27, 28. *"When the established the heavens, I was there… when he made firm the skies above."*

    Job 26:11. *"The pillars of heaven tremble."*

4. Plurality of heavens.

    Deut. 10:14. *"Behold, to the Lord your God belong heaven and the heaven of heavens."*

    Neh. 9:6. *"Thou hast made heaven, the heaven of heavens, with all their host."*

5. The Hebrews believed in seven heavens. God's throne was in the seventh heaven.

    Ps. 11:4. *"The Lord's throne is in heaven."*

    1 King 8:49. *"Hear thou in heaven thy dwelling place."*

6. Paradise was regarded as the third heaven.

    2 Cor. 12:2. *"I know a man in Christ who…was caught up to the third heaven."*

7. The second heaven was the abode of evil spirits and fallen angels.

    Eph. 6:12. *"Against the spiritual hosts of wickedness in the heavenly places."*

8. But heaven was not sensuous like the heaven of Islam.

    Mark 12:25. *"When they rise from the dead, they neither marry nor are given in marriage, but are like angels in heaven."*

9.   God fills all heaven.

2 Chron. 2:6. *"Heaven, even highest heaven cannot contain him."*

Jer. 23:24. *"Do I not fill heaven and earth? says the Lord."*

10.   Heaven—the residence of Deity.

Deut. 26:15. *"Look down from thy holy habitation, from heaven, and bless thy people."*

Rev. 11:19. *"Then God's temple in heaven was opened."*

11.   Heaven was associated with atmospheric phenomena.

Gen. 1:8. *"And God called the firmament Heaven."*

Gen. 7:11. *"The fountains of the great deep burst forth, and the windows of the heavens were opened."*

Exod. 16:4. *"Then the Lord said to Moses, 'Behold, I will rain bread from heaven.'"*

2 Sam. 22:14. *"The Lord thundered from heaven."*

12.   War in heaven.

Rev. 12:7. *"Now war arose in heaven."*

Isa. 14:12. *"How you are fallen from heaven, O Day Star, son of Dawn."*

Luke 10:18. *"'I saw Satan fall like lightning from heaven.'"*

13.   As related to astronomy.

Jer. 33:22. *"As the host of heaven cannot be numbered."*

Ps. 19:1. *"The heavens are telling the glory of God; and the firmament proclaims his handiwork."*

14.   Guardian angels are stationed in heaven.

Matt. 18:10. *"I tell you that in heaven their angels always behold the face of my Father."*

Gen. 22:15. *"And the angel of the Lord called to Abraham…from heaven."*

II. HELL

1.   **Sheol**—the pit.

HADES is the Latin word for Sheol. The Hebrew underworld of the dead.

A. Hebrew concept of Hades.

The Greeks thought of Hades as a place of activity. The Hebrews thought it was a place of inactivity. **See Ps. 94:17.** *"If the Lord had not been my help, my soul would soon have dwelt in the land of silence."*

B. Sheol had four levels.

(1) The abode of martyrs. These martyrs were sure of a resurrection.

(2) The level of the righteous. They also were sure of resurrection.

(3) Level of prosperous sinners. These had a chance of salvation.

(4) The level of poor sinners. Not much hope for them. Poverty and sickness were indications of God's frown.

C. Hebrews thought that the dead might possibly come back to earth.

1 Sam. 2:6. *"The Lord kills and brings to life; he brings down to Sheol and raises up."*

Saul and the Endor medium.

1 Sam. 28:11. *"Then the woman said, 'Whom shall I bring up for you?' He said, 'Bring up Samuel for me.'"*

D. State in Sheol.

Job 14:21. *"His sons come to honor, and he does not know it."*

Ps. 115:17. *"The dead do not praise the Lord, nor do any that go down into silence."*

Eccl. 9:10. *"There is no work or thought or knowledge or wisdom in Sheol."*

E. Fire connected with Sheol.

Deut. 32:22. *"For a fire is kindled by my anger, and it burns to the depths of Sheol."*

Rev. 20:14. *"Then Death and Hades were thrown into the lake of fire."*

F. Sheol—destiny of the wicked.

Ps. 9:17. *"The wicked shall depart to Sheol."*

Prov. 7:27. *"Her house is the way to Sheol."*

Matt. 10:28. *"Rather fear him who can destroy both soul and body in hell."*

Luke 12:5. *"Fear him who...has power to cast into hell."*

G. The PIT means hell.

Eze. 31:16. *"I cast it down to Sheol with those who go down to the Pit."*

H. Deliverance from hell.

Rev. 1:18. *"And I have the keys of Death and Hades."*

Ps. 86:13. *"Thou hast delivered my soul from the depths of Sheol."*

I. The two resurrections.

John 5:29. *"And come forth, those who have done good, to the resurrection of life, and those who have done evil, to the resurrection of judgment."*

2. **Gehenna**

This was the Hinnom valley, where there may have been a sanctuary of MOLECH, where human sacrifices were offered. (**Jer. 7:31**.)

A. It was defiled by King Josiah. (**2 Kings 23:6**.)

B. Gehenna is often used as a synonym for Hell.

C. The Jews thought the souls in Gehenna might somehow be purified by fire—they held ideas somewhat like those of the Catholic concept of purgatory.

D. This concept is also suggested by Jesus' preaching to the spirits in prison.

1 Peter 3:19. *"In which he went and preached to the spirits in prison."*

PAPER 12
The Universe of Universes

PAPER 12
The Universe of Universes

INTRODUCTION

I. *REFERENCE*: Page 128, ¶1 - "The immensity of..."

COMMENT

The immensity of the cosmos does not prevent our learning something about it and the persons who live in it.

II. *REFERENCE*: Page 128, ¶2 - "In principle..."

COMMENT

In potential, the universe may be infinite, but in actuality it is space limited.

III. *REFERENCE*: Page 128, ¶3 - "We are convinced..."

COMMENT

1. The cosmos is unfinished—the potential of the Infinite is not wholly revealed.

2. The revelation of the eternal purpose is still in progress.

1. SPACE LEVELS OF THE MASTER UNIVERSE

I. *REFERENCE*: Page 128, ¶4 - "The universe of universes..."

COMMENT

1. The cosmos has dimensions. The universe is a limited and co-ordinate whole.

2. This delimited universe is under the control of Paradise gravity.

II. *REFERENCE*: Page 128, ¶5 - "The successive space levels..."

COMMENT

1. The outer space levels constitute the major divisions of the master universe.
2. The cosmos keeps control of its energies—they do not escape.
3. Energy whirls and swings onward in the great space circuits.

III. *REFERENCE*: Page 129, ¶2 - "Proceeding outward..."

COMMENT

Proceeding outward from Paradise, we encounter six space levels:

1. The Central Universe—Havona.
2. The Seven Superuniverses.
3. First Outer Space Level.
4. Second Outer Space Level.
5. Third Outer Space Level.
6. Fourth Outer Space Level.

IV. *REFERENCE*: Page 129, ¶3 - "*Havona*, the central universe..."

COMMENT

A description of Havona.

V. *REFERENCE*: Page 129, ¶4 - "*The Paradise-Havona System...*"

COMMENT

The seven superuniverses revolve around the Havona creation and Paradise.

VI. *REFERENCE*: Page 129, ¶5 - "*The Seven Superuniverses...*"

COMMENT

1. Superuniverses do not divide a nebula or cross local universes.
2. Each superuniverse embraces about one seventh of the inhabited cosmos.
3. Nebadon is one of the newer universes in Orvonton.

VII. *REFERENCE*: Page 129, ¶6 - "The Grand Universe..."

COMMENT

1. A bird's-eye view of the grand universe.

2. Evidences of an unfinished creation—limits of habitation.

3. Location of the local universe of Nebadon.

VIII.REFERENCE: Page 129, ¶7 - "The Outer Space Levels..."

COMMENT

1. Vast systems of force and materializing energy are organizing in outer space.

2. The quiet space zone intervening is about 400,000 light years.

3. Semiquiet space zones are free from cosmic fog.

4. The galaxies of the first outer space level appear at about 500,000 light years from the outer borders of the grand universe.

5. This outer belt of creation, the first outer space zone, encircles the whole organized and inhabited cosmos.

IX. REFERENCE: Page 130, ¶2 - "Still greater activities..."

COMMENT

Fifty million light years beyond the first outer space level still greater cosmic activities are in progress.

X. REFERENCE: Page 130, ¶3 - "The central universe is..."

COMMENT

1. Havona is the creation of eternity; the superuniverses, of time; the outer space cosmos, of eventuated ultimacy.

2. There are those who believe in an ever-expanding universe of infinity.

3. The present master universe is delimited—bounded on its outer margins by open space.

2. THE DOMAINS OF THE UNQUALIFIED ABSOLUTE

I. REFERENCE: Page 130, ¶4 - "When Urantia astronomers..."

COMMENT

1. What astronomers see in outer space is the mighty outworking of the plans of the Architects of the Master Universe.

2. In general, these activities beyond the borders of the grand universe represent the domains of the Unqualified Absolute.

II. *REFERENCE*: Page 130, ¶5 - "Although the unaided..."

COMMENT

1.   The eye can see only two or three nebulae beyond Orvonton, but the telescope reveals billions of universes in formation.

2.   And there are other millions of universes beyond the range of our most powerful telescopes.

III. *REFERENCE*: Page 130, ¶6 - "In the not-distant future..."

COMMENT

1.   New telescopes will reveal 375 million new galaxies in outer space.

Note: Galaxies, not nebulae or universes. Orvonton, the Milky Way, is a galaxy.

2.   Many island universes thought to be in outer space belong to Orvonton.

3.   The superuniverses are all enlarging. New nebulae are being organized.

IV. *REFERENCE*: Page 131, ¶2 - "The Uversa star students..."

COMMENT

1.   The grand universe is surrounded by an ever-expanding creation of the master universe.

2.   The energy and matter of these outer regions equal many times the total mass of the grand universe.

3.   These outer space phenomena are the work of the Paradise force organizers.

4.   The Orvonton power directors have nothing to do with these outer space realms.

V. *REFERENCE*: Page 131, ¶3 - "We know very little..."

COMMENT

1.   Very little is known about what is really going on in these outer realms.

2.   It is thought that no beings like mortals or angels exist on the spheres of these outer regions.

VI. *REFERENCE*: Page 131, ¶4 - "Throughout Orvonton..."

COMMENT

A new order of creation is taking place in outer space. The Corps of the Finality is destined to serve on these new spheres.

3. UNIVERSAL GRAVITY

I. *REFERENCE*: Page 131, ¶5 - "All forms of force-energy..."

COMMENT

1. All forms of reality are subject to the grasp of the universal gravity circuits.

2. The Universal Father functions over all four of the gravity circuits of the master universe:
   A. Personality Gravity of the Father.
   B. Spirit Gravity of the Eternal Son.
   C. Mind Gravity of the Conjoint Actor.
   D. Cosmic Gravity of Paradise.

II. *REFERENCE*: Page 131, ¶6 - "These four circuits..."

COMMENT

These circuits are not related to nether Paradise—they are *presence* circuits.

III. *REFERENCE*: Page 132, ¶1 - "In this connection..."

COMMENT

Report concerning a study of gravity systems.

IV. *REFERENCE*: Page 132, ¶1 - "1. Physical Gravity..."

COMMENT

1. After computing the total gravity active from Paradise, it is found that the grand universe is making use of only five per cent of such gravity.

2. These calculations refer to absolute gravity.

V. *REFERENCE*: Page 132, ¶3 - "2. Spiritual Gravity..."

COMMENT

1. In the case of spirit gravity it is found that the spirit gravity of the grand universe is about the same as the estimated total for the active function of the Eternal Son.

2. This suggests that the now forming universes of outer space are nonspiritual.

VI. *REFERENCE*: Page 132, ¶4 - "3. Mind Gravity..."

COMMENT

1. It is more difficult to estimate total mind gravity, but it has been attempted.

2. It is found that about 85 per cent of mind gravity is accounted for by the grand universe.

3. This suggests that 15 per cent of mind gravity may be functioning in outer space. These intelligences are apparently nonspiritual in nature.

VII. *REFERENCE*: Page 133, ¶2 - "But all these..."

COMMENT

These deductions are estimates but they are fairly reliable.

VIII. *REFERENCE*: Page 133, ¶3 - "Personality Gravity..."

COMMENT

Personality gravity is noncomputable.

4. SPACE AND MOTION

I. *REFERENCE*: Page 133, ¶4 - "All units of cosmic energy..."

COMMENT

1. All energy units are in primary revolution while swinging around the Paradise orbit.

2. In all the cosmos, nothing is stationary except Paradise.

II. *REFERENCE*: Page 133, ¶5 - "The Unqualified Absolute..."

COMMENT

1. The Unqualified Absolute is functionally limited to space. His relation to motion is uncertain.

2. Motion is not inherent in space—not even the motion of space.

3. There are three opinions regarding the origin of motion.

III. *REFERENCE*: Page 133, ¶6 - "In outer space..."

COMMENT

The Unqualified Absolute must prepare space for the functioning of the force organizers.

IV. *REFERENCE*: Page 133, ¶7 - "Space is..."

Comment

Space is real, it even moves. Space motions may be classified as follows:

1. Primary motion.
2. Secondary motion.
3. Relative motions.
4. Compensatory or correlating movement.

V. *REFERENCE*: Page 134, ¶1 - "The present relationship..."

Comment

1. The idea of an "exploding" cosmos is not true. Outward expansion is uniform.
2. The entire master universe participates in this space respiration.

VI. *REFERENCE*: Page 134, ¶2 - "When the universes..."

Comment

The work of cosmic respiration is *space* work—not power-energy work.

VII. *REFERENCE*: Page 134, ¶3 - "Although your spectroscopic..."

Comment

1. Spectroscopic estimations of outer space velocities are unreliable.
2. The theory of increased velocity according to distance is false. This error is due to angles of observation and other time-space distortions.

VIII. *REFERENCE*: Page 134, ¶4 - "But the greatest..."

Comment

The greatest distortion is due to the alternating direction of the space paths around Paradise.

IX. *REFERENCE*: Page 134, ¶5 - "It is probable..."

Comment

These alternate directions of the space paths around Paradise are concerned in the gravity control of the cosmos.

5. SPACE AND TIME

I. *REFERENCE*: Page 134, ¶6 - "Like space..."

COMMENT

1. Time is a bestowal of Paradise, but not like space. Time comes from motion because mind is aware of sequentiality.

2. Motion is essential to time, but the only universal time unit is the Paradise day.

II. *REFERENCE*: Page 135, ¶2 - "Space is not infinite..."

COMMENT

Space is neither infinite nor absolute, but the absolute of time is eternity.

III. *REFERENCE*: Page 135, ¶3 - "Time and space..."

COMMENT

Time and space are inseparable only in the finite cosmos. Nonspatial time exists only in the Paradise mind.

IV. *REFERENCE*: Page 135, ¶4 - "The relatively motionless..."

COMMENT

1. The relatively motionless midspace zones impinging on Paradise are the transition zones from tine to eternity.

2. Time-conscious beings can visit Paradise, but unconsciousness precedes Paradise citizenship.

V. *REFERENCE*: Page 135, ¶5 - "Relationships to time..."

COMMENT

1. Motion is essential to space relationships, but consciousness of time can exist without motion.

2. Man's mind is less time-bound than space-bound. Imagination is comparatively time free.

VI. *REFERENCE*: Page 135, ¶6 - "There are three..."

COMMENT

There are three levels of time recognition.

VII.*REFERENCE*: Page 135, ¶7 - "Unspiritual animals know..."

COMMENT

1. Animals know only the past; man has insight—may know the future.

2. Reality is progressive—static morality is but slightly superanimal.

3. Stoicism is not a high order of self-realization. Human ethics are dynamic.

VIII.*REFERENCE*: Page 135, ¶8 - "The human personality..."

COMMENT

Personality is not merely a concomitant of time-space events; personality can cause cosmic events.

6. UNIVERSAL OVERCONTROL

I. *REFERENCE*: Page 135, ¶9 - "The universe is nonstatic..."

COMMENT

The universe is nonstatic—stability is proportional to divinity—it is not due to inertia, but results from:

1. Balanced energies.

2. Co-operative minds.

3. Co-ordinated morontias.

4. Spirit overcontrol.

5. Personality unification.

II. *REFERENCE*: Page 135, ¶10 - "In the physical control..."

COMMENT

The master universe is controlled by the Universal Father through:

1. Physical—the Isle of Paradise.

2. Spiritual—the Eternal Son.

3. Mindal—the Conjoint Actor.

III. *REFERENCE*: Page 136, ¶1 - "The Third Source..."

COMMENT

1. The Conjoint Actor contributes to the co-ordination of the cosmos by:

    A. Absoluteness of cosmic mind control.

B.   Physical- and spiritual-gravity complements.

2.   Mind functions wherever the material and the spiritual become interassociated.

IV. REFERENCE: Page 136, ¶2 - "In all your contemplation..."

COMMENT

When physical, mindal, and spiritual energies are associated, you must reckon with:

1.   Unification by personality.

2.   Reactions of experiential Deity.

3.   Actions of the Absolutes.

V. REFERENCE: Page 136, ¶3 - "The universe is..."

COMMENT

1.   The universe is predictable only in the quantative or gravity-measurement sense.

2.   Primal energies, mind meanings, and spirit values are not subject to linear gravity.

3.   Qualitatively, the cosmos is only partially predictable.

4.   We can never fully predict the decisions of freewill beings.

VI. REFERENCE: Page 136, ¶4 - "All phases..."

COMMENT

1.   Even nonpersonal realities react with more or less elesticity in any given isolated situation.

2.   These unpredictable reactions of energy, mind, or other phenomena are probably due to the Ultimate and the Absolutes.

VII. REFERENCE: Page 136, ¶5 - "We do not really know..."

COMMENT

Diversity of reaction in the presence of uniform causation suggests the action of the Absolutes.

VIII. REFERENCE: Page 136, ¶6 - "Individuals have..."

COMMENT

Individuals, planets, and universes have their guardians—but who looks after the master universe? Probably—

1.   The Absolutes in potential.

2. The Ultimate in direction.

3. The Supreme in evolutionary co-ordination.

4. The Architects of the Master Universe in administration prior to the appearance of specific rulers.

IX. REFERENCE: Page 137, ¶2 - "The Unqualified Absolute..."

COMMENT

1. The Unqualified Absolute pervades all space.

2. The Universal Absolute functions wherever the other two Absolutes perform.

3. The Ultimate has a space presence co-existent with the master universe.

4. The Ultimate is progressively integrating the potentials of the three Absolutes.

7. THE PART AND THE WHOLE

I. REFERENCE: Page 137, ¶3 - "There is operative..."

COMMENT

1. There is operative throughout the cosmos an impersonal law which is equivalent to providence.

2. God shows mercy to the individual; he is impartial toward the total.

3. The will of God may not prevail in the part, but it always does in the whole.

II. REFERENCE: Page 137, ¶4 - "In all his dealings..."

COMMENT

1. Owing to a finite viewpoint, God's acts may appear to be arbitrary.

2. The laws of God are the habits of God—good habits.

3. Nature is not always an act of Deity. Other factors are present.

III. REFERENCE: Page 137, ¶5 - "It is repugnant..."

COMMENT

1. No personal act of Deity is ever inferior.

2. If God so wills, he can act in a different manner at any time.

3. This would be the action of a higher law, not the reversal of a lower law.

IV. *REFERENCE*: Page 137, ¶6 – "God is not..."

COMMENT

1. God is not a habit-bound slave to his own laws.

2. All the acts of God are volitional, notwithstanding their apparent sameness.

3. But this perfection of performance is not true of all his subordinates.

V. *REFERENCE*: Page 137, ¶7 – "Because God is changeless..."

COMMENT

Because God is changeless, we can depend upon his management of the cosmos.

VI. *REFERENCE*: Page 138, ¶2 – "And all this steadfastness..."

COMMENT

1. God's acts are volitional. He is not a slave to perfection and infinity.

2. God is not:

   A. A self-acting, automatic force.
   B. A slavish law-bound power.
   C. A mathematical equation.
   D. A chemical formula.

3. God is a freewill and primal personality.

VII. *REFERENCE*: Page 138, ¶3 – "The will of God..."

COMMENT

1. Increasingly, in the lives of spirit-led beings, the will of God prevails.

2. Still more in the morontia life does the divine way shine forth.

VIII.*REFERENCE*: Page 138, ¶4 – "The Fatherhood of God..."

COMMENT

God loves *each* person—and all persons—the paradox of the part and the whole.

IX. *REFERENCE*: Page 138, ¶5 - "The love of the Father..."

COMMENT

1.   Each person is unique—without duplicate and irreplaceable.

2.   The divine love glorifies each child in the Father's personality circuit

3.   God's love reveals the high regard of the Father for all his creatures —from the highest to the lowest.

X. *REFERENCE*: Page 138, ¶6 - "This very love of God..."

COMMENT

1.   God loves all his creatures—and this reveals the *all* relationship as well as the *each* relationship.

2.   Brotherhood has to do with the whole in contradistinction to the qualities of the part.

XI. *REFERENCE*: Page 138, ¶7 - "Brotherhood constitutes..."

COMMENT

1.   We cannot escape the benefits or the penalties of brotherhood — relationship to other persons.

2.   The part profits or suffers with the whole. They exist and progress together.

3.   The part can be retarded by the inertia of the whole or carried forward by the momentum of the cosmic brotherhood.

XII. *REFERENCE*: Page 139, ¶1 - "It is a mystery..."

COMMENT

1.   The mystery of God's residence on Paradise and presence in the creatures of a far-flung cosmos should not lessen our faith.

2.   God lives with us notwithstanding:

    A.   The magnitude of his infinity.
    B.   The immensity of his eternity.
    C.   The grandeur of his matchless character.

3.   The last part of the last sentence is a paraphrase of **Acts 17:28**. *"In him we live and move and have our being."*

XIII. *REFERENCE*: Page 139, ¶2 - "Even though the..."

COMMENT

1. Though God functions through many high beings, his Father fragments commune with human souls.

2. While the Father abides on Paradise, his divine presence dwells in the minds of men.

XIV. *REFERENCE*: Page 139, ¶3 - "Even though the..."

COMMENT

While the Son and the Spirit minister to us, God has given a part of himself to live within us.

8. MATTER, MIND, AND SPIRIT

I. *REFERENCE*: Page 139, ¶4 - "'God is spirit...'"

COMMENT

1. "God is spirit," but Paradise is not. **John 4:24.** *"God is spirit."*

2. Spirit beings do not live in empty space. They live and work on material worlds.

II. *REFERENCE*: Page 139, ¶5 - "The bestowal of..."

COMMENT

Paradise bestows and controls the force-charge of pervaded space.

III. *REFERENCE*: Page 139, ¶6 - "Whatever the transformations..."

COMMENT

1. No matter what the changes, force goes out from Paradise and swings on forever around the eternal space paths.

2. Energy always obeys the law. Only in creature volition is there deviation from the divine plans.

3. Energy is the proof of the stability and eternity of Paradise.

IV. *REFERENCE*: Page 139, ¶7 - "The bestowal of spirit..."

COMMENT

1. The spiritual gravity of the Eternal Son is just as real as the physical gravity of Paradise.

2. But these matters of spirit are discerned only by the spiritual insight of the soul.

V. REFERENCE: Page 140, ¶2 - "As the mind..."

COMMENT

1. As mortal mind becomes more spiritual it is less subject to material gravity.

2. As physical gravity measures quantitative energy, spirit gravity measures qualitative energies of divinity.

VI. REFERENCE: Page 140, ¶3 - "What Paradise is..."

COMMENT

What Paradise is to the cosmos, and what the Eternal Son is to the spirit creation, the Conjoint Actor is to the realm of mind.

VII. REFERENCE: Page 140, ¶4 - "The Conjoint Actor..."

COMMENT

1. The Conjoint Actor reacts to both material and spiritual realities.

2. In this mind ministry the Conjoint Actor becomes:
    A. Partner of the spiritual mind.
    B. Essence of the morontia mind.
    C. Substance of the material mind.

VIII. REFERENCE: Page 140, ¶5 - "Mind is the..."

COMMENT

1. Mind is the technique for making spirit realities experiential.

2. Co-ordination of things, ideas, and values is supermaterial.

IX. REFERENCE: Page 140, ¶6 - "Though it is hardly..."

COMMENT

Mortal mind can understand much of three levels of finite reality—matter, mind, and spirit.

X. REFERENCE: Page 140, ¶7 - "The goal of existence..."

COMMENT

1. The goal of existence is spirit. Mind intervenes between the material and the spiritual.

2.   Total Deity is not mind—but mind-spirit unified by personality.

XI. *REFERENCE*: Page 140, ¶8 - "On Paradise..."

COMMENT

1.   On Paradise all three energies—material, mindal, and spiritual—are co-ordinate.

2.   In the cosmos energy-matter is dominant, except in personality, were spirit, through mind, strives for the mastery.

3.   Spirit is the fundamental of personality—transcending both mind and matter.

XII. *REFERENCE*: Page 140, ¶9 - "In cosmic evolution..."

COMMENT

1.   In the cosmos matter becomes a philosophic shadow cast by mind in the presence of spirit reality.

2.   Mind, matter, and spirit are real, but not of equal value in personality.

3.   Consciousness of divinity is a progressive spiritual experience.

XIII. *REFERENCE*: Page 141, ¶2 - "The brighter the shining..."

COMMENT

1.   The brighter the spirit shining (the Father in the universe, the fragment in the creature), the greater the shadow cast by mind.

2.   In time the body is real, but in death only the mind and spirit survive.

3.   A cosmic reality can be nonexistent in personality experience.

9. PERSONAL REALITIES

I. *REFERENCE*: Page 141, ¶3 - "Spirit is the basic..."

COMMENT

1.   Spirit is the basic reality of all personality experience and progress.

2.   Man's destiny consists in the creation and attainment of spirit goals.

II. *REFERENCE*: Page 141, ¶4 – "Love is the secret..."

COMMENT

1. Love is the secret of beneficial association between personalities. But you must really *know* such persons.

2. A telephone number does not identify the subscriber.

III. *REFERENCE*: Page 141, ¶5 – "Mathematics, material science..."

COMMENT

1. Mathematics is indispensable to an understanding of the cosmos, but it is not a part of spiritual realities.

2. As regards both energy and life, the sum of two things is often more than their additive result.

3. That hydrogen and oxygen could make water could not be predicted by combined physics, chemistry, and philosophy.

4. Such things should prevent a mechanistic cosmology.

IV. *REFERENCE*: Page 141, ¶6 – "Technical analysis..."

COMMENT

Analysis of a thing does not reveal what it can do. Water puts out fire, but oxygen is a supporter of combustion.

V. *REFERENCE*: Page 141, ¶7 – "Your religion is..."

COMMENT

1. Religion is enhanced by escape from the bondage of fear. Philosophy is trying to escape tradition.

2. Science is concerned with:
    A. Contest of truth and error.
    B. Deliverance from abstraction.
    C. Deliverance from slavery of mathematics.
    D. Deliverance from blindness of materialism.

VI. *REFERENCE*: Page 142, ¶1 – "Mortal man has..."

COMMENT

1. Man's mind is an energy system surrounding a spirit nucleus, and this is the potential of eternal personality.

2. Serious trouble or real death can come only when self fully displaces the spirit nucleus, thus destroying the cosmic scheme of personality identity.

PAPER 13
The Sacred Spheres of Paradise

PAPER 13
The Sacred Spheres of Paradise

1. **THE SEVEN SACRED WORLDS OF THE FATHER**
2. **FATHER-WORLD RELATIONSHIPS**
3. **THE SACRED WORLDS OF THE ETERNAL SON**
4. **THE WORLDS OF THE INFINITE SPIRIT**

INTRODUCTION

I. *REFERENCE*: Page 143, ¶1 - "Between the central Isle..."

COMMENT

Between Paradise and Havona we find the three circuits of the secret spheres of the Deities.

II. *REFERENCE*: Page 143, ¶2 - "These three seven-world circuits...

COMMENT

1. These worlds are unique in their grandeur. They are all different, except the worlds of the Son, which are alike.
2. Like Paradise they are eternal—they always have been.

III. *REFERENCE*: Page 143, ¶3 - "The seven secret spheres..."

COMMENT

The seven worlds of the Father are reflective of spiritual luminosity— illuminating all of Paradise and Havona.

DISCUSSION OF LIGHT

1. *Physical Light*
   A. Light with heat—sunlight.
   B. Light without heat. (Firefly?)
2. *Intellectual Light*—Understanding

   Dan. 5:14. *"I have heard of you that the spirit of the holy gods is in you, and that light and understanding and excellent wisdom is found in you."*

   Ps. 119:105. *"Thy word is a lamp to my feet and a light to my path."*

3. **Human Leadership**

   Eph. 5:8. *"For once you were darkness, but now you are light in the Lord."*

Matt. 5:14. 16. *"You are the light of the world. A city set on a hill cannot be hid." "Let your light so shine before men, that they may see your good works and give glory to your Father who is in heaven."*

4. *Spiritual Light*—Spirit Illumination

John 1:9. *"The true light that enlightens every man was coming into the world."*

John 8:12. *"Again Jesus spoke to them, saying, 'I am the light of the world; he who follows me will not walk in darkness, but will have the light of life.'"*

5. *Salvation*—Survival

John 9:41. *"Jesus said to them, 'If you were blind, you would have no guilt; but now that you say, "We see," your guilt remains.'"*

John 15:22. *"If I had not come and spoken to them, they would not have sin; but now they have no excuse for their sin."*

Ps. 27:1. *"The Lord is my light and my salvation; whom shall I fear?"*

Job 33:27, 28. *"'I have sinned and perverted that which was right, and it was not requited to me. He has redeemed my soul from going down into the Pit, and my life shall see the light.'"*

Ps. 36:9. *"For with thee is the fountain of life; in thy light do we see light."*

6. *Light and Life*—Universe Status

John 1:4. *"In him was life, and the life was the light of men."*

John 8:12. *"He who follows me...will have the light of life."*

7. *Deity Luminosity*

1 John 1:5. *"That God is light and in him is no darkness at all."*

1 Tim. 6:16. *"Who alone has immortality and dwells in unapproachable light, whom no man has ever seen or can see."*

Ps. 104:2. *"Who coverest thyself with light as with a garment."*

Rev. 22:5. *"They need no light of lamp or sun, for the Lord God will be their light."*

IV. REFERENCE: Page 143, ¶4 - "On the seven sacred..."

COMMENT

1. On the worlds of the Son, the energies of impersonal spirit luminosity take origin—light without heat.

2. No personal beings sojourn on these seven worlds.

V. REFERENCE: Page 143. ¶4 – "The seven worlds..."

COMMENT

1. The seven worlds of the Infinite Spirit are the headquarters of the Seven Master Spirits.

2. All the grand universe, but not Paradise, is bathed in the spiritualizing influences of the Third Person of Deity.

VI. REFERENCE: Page 143, ¶5 – "Although the worlds..."

COMMENT

1. While the Father's worlds are personal status spheres, many entities other than personal sojourn thereon.

2. Each of these Father and Spirit worlds has a special type of permanent citizenship.

3. The Son's worlds harbor uniform types of other-than-personal beings.

VII. REFERENCE: Page 143, ¶7 – "The twenty-one Paradise..."

COMMENT

1. On these twenty-one Paradise satellites thousands of unrevealed activities are going on.

2. These spheres embrace the potentials of the master universe.

3. The Urantia papers present but a fleeting glimpse of these worlds as pertaining to the present age of the grand universe.

1. THE SEVEN SACRED WORLDS OF THE FATHER

I. REFERENCE: Page 144, ¶2 – "The Father's circuit..."

COMMENT

1. The Father's sacred worlds contain the universe secrets of personality and certain parts are closed to personalities.

2. The only other realms closed to personality are nether Paradise and the sacred worlds of the Son.

3. One Bible reference bears out the idea of secrecy.
   Deut. 29:29. *"'The secret things belong to the Lord our God; but the things that are revealed belong to us and to our children forever.'"*

II. *REFERENCE:* Page 144, ¶3 - "The Paradise worlds..."

COMMENT

1. The Father's worlds are ruled by the highest order of Trinity Sons— the Trinitized Secrets of Supremacy.

2. In another age will they be "Secrets of Ultimacy"? Yes—probably.

III. *REFERENCE:* Page 144, ¶4 - "One of the reasons..."

COMMENT

1. One reason for secrecy on these worlds is the presence of specialized Deity manifestations.

2. The Secrets of Supremacy are the special agents of these impersonal specialized presences of Divinity.

IV. *REFERENCE:* Page 144, ¶5 - "1. DIVININGTON..."

COMMENT

1. This is the personal-communion sphere of the Father—the "bosom of the Father." **See John 1:18.** *"No one has ever seen God; the only Son, who is in the bosom of the Father, he has made him known."*

2. Many other beings, unrevealed, created by the Father, dwell on Divinington.

3. Divinington is the rendezvous of the Thought Adjusters.

DISCUSSION OF GOD INDWELLING MAN

Job 32:8. *"But it is the spirit in a man, the breath of the Almighty, that makes him understand."*

Prov. 20:27. *"The spirit of man is the lamp of the Lord, searching all his innermost parts."*

Eccl. 12:7. *"And the spirit returns to God who gave it."*

Eze. 36:27. *"And I will put my spirit within you, and cause you to walk in my statutes."*

Zech. 12:1. *"Thus says the Lord, who...formed the spirit of man within him."*

Rom. 8:16. *"It is the Spirit himself bearing witness with our spirit that we are the children of God."*

1 Cor. 2:11. *"What person knows a man's thoughts except the spirit of the man which is in him?"*

1 John 3:24. *"And by this we know that he abides in us, by the Spirit which he has given us."*

V. *REFERENCE*: Page 144, ¶6 - "The *secrets of...*"

COMMENT

1. Among the secrets of Divinington is that of the bestowal of the Thought Adjusters.

2. Various orders of personality have innate secrets which are withheld from all other orders of personality.

VI.*REFERENCE*: Page 145, ¶1 - "This sphere also holds..."

COMMENT

1. Divinington holds the secrets of other Father fragments and of the Gravity Messengers.

2. Probably the secrets of these spheres would not be understood by those from whom they are withheld.

VII. *REFERENCE*: Page 145, ¶2 - "2. SONARINGTON..."

COMMENT

1. This world is the "bosom of the Son"—the headquarters of the ascending and descending Sons.

2. Many unrevealed orders of Sons make this sphere their home.

VIII.*REFERENCE*: Page 145, ¶3 - "The *secrets of...*"

COMMENT

1. Among the secrets of Sonarington are those of the bestowal of the incarnated Paradise Sons.

2. Only incarnated Sons penetrate that sector relating to the incarnation of the Divine Sons.

3. But there are many other mysteries hidden on this world.

IX. *REFERENCE*: Page 145, ¶4 - "3. SPIRITINGTON..."

COMMENT

1. This world is the "bosom of the Spirit," home for the Seven Master Spirits and many of their offspring.

2. This is home for many unrevealed orders of spirit beings.

X. *REFERENCE*: Page 145, ¶5 - "The *secrets of...*"

COMMENT

1. Reflectivity is the secret of Spiritington. Reflectivity concerns many activities not revealed.

2. And there are other secrets of this sacred world.

XI. *REFERENCE*: Page 145, ¶6 - "4. VICEGERINGTON..."

COMMENT

This world is the "bosom of the Father and the Son." Many unrevealed beings forgather on this sphere.

XII. *REFERENCE*: Page 146, ¶2 - "The secrets of..."

COMMENT

1. This world holds the secrets of trinitization.

2. This is home for numerous beings trinitized or eventuated by both Deity and other orders of personality.

XIII. *REFERENCE*: Page 146, ¶3 - "Nontrinitized beings..."

COMMENT

All sectors of Vicegerington are open to all orders of trinitized beings.

XIV. *REFERENCE*: Page 146, ¶4 - "There are still other..."

COMMENT

There are many forms of trinitization which have not been revealed to us.

XV. *REFERENCE*: Page 146, ¶5 - "5. SOLITARINGTON..."

COMMENT

This world is the "bosom of the Father and the Spirit," and the home of many unrevealed orders.

XVI. *REFERENCE*: Page 146, ¶6 - "This is also..."

COMMENT

This is the home of many orders, including Solitary Messengers and the Power Directors.

XVII.REFERENCE: Page 146, ¶7 - "There are numerous..."

COMMENT

Many orders of spirit beings not connected with the ascension plan make their home on Solitarington.

XVIII.REFERENCE: Page 146, ¶8 - "The *secrets of...*"

COMMENT

Secrets belonging to many orders of Deity-fathered personalities are held on this world—even of beings of origin in the Trinity, the Supreme, and the Ultimate.

XIX.REFERENCE: Page 146, ¶9 - "6. SERAPHINGTON..."

COMMENT

1. This world is the "bosom of the Son and the Spirit."

2. It is the home of all ministering spirits and a host of unrevealed beings created by the Son and the Spirit.

XX. REFERENCE: Page 147, ¶2 - "*The secrets of...*"

COMMENT

1. Of the threefold mystery of Seraphington, only one—the mystery of seraphic transport—is noted.

2. The other mysteries pertain to unrevealed orders of beings.

XXI.REFERENCE: Page 147, ¶3 - "7. ASCENDINGTON..."

COMMENT

1. Ascendington is the "bosom of the Father, Son, and Spirit." It is the home of ascenders before attaining Paradise status.

2. Havona ascenders spend most of their "vacations" on Ascendington.

XXII.REFERENCE: Page 147, ¶4 - "*The secrets of...*"

COMMENT

The great secret of Ascendington pertains to the mystery of the evolution of the immortal soul within the mortal mind.

XXIII. *REFERENCE*: Page 147, ¶5 - "You will never fully..."

COMMENT

1. The mystery of the soul's evolution will not be understood by mortals until they reach Ascendington.

2. Even after the mortal comprehends this mystery, he never reveals it to other orders of personality.

2. FATHER-WORLD RELATIONSHIPS

I. *REFERENCE*: Page 147, ¶6 - "These home worlds..."

COMMENT

1. These Paradise worlds are reunion spheres and serve as permanent cosmic addresses.

2. Finaliters live on Paradise, but Ascendington is their eternal home address.

3. Seventh-stage spirits may give up their residence on Paradise.

II. *REFERENCE*: Page 148, ¶2 - "If outer universes..."

COMMENT

Ascenders from outer space will regard Ascendington as their home world.

III. *REFERENCE*: Page 148, ¶3 - "Ascendington is..."

COMMENT

Ascendington is the only Paradise world unreservedly open to the inspection of mortal ascenders.

IV. *REFERENCE*: Page 148, ¶4 - "The Trinity-origin beings..."

COMMENT

Trinity-origin beings are residential on Paradise, but fraternize with ascenders on Ascendington.

V. *REFERENCE*: Page 148, ¶5 - "You might assume..."

COMMENT

1. There are many questions difficult of understanding relating to these sacred worlds of Paradise.

2. Status on the Father's worlds is determined by:

    A.   The universe age.

    B.   Nature of origin.

    C.   Actuality of service.

VI. *REFERENCE*: Page 148, ¶6 - "The worlds of the..."

COMMENT

1.   The Father's worlds are more status worlds than actual residential spheres.

2.   Finaliters are admitted to Sonarington, except for the one-seventh concerned with the incarnation of the divine Sons.

VII. *REFERENCE*: Page 148, ¶7 - "Eventually you will have..."

COMMENT

1.   Eventually finaliters have full access to Ascendington, relative access to the other Father worlds, except Divinington.

2.   Throughout all eternity you will be denied access to Divinington—the "bosom of the Father."

VIII. *REFERENCE*: Page 149, ¶1 - "These rendezvous worlds..."

COMMENT

1.   Only those things are forbidden which are wholly outside our personal experience.

2.   You may become creature perfect even as the Father is deity perfect, but you may not share the personality secrets of other orders of personality.

IX. *REFERENCE*: Page 149, ¶2 - "All these secrets..."

COMMENT

1.   All secrets are known to the collective body of Trinitized Secrets of Supremacy.

2.   Ascenders fully know the ten Secrets of Supremacy on Ascendington, but not so fully those on the other worlds, least of all those on Divinington.

X. *REFERENCE*: Page 149, ¶3 - "The Trinitized Secrets..."

COMMENT

The Secrets of Supremacy are related to the Supreme, the Ultimate, and to the Supreme-Ultimate.

3. THE SACRED WORLDS
OF THE ETERNAL SON

I. *REFERENCE*: Page 149, ¶4 – "The seven luminous spheres..."

COMMENT

The luminous spheres of the Son are the source of the threefold light of the central universe and the worlds of the seven phases of pure-spirit reality.

II. *REFERENCE*: Page 149, ¶5 – "Personality is not..."

COMMENT

1. No personalities are resident on these worlds—only other-than-personal beings.

2. These beings probably pertain to service on the projected worlds of outer space.

3. Every two-billion-year cycle witnesses the creation of new reserves of this order.

III. *REFERENCE*: Page 149, ¶6 – "As far as I am..."

COMMENT

1. Even the personalities created by the Eternal Son do not go to these worlds.

2. All types of impersonal spirits are admitted to these luminous worlds.

3. High spirit personalities do not indulge idle curiosity—therefore refrain from visiting these secret worlds.

4. THE WORLDS OF THE INFINITE SPIRIT

I. *REFERENCE*: Page 149, ¶7 – "Between the inner..."

COMMENT

1. The secret worlds of the Infinite Spirit are found between the worlds of the Son and the inner circuit of Havona.

2. The worlds of the Spirit are occupied by:

    A. Offspring of the Infinite Spirit.
    B. Trinitized sons of glorified personalities.
    C. Unrevealed universe administrators.

II. *REFERENCE*: Page 150, ¶2 - "The Seven Master Spirits..."

COMMENT

1. The administration cf the grand universe is conducted from these seven executive spheres.

2. The Seven Master Spirits are the mind-spirit co-ordinators of the master cosmos.

III. *REFERENCE*: Page 150, ¶3 - "From these seven..."

COMMENT

1. The Master Spirits equalize the cosmic-mind circuits and differentiate the presence of the Deities.

2. Physical reactions are uniform, but spiritual presence is determined by individual capacity for receptivity.

IV. *REFERENCE*: Page 150, ¶4 - "Physical authority..."

COMMENT

1. Physical realities are unvarying in the universe, but things spiritual are dependent on attitudes of will creatures.

2. The spiritual presence of absolute Deity is not influenced by creature attitude, but the work of subabsolute Deity is influenced by the creature attitude.

3. The presence of divinity is not whimsical; it is determined by the free will of personality.

V. *REFERENCE*: Page 150, ¶5 - "The determiner of..."

COMMENT

1. The determiner of the spiritual presence consists in the choosing of the freewill creature.

2. Thus does the spirit of divinity become obedient to the choosing of the creature.

VI. *REFERENCE*: Page 150, ¶6 - "The executive abodes..."

COMMENT

1. The Master Spirit on each world presides over one of the seven superuniverses.

2. These executive worlds are open to all beings who desire to visit thereon.

VII. *REFERENCE*: Page 151, ¶2 - "To me..."

1. These executive worlds are the most intriguing spheres outside of Paradise—the activities being material, intellectual, and spiritual.

2. These worlds are favorite spheres for "vacations" by numerous celestial beings.

3. In no other place can you observe such a revelation of the seven levels of universe reality.

PAPER 14
The Central and Divine Universes

PAPER 14
The Central and Divine Universes

1. **THE PARADISE-HAVONA SYSTEM**
2. **CONSTITUTION OF HAVONA**
3. **THE HAVONA WORLDS**
4. **CREATURES OF THE CENTRAL UNIVERSE**
5. **LIFE IN HAVONA**
6. **THE PURPOSE OF THE CENTRAL UNIVERSE**

INTRODUCTION

I. *REFERENCE*: Page 152, ¶1 - "The perfect and..."

COMMENT

1. Paradise is the motionless and stable nuclear Isle at the heart of the master universe.

2. The central universe of Havona is of unbelievable mass and is beyond human understanding.

II. *REFERENCE*: Page 152, ¶2 - "This is the one..."

COMMENT

1. This is a perfect and eternal universe—it is not an evolutionary creation.

2. This is the eternal core around which the universe of universes revolves.

3. The Creator Sons are striving to reproduce the pattern universe as:

    A. Ideal of divine completeness.
    B. Supreme finality.
    C. Ultimate reality.
    D. Eternal perfection.

1. THE PARADISE-HAVONA SYSTEM

I. *REFERENCE*: Page 152, ¶3 - "From the periphery..."

COMMENT

Seven space conditions and motions occur between Paradise periphery and the superuniverse level.

II. *REFERENCE*: Page 152, ¶4 - "The billion worlds..."

COMMENT

1. Havona is arranged in seven concentric circuits swinging around Paradise.

2. These circuits are different, but each is pervaded by one of the Seven Spirits of the Circuits—a specialization of the Infinite Spirit.

III. *REFERENCE*: Page 153, ¶2 - "The Havona planetary..."

COMMENT

1. The Havona circuits are not superimposed—the worlds revolve in linear procession.

2. Aside from administration, the whole Paradise-Havona system functions as one unit.

IV. *REFERENCE*: Page 153, ¶3 - "Time is not...

COMMENT

1. Time does not exist on Paradise, but time is reckoned in Havona.

2. Havona time is determined by the length of each circuit and therefore is different on the worlds of each circuit.

V. *REFERENCE*: Page 153, ¶4 - "Besides Havona-circuit time..."

COMMENT

1. There are numerous time reckonings in the central universe:
   A. Havona circuit time.
   B. Paradise-Havona standard day.
   C. Other time designations.

2. The Paradise-Havona day is 7 minutes, 3-1/8 seconds less than one thousand years of Urantia time.

   2 Peter 3:8. *"With the Lord one day is as a thousand years, and a thousand years as one day."*

   Ps. 90:4. *"For a thousand years in thy sight are but as yesterday when it is past, or as a watch in the night."*

VI. *REFERENCE*: Page 153, ¶5 - "This Paradise-Havona..."

COMMENT

The Paradise-Havona day is the standard time of the seven superuniverses.

VII. *REFERENCE*: Page 153, ¶6 – "On the outskirts..."

COMMENT

1. The dark gravity bodies which surround the Havona worlds are unique.

2. These bodies neither reflect nor absorb light, and they conceal Havona from the cosmos.

VIII. *REFERENCE*: Page 153, ¶7 – "The great belt..."

COMMENT

This is a description of the mechanism and function of the belt of dark gravity bodies.

IX. *REFERENCE*: Page 153, ¶8 – "The inner procession..."

COMMENT

This describes the arrangement of the dark gravity bodies.

X. *REFERENCE*: Page 154, ¶2 – "The intervening space..."

COMMENT

The space between the two circuits of gravity bodies is unique—nothing like it in the master universe.

XI. *REFERENCE*: Page 154, ¶3 – "In our opinion..."

COMMENT

The dark gravity bodies are also unique—outer space contains nothing like them.

2. CONSTITUTION OF HAVONA

I. *REFERENCE*: Page 154, ¶4 – "Spirit beings do not..."

COMMENT

Spirit beings live on real, material worlds.

II. *REFERENCE*: Page 154, ¶5 – "The physical realities..."

COMMENT

1. Havona energies are threefold in nature and differ from all other energy systems.

2. Havona creation is of Trinity origin—threefold. A local universe is twofold in origin.

III. *REFERENCE*: Page 154, ¶6 - "The material of Havona..."

COMMENT

1. Havona material consists of one thousand chemical elements and seven forms of energy.

2. Each form of energy has seven phases of excitation. This yields forty-nine specialized forms of sensation.

3. Morontia senses are seventy. Higher spiritual responses vary from seventy to two hundred ten.

IV. *REFERENCE*: Page 154, ¶7 - "None of the..."

COMMENT

A human being on a Havona world would be utterly lacking in all sensory responses to the environment.

V. *REFERENCE*: Page 154, ¶8 - "There are numerous..."

COMMENT

In Havona both physical and spiritual phenomena occur which are unknown on such worlds as Urantia.

VI. *REFERENCE*: Page 154, ¶9 - "All natural law..."

COMMENT

1. The entire central universe is organized on the basis of the threefold energy system.

2. The physical and spiritual energies of Havona are maintained in perfect balance.

VII. REFERENCE: Page 155, ¶2 - "The universal spiritual..."

COMMENT

1. The universal spirit gravity of the Eternal Son draws all spirit values and personalities Godward.

2. Spirit gravity pull is proportionate to the actual spiritual values concerned.

VIII. REFERENCE: Page 155, ¶3 - "Likewise does the..."

COMMENT

1. The mind gravity of the Infinite Spirit draws all intellectual values toward Paradise.

2. In liaison with the spirit gravity this draws all ascendant souls to God.

IX. REFERENCE: Page 155, ¶4 - "Havona is a..."

COMMENT

1. Havona is a spiritually perfect, balanced, and stable universe.

2. Sin has never appeared in Havona, in either native beings or those admitted to its borders.

3. The methods of selection are so perfect that no being has ever been prematurely admitted to the central universe.

3. THE HAVONA WORLDS

I. REFERENCE: Page 155, ¶5 - "Concerning the government..."

COMMENT

1. There is no government in perfect Havona.

2. Havona has ideal self-government—no courts or legislatures.

II. REFERENCE: Page 155, ¶5 - "There is no need..."

COMMENT

The perfect and perfected beings of Havona stand in no need of any sort of governmental regulation.

III. REFERENCE: Page 155, ¶6 - "The administration of..."

COMMENT

1. The administration of Havona, while not automatic, is both perfect and efficient.

2. The Eternals of Days are not creators, but they are perfect administrators—bordering on absoluteness.

IV. *REFERENCE*: Page 156, ¶2 - "The billion spheres..."

COMMENT

1. The perfect worlds of Havona are the training worlds for Paradise personalities and ascending mortals.

2. Ascending creatures progress from the outer to the inner circuits of Havona on their way to Paradise.

V. *REFERENCE*: Page 156, ¶3 - "At present..."

COMMENT

1. Only one per cent of Havona is utilized in the work of mortal progression.

2. One tenth of one per cent of Havona is dedicated to the Corps of the Finality.

3. The Finality Corps have their personal residences on Paradise.

VI. *REFERENCE*: Page 156, ¶4 - "The planetary construction..."

COMMENT

1. Havona construction is not like the other universes. This is why such enormous spheres can be inhabited.

2. The physical aspects of Havona are balanced by triata and the surrounding dark gravity bodies.

3. Antigravity is also utilized in the control of Havona functions.

VII. *REFERENCE*: Page 156, ¶5 - "The architecture..."

COMMENT

The organization and embellishment of Havona are beyond human imagination. But there are real rivers and lakes.

VIII. *REFERENCE*: Page 156, ¶6 - "Spiritually these worlds..."

COMMENT

The Havona worlds are ideally appointed to harbor a vast range of personalities who function thereon.

4. CREATURES OF THE CENTRAL UNIVERSE

I. *REFERENCE*: Page 156, ¶7 - "There are seven..."

COMMENT

1. There are seven forms of life on Havona of three phases each.

2. Each phase is divided into seventy major divisions of one thousand minor subdivisions.

II. *REFERENCE*: Page 157, ¶1 - "Decay and death..."

COMMENT

Decay and death do not occur in Havona. Life continues by a process of transmutation.

III. *REFERENCE*: Page 157, ¶2 - "The Havona natives..."

COMMENT

1. Havona natives are children of the Trinity—they are nonreproducing. They never were created.

2. Havona is an eternal existence. The story of Havona creation is an effort to afford finite creatures a concept of "beginnings."

IV. *REFERENCE*: Page 157, ¶5 - "The natives of Havona..."

COMMENT

1. Havona natives are the permanent citizens of their respective spheres.

2. As material creatures function on the worlds of space, so do Havona natives function on their worlds.

3. In a sense, Havona natives may be regarded as material beings.

V. *REFERENCE*: Page 157, ¶4 - "There is a life..."

COMMENT

While Havoners minister to both Paradise descenders and mortal ascenders, they also live a life of their own.

VI. *REFERENCE*: Page 157, ¶5 - "As the worship..."

COMMENT

1. Worship of Havoners pleases Deity even as does the worship of finite beings.

2. As mortals strive to do the will of God, Havoners gratify the ideals of the Trinity.

3. Havoners are in their very nature the will of God.

VII. *REFERENCE*: Page 157, ¶6 - "Havoners have both..."

COMMENT

1. Havoners have unrevealed destinies.

2. Havoners progress within Havona—inward, outward, and within a circuit.

VIII.*REFERENCE*: Page 157, ¶7 - "In addition to..."

COMMENT

1. Havona contains numerous pattern beings—directors and teachers—for the edification of all creatures.

2. The creatures of finite creation are fashioned after these Havona pattern personalities.

IX. *REFERENCE*: Page 157, ¶8 - "Then there are..."

COMMENT

1. Father attainers come and go from Havona on sundry missions.

2. Havona is home for numerous groups of candidates for Paradise residence.

X. *REFERENCE*: Page 158, ¶2 - "The Infinite Spirit..."

COMMENT

1. The Infinite Spirit has a host of representatives ministering throughout Havona.

2. They perform their tasks while ministering to the ascending mortals.

XI. *REFERENCE*: Page 158, ¶3 - "There are numerous groups..."

COMMENT

Many groups of Havoners are in no way associated with the scheme of mortal ascension.

XII. *REFERENCE*: Page 158, ¶4 - "Havona teems..."

COMMENT

Havona teems with diverse beings who are striving for higher levels of divinity realization.

5. LIFE IN HAVONA

I. *REFERENCE*: Page 158, ¶5 – "On Urantia..."

COMMENT

1. On Urantia we pass through a short and intense test and further progress through the mansion worlds.

2. In the superuniverse we pass through our spiritual training.

3. Our education continues on each of the billion worlds of Havona.

II. *REFERENCE*: Page 158, ¶6 – "Life on the divine worlds..."

COMMENT

1. Life in Havona transcends all human concepts.

2. Social and economic activities in Havona are wholly unlike those of Urantia. Even the method of thinking is different.

III. *REFERENCE*: Page 158, ¶7 – "The regulations of the..."

COMMENT

1. The regulations of Havona are in accordance with the reason of righteousness and the rule of justice.

2. These two factors equal fairness. Havoners like to do things the way they should be done.

IV. *REFERENCE*: Page 158, ¶8 – "When intelligent beings..."

COMMENT

1. When Havona new arrivals attain comprehension of their Master Spirit, they are promoted from the seventh to the sixth circuit.

2. The circles of the human mind take their designations from these Havona arrangements.

3. After attaining realisation of Supremacy, ascenders are transferred to the fifth circuit.

4. After attaining the Infinite Spirit, they progress to the fourth circuit.

5. On attaining the Eternal Son, they go to the third circuit.

6. On recognition of the Universal Father, they go to the second circuit.

7. Arrival on the first circuit signifies acceptance into Paradise service.

8. From the first circuit pilgrims attain Paradise residence and acceptance into the Corps of the Finality.

V. REFERENCE: Page 159, ¶2 - "During your sojourn..."

COMMENT

1. Ascenders visit freely among the worlds of the circuit of sojourn and among those already traversed.

2. A pilgrim can traverse "achieved" space, but must have a transport supernaphim to traverse "unachieved" space.

VI. REFERENCE: Page 159, ¶3 - "There is a..."

COMMENT

1. Each Havona world is unique—refreshingly original.

2. This diversity extends to all features—physical, intellectual, and spiritual.

VII. REFERENCE: Page 159, ¶4 - "Not until you..."

COMMENT

The tonic of adventure extends to the traversal of the last Havona world. Then the eternity impulse appears.

VIII. REFERENCE: Page 159, ¶5 - "Monotony is indicative..."

COMMENT

Monotony is indicative of immaturity. Havona ascenders have attained all-round maturity.

IX. REFERENCE: Page 159, ¶6 - "Not only will you..."

COMMENT

1. Undreamed-of changes confront you as you go from world to world and from circuit to circuit.

2. Each Havona world is a university of surprises. Monotony is no part of the Havona career.

X. REFERENCE: Page 159, ¶7 - "Love of adventure..."

COMMENT

This life is only the beginning of a long career of discovery.

XI. REFERENCE: Page 160, ¶1 - "Curiosity—the spirit..."

COMMENT

1. Curiosity—the exploratory urge—is innate in evolutionary creatures.

2. This urge suffers disappointment on earth but will be fully realized in the age to come.

6. THE PURPOSE OF THE CENTRAL UNIVERSE

I. REFERENCE: Page 160, ¶2 - "The range of..."

COMMENT

The great range of Havona activities can be described as Havonal, Paradisiacal, and Supreme-Ultimate evolutional.

II. REFERENCE: Page 160, ¶3 - "Many superfinite..."

COMMENT

The superfinite activities of Havona are numerous and embrace many unrevealed functions.

III. REFERENCE: Page 160, ¶4-9 - "1. The Universal Father..."

COMMENT

The Universal Father derives many satisfactions from the perfect Havona creation:

1. Parental satisfaction.
2. Adoration leading to love satiety.
3. Achievement gratification.
4. Reciprocation of beauty and harmony.
5. Worthy revelation of spirit reality.
6. Power nucleus for universe expansion.
7. Goal of finite ascenders.
8. The eternal home of Deity.

IV. REFERENCE: Page 161, ¶10 - 161, ¶4 - "2. *The Eternal Son...*"

COMMENT

The Eternal Son derives satisfactions from Havona:

1. Partnership effectiveness of the Trinity.
2. Basis of absolute confidence in the Father.
3. A base for expanding spirit power.
4. An arena for demonstration of ministry.

5. Foundation for spirit gravity control.
6. Gratification of parental craving.
7. Demonstration that the Son is the World of the Father.
8. Reciprocation of equality of fraternity.

V. REFERENCE: Page 161, ¶5-10 - "3. *The Infinite Spirit...*"

COMMENT

How the Havona universe affords satisfaction to the Infinite Spirit:

1. Proof of being the Conjoint Actor.
2. Pleasure of creative activity with coexistence.
3. An arena of potential mercy ministry.
4. Partnership universe administration.
5. Laboratory of the cosmic mind.
6. Graduate schools of his mind creatures.
7. Compensation for his space ministry.

VI. REFERENCE: Page 161, ¶6 - 162, ¶1 - "4. *The Supreme Being...*"

COMMENT

How the Supreme Being derives satisfaction from Havona:

1. Proof of pre-finite reality of the Supreme.
2. Unification of power potentials and spirit nature of the Supreme.
3. Perfect pattern of potential Supremacy.
4. Finality of spirit values.
5. Intelligence with unlimited potential.

VII. REFERENCE: Page 162, ¶2-6 - "5. *The Co-ordinate Creator Sons...*"

COMMENT

Havona as satisfaction to the Co-ordinate Creator Sons:

1. Pattern for the Creator Sons.
2. Educational training for bestowal Sons.
3. Personality patterns for their own creations.
4. Destiny for their own creatures.
5. Vital "overcontrol" of their universes.
6. The source of the Supreme and Ultimate.
7. The source of creative power.
8. Home of their parents—their home.

VIII.REFERENCE: Page 162, ¶7-11 - "6. The Co-ordinate Ministering Daughters..."

COMMENT

Havona as satisfaction to the Co-ordinate Ministering Daughters:

1. Prepersonal training of Creative Spirits.
2. Learning co-operation with Creator Sons.
3. Mind patterns for their creatures.
4. Home of the Infinite Spirit.
5. Source of their creative powers.
6. The reflective phenomena.

IX. REFERENCE: Page 162, ¶12 - 163, ¶2 - "7. The Evolutionary Mortals..."

COMMENT

Havona satisfactions to evolutionary mortals:

1. Home of our pattern personalities.
2. Home of our superfinite helpers.
3. Source of high spirit stimulus.
4. Pre-Paradise training goal.
5. The portal to Paradise and God.
6. The home of finaliters.
7. Destiny of finite ascenders.
8. Beginning of eternity careers.

X. REFERENCE: Page 163, ¶3 - "Havona will..."

COMMENT

1. Havona will probably be the training universe for absonite beings, and finishing school for outer-spacers.

2. Potentials of Havona are unlimited.

EXPLANATION

The first fourteen papers of Part I have been analyzed paragraph by paragraph.

From Paper 15 on, only selected paragraphs from each paper will be analyzed and Papers 23 through 30 have been omitted.

This study ends with Paper 31, the last paper in Part I of *The Urantia Book*.

PAPER 15

The Seven Superuniverses

PAPER 15
The Seven Superuniverses

INTRODUCTION
I. *REFERENCE*: Page 164, ¶1 - "As far as..."

COMMENT

1. God as a father deals with individuals. Practically speaking, the universes are nonexistent.

2. The Son and the Spirit deal more directly with the local universes.

3. The Trinity is concerned more with the seven superuniverses.

4. A Master Spirit is concerned with a single superuniverse.

The Ancients of Days maintain intelligent control of both physical and spiritual forces designed to facilitate intellectual advancement and spiritual growth of all will creatures.

1. THE SUPERUNIVERSE SPACE LEVEL
I. *REFERENCE*: Page 164, ¶4 - "Within the limited range..."

COMMENT

1. Urantia and its universe are not plunging into new and uncharted space.

2. The galaxies are controlled and are swinging in majestic grandeur around Paradise.

Our local universe pursues a definite space path. It is a comparatively recent creation. Its position in the Milky Way galaxy is well known.

2. ORGANIZATION OF THE SUPERUNIVERSES

I. *REFERENCE*: Page 165, ¶6 – "Only the Universal Father..."

COMMENT

Only God the Father knows the number and name of all the inhabited worlds in the grand universe.

This section presents the organization plan of the grand universe—from the local system to the superuniverse capital.

3. THE SUPERUNIVERSE OF ORVONTON

II. *REFERENCE*: Page 167, ¶7 – "Of the ten major..."

COMMENT

Of the ten major divisions of Orvonton, Urantia astronomers have identified eight.

III. *REFERENCE*: Page 168, ¶1 – "The rotational center..."

COMMENT

Our minor sector (Ensa) revolves around the center of the Sagittarius star cloud.

Description of the Milky Way. The astronomical position of Urantia. Dimensions of the Milky Way like a watch. Paradise lies beyond the area of greatest density of the Milky Way. Story of the Andronover nebula and the birth of the solar system. Nebadon and associated universes revolve around Sagittarius. Story of the seven different stellar movements. Orvonton moves counterclockwise around Paradise. Physical organization of a local universe.

4. NEBULAE—THE ANCESTORS OF UNIVERSES

Mystery of the ultimatons and the force charge of space. Universe organization. Paradise force organizers transmute space potency and power directors organize it. The mystery of energy segmentation. Paradise force organisers are nebulae originators. Suns originate in these mother wheels of space. A mother wheel may give origin to one hundred million suns. Administrative units are not related to nebulae organization. Story of spiral nebulae. Andromeda. Constitution of the Milky Way. Magellanic cloud. Stellar gas clouds.

5. THE ORIGIN OF SPACE BODIES

Origin of planets—ten different methods. One hundred ways of sun formation.

6. THE SPHERES OF SPACE

The spheres of space—suns, dark islands, minor space bodies, planets. Architectural spheres. Suns that shine without heat. Solar dynamos. More than ten million blazing suns in Orvonton. Dark islands are gravity controllers. Comets. Inhabited planets. Dead suns. Three inhabitable planets in our solar system.

7. THE ARCHITECTURAL SPHERES

Architectural capitals independently lighted and heated. Standard Orvonton time. Economy of headquarters worlds is material, morontial, and spiritual. Jerusem and seven cultural worlds. Edentia and 70 satellites. Salvington and 490 worlds. Uminor the third and Umajor the fifth. Uversa and 490 worlds.

8. ENERGY CONTROL AND REGULATION

Energy control and regulation. Superuniverse capitals centers of energy control—power centers and physical controllers. Physical energy circuits take 968 million years to complete circuit of superuniverse. Velocity and mass are determining factors. Gravity and antigravity. Stellar collisions. Energy regulation. The Absolutes and experiential Deities. The universe does not run down.

9. CIRCUITS OF THE SUPERUNIVERSES

Universal gravity circuits. The seven superuniverse circuits. The three local universe circuits. Blending circuits—settling a universe in light and life. Essentials of superuniverse membership.

10. RULERS OF THE SUPERUNIVERSES

I. *REFERENCE*: Page 178, ¶2 - "The headquarters..."

COMMENT

1. The executive branch of superuniverse government is directed by one of the Seven Master Spirits.

2. The Master Spirits administer the superuniverses through their Seven Supreme Executives stationed on the seven special worlds of the Infinite Spirit.

II. *REFERENCE*: Page 178, ¶3 - "The superuniverse headquarters..."

COMMENT

The reflectivity mechanism of the grand universe operates from the capitals of the seven superuniverses.

III. *REFERENCE*: Page 178, ¶4 and 5 - "Each superuniverse is..." and "The three..."

COMMENT

The three Ancients of Days rule a superuniverse, assisted by:

1. One billion Perfectors of Wisdom.

2. Three billion Divine Counselors.

3. One billion Universal Censors.

IV. *REFERENCE*: Page 178, ¶6 - "The remaining three orders..."

COMMENT

1. The Ancients of Days are also assisted by three orders of glorified ascendant mortals:

   A. Mighty Messengers.
   B. Those High in Authority.
   C. Those Without Name and Number.

2. These three groups are known as Trinitized Sons of Attainment.

3. They are all dual-origin mortals who became finaliters and were then embraced by the Trinity.

V. *REFERENCE*: Page 179, ¶2 - "The Reflective Image Aids..."

COMMENT

On the superuniverse capitals, the Reflective Image Aids function as representing numerous groups who are related to the superuniverse governments—such as:

1. Manifestations of the Supreme Being.

2. Unqualified Supervisors of the Supreme.

3. Qualified Vicegerents of the Ultimate.

4. Liaison reflectivators of Majeston.

5. Superpersonal spirit representatives of the Eternal Son.

11. THE DELIBERATIVE ASSEMBLY

I. *REFERENCE*: Page 179, ¶5 – "It is on such worlds..."

COMMENT

1. On Uversa the autocracy of perfection and the democracy of evolution meet face to face.

2. The superuniverse government is constituted as follows:

    A. Executive branch originates in the realms of perfection.
    B. The legislative branch derives from the flowering of the evolutionary universes.

II. *REFERENCE*: Page 180, ¶2 – "Never have I known..."

COMMENT

1. In superuniverse government, the executive and legislative branches never disagree.

2. All this proves that evolutionary beings can attain to heights of perfected wisdom.

3. It also demonstrates the wisdom of the Father's plan of the Paradise ascension.

12. THE SUPREME TRIBUNALS

I. *REFERENCE*: Page 180, ¶4 – "The courts of the..."

COMMENT

1. The tribunals of the Ancients of Days are the supreme courts for all component local universes.

2. Local universe courts are well-nigh supreme except in matters involving the extinction of will creatures.

3. Mandates for the extinction of will creatures originate on, and are executed from, the headquarters of the superuniverses.

13. THE SECTOR GOVERNMENTS

This section deals with the organization and conduct of the minor and major sector governments of the seven superuniverses.

14. PURPOSES OF THE SEVEN SUPERUNIVERSES

I. *REFERENCE*: Page 182, ¶2 - "Orvonton, the seventh..."

COMMENT

Orvonton is renowned for:

1. Lavish bestowal of mercy.
2. Justice tempered by mercy.
3. Power conditioned by patience.
4. Time sacrificed to secure eternal stabilizations.

Further summary of Section 14. The seven major purposes of the superuniverses. The seventh superuniverse is something like a "meaning-of-the-whole." Much going on in Orvonton remains unrevealed. Urantia is No. 606 in Satania which now has 619 inhabited worlds. Relation of system to other superuniverse divisions.

DISCUSSION OF THE NUMBER SEVEN IN THE BIBLE

1. The seven-day week origin in Eden. (**See Gen. creation week.**)
2. Noah waited seven days to send the dove out the second time. *"He waited another seven days, and again he sent forth the dove."* **Gen. 8:10**.
3. Moses waited seven days after smiting the Nile. *"Seven days passed after the Lord had struck the Nile."* **Ex. 7:25**.
4. Samuel tarries seven days at Gilgal. *"Seven days you shall wait, until I come to you and show you what you shall do."* **1 Sam. 10:8**.
5. After seven days the word of the Lord came to Ezekiel. *"And I sat there overwhelmed among them seven days."* **Eze. 3:15**.
6. Paul stopped seven days at Troas. *"We came to them at Troas, where we stayed for seven days."* **Acts 20:6**.
7. He did the same thing at Tyre. *"And having sought out the disciples, we stayed there for seven days."* **Acts 21:4**.
8. Also at Puteoli. *"There we found brethren, and were invited to stay with them for seven days."* **Acts 28:14**.
9. The feasts lasted seven days. *"Seven days you shall eat unleavened bread."* **Ex. 12:15**. *"And the king gave...a banquet lasting for seven days."* **Esther 1:5**.
10. Priests and altars were consecrated for seven days. *"The son who is priest in his place shall wear them seven days."* **Ex. 29:30**. *"Through seven days shall you ordain them."* **Ex. 29:35**. *"Seven days you shall make atonement for the altar."* **Ex. 29:37**.

11. Defilement lasted seven days. *"Then she shall be unclean seven days."* **Lev. 12:2.**

12. Fasting for seven days. *"And they...fasted seven days."* **1 Sam. 31:13.**

13. Mourning for seven days. *"And he made a mourning for his father seven days."* **Gen. 50:10.**

14. Seven years of service. *"I will serve you seven years for your younger daughter."* **Gen. 29:18.**

15. Seven animals offered. *"Abraham set seven ewe lambs of the flock apart."* **Gen. 21:28.**

16. The seven altars. *"Build for me here seven altars."* **Num. 23:1.**

17. Sprinkled blood and oil seven times. *"And the priest shall...sprinkle part of the blood seven times before the Lord."* **Lev. 4:6.**

18. Marched around Jericho seven times on the seventh day and blew seven trumpets. *"And seven priests shall bear seven trumpets...and on the seventh day you shall march around the city seven times."* **Josh. 6:4.**

19. Naaman dips seven times. *"Go and wash in the Jordan seven times."* **2 Kings 5:10.**

20. Bowing seven times. *"He himself went on before them, bowing himself to the ground seven times."* **Gen. 33:3.**

21. Praise God seven times. *"Seven times a day I praise thee."* **Ps. 119:164.**

22. Restoration sevenfold. *"And if he is caught, he will pay sevenfold."* **Prov. 6:31.**

23. Forgiveness seven times. *"Jesus said to him, 'I do not say to you seven times, but seventy times seven.'"* **Matt. 18:22.**

24. Seven deacons. *"Pick out from among you seven men of good repute."* **Acts 6:3.**

25. The seven churches. *"John to the seven churches."* **Rev. 1:4.**

26. Job's seven troubles. *"He will deliver you from six troubles; in seven there shall no evil touch you."* **Job 5:19.**

27. The seven lamps. *"And you shall make the seven lamps for it."* **Ex. 25:37.**

28. Seven evil spirits. *"Then he goes and brings with him seven other spirits more evil than himself."* **Matt. 12:45.**

29. The seven trumpet angels. *"Then I saw the seven angels...and seven trumpets were given to them."* **Rev. 8:2**.

30. The seven last plagues. *"Then I saw...seven angels with seven plagues."* **Rev. 15:1**.

31. The seven seals. *"Then I saw...a scroll...sealed with seven seals."* **Rev. 5:1**.

32. The seven thunders. *"The seven thunders sounded."* **Rev. 10:3**.

33. The sabbatical year.

Note: All of this seven business could hardly be derived from the seven-day week. You should also recall how the number seven appears in the periodic arrangement of chemistry.

PAPER 16
The Seven Master Spirits

PAPER 16
The Seven Master Spirits

INTRODUCTION

I. *REFERENCE:*Page 184, ¶1 – "The Seven Master Spirits..."

COMMENT

1. The Seven Master Spirits are the primal agents of the Infinite Spirit.

2. The Seven Master Spirits represent all possible associations and interassociations of the three Deities.

3. This explains why the inhabited universe exists and is administered in seven grand divisions.

The Seven Master Spirits derive their individual characteristics from these seven likenesses:

1. The Universal Father.
2. The Eternal Son.
3. The Infinite Spirit.
4. The Father and the Son.
5. The Father and the Spirit.
6. The Son and the Spirit.
7. The Father, Son, and Spirit.

Father and Son are both ancestors of the Master Spirits, in addition to the Infinite Spirit. The diversity of the Master Spirits is manifested throughout all creation. Each Master Spirits maintains force-focal headquarters on the periphery of Paradise.

1. RELATION TO TRIUNE DEITY

I. *REFERENCE*: Page 185, ¶1, last sentence - "We have come to speak..."

COMMENT

1.   The Trinity is the absolute inevitability.

2.   The Seven Master Spirits are the subabsolute inevitability.

II. *REFERENCE*: Page 185, ¶3 - "But when the Seven..."

COMMENT

When the Seven Master Spirits assemble and function as a group, they are representative of the power, wisdom, and authority of the Trinity. Master Spirits portray sevenfold Deity.

2. RELATION TO THE INFINITE SPIRIT

I. *REFERENCE*: Page 185, ¶5, 2nd sentence - "At the center of centers..."

COMMENT

1.   Not all who attain Paradise are able immediately to discern the Infinite Spirit.

2.   But all are able to commune with the Master Spirit who presides over the superuniverse of their origin.

II. *REFERENCE*: Page 186, ¶1 - "To the universe..."

COMMENT

Outside of Paradise and Havona, the Infinite Spirit speaks only by and through the Seven Master Spirits.

Outside Havona, the Infinite Spirit works through the Master Spirits. Collectively they mainfest attributes of the Infinite Spirit.

3. IDENTITY AND DIVERSITY OF THE MASTER SPIRITS

I. *REFERENCE*: Page 186, ¶5 - "The Seven Master Spirits..."

COMMENT

1.   Master Spirits are personal and indescribable. They are akin, but also diverse.

2.   Each conducts his superuniverse in accordance with his unique nature.

II.*REFERENCE*: Page 188, ¶7 - "The inability of the Havona..."

COMMENT

1. During this age, the Seventh Master Spirit compensates the inability of Havona pilgrims to find God the Supreme.

2. All ascenders will be able to recognize and communicate with Master Spirit Number Seven.

Detailed description of the nature and function of the Seven Master Spirits as representing the seven associations of Deity, and as related to the seven superuniverses. When all Seven Master Spirits are associated they are representative of the Trinity. The Seventh Master Spirit acts for the evolving God the Supreme and is also in liaison with the Reflective Spirits of Uversa.

DISCUSSION

John saw seven spirits. **See Rev. 1:4**. *"And from the seven spirits who are before his throne."*

This passage probably refers to the seven Image Aids on Uversa.

See also Rev. 2:7. *"He who has an ear, let him hear what the Spirit says to the churches."*

One of these spirits says: *"To him who conquers I will grant to eat of the tree of life, which is in the paradise of God."* **Rev. 2:7**.

4. ATTRIBUTES AND FUNCTIONS OF THE MASTER SPIRITS

I. *REFERENCE*: Page 189, ¶3, last sentence—"It is literally true..."

COMMENT

1. The Seven Master Spirits are:
   A. Personalized physical power.
   B. Cosmic mind.
   C. Spiritual presence of triune Deity.

2. This seems to be **Rev. 5:6**. *"Which are the seven spirits of God sent out into all the earth."*

II. *REFERENCE*: Page 189, ¶5 - "The Seven Master Spirits are the creators..."

COMMENT

1. The Master Spirits are the creators of the Universe Power Directors and their associates.

2. They also assist the Creator Sons in the organization of local universes.

III. *REFERENCE*: Page 189, ¶8 – "Much of the reality..."

COMMENT

1. Always does the morontia intervene between the material and spirit realms.

2. It is in the morontia that the Master Spirits contribute so much to man's ascension experience.

The Master Spirits represent the Third Source and Center in all relationships of energy, mind, and spirit. They function on all universe levels below the absolute. They are creators of the cosmic mind and the Universe Power Directors. Cannot connect energy manifestations of the Master Spirits with force functions of the Unqualified Absolute.

Relation to Morontia Power Supervisors is unrevealed.

The seven spheres of functional activity.

5. RELATION TO CREATURES

I. *REFERENCE*: Page 190, last ¶ – "Through this personal influence..."

COMMENT

1. Every ascendant mortal bears the characteristic stamp of one of the Master Spirits.

2. Each creature, man or angel, will eternally carry this badge of natal identification.

II. *REFERENCE*: Page 191, ¶3, last 2 sentences – "Throughout all eternity..."

COMMENT

1. Even in the Corps of the Finality these Master Spirit traits are in evidence.

2. To portray a complete Trinity relationship requires seven finaliters— one from each superuniverse.

A superuniverse has the counsel of all Seven Master Spirits—but the personal touch of only one. The personal stamp of the Master Spirit persists eternally.

6. THE COSMIC MIND

I. *REFERENCE*: Page 191, ¶4 - "The Master Spirits are the sevenfold..."

COMMENT

1. The Master Spirits are the source of the cosmic mind.

2. The cosmic mind is a subabsolute derivation from the Infinite Spirit.

3. Cosmic mind is functionally related to the mind of the Supreme Being.

II. *REFERENCE*: Page 191, ¶7 - "There exists in all..."

COMMENT

1. The "reality response" is a quality of cosmic mind which saves us from the false assumptions of science, philosophy, and religion.

2. This reality sensitivity responds to cosmic reality just as energy material responds to gravity.

III. *REFERENCE*: Page 192, ¶2 - "The cosmic mind..."

COMMENT

The cosmic mind unfailingly responds to three levels of reality:

1. Causation—mathematical response.
2. Duty—judicial response.
3. Worship—spiritual response.

IV. *REFERENCE*: Page 192, ¶8 - "It is the purpose of education..."

COMMENT

It is the purpose of:

1. *Education*—to develop and sharpen these endowments.
2. *Civilisation*—to express them.
3. *Life Experience*—to realise them.
4. *Religion*—to ennoble them.
5. *Personality*—to unify them.

On evolutionary worlds Master Spirits work through local universe Mother Spirits. Creature kinship is explained by the common cosmic mind. The levels of reality (causation, duty, worship) pertain to science, philosophy, and religion. This represents man's experience with things, meanings, and values.

7. MORALS, VIRTUE, AND PERSONALITY

I. *REFERENCE*: Page 193, ¶3 - "Only a personality..."

COMMENT

1. Personality has insight and foresight—can look before it leaps.
2. Personality can learn from looking as well as from leaping.
3. Animals can learn only by leaping.

II. *REFERENCE*: Page 193, ¶9 - "Morality can never be..."

COMMENT

1. Morality cannot be advanced by force.
2. Moral fragrancy is contagious. Right-minded persons will be attracted.

Moral duty, scientific curiosity, and spiritual insight are human inalienables. Animal response is on motor level of experience with trial and error. Moral beings can choose between ends as well as between means. Virtue is choosing between good and evil. Choice is affected by ignorance and immaturity. Supreme virtue is to do the will of the Father.

8. URANTIA PERSONALITY

I. *REFERENCE*: Page 194, ¶3 - "Personality is a unique..."

COMMENT

1. Personality is unique and always precedes the coming of the Thought Adjuster.
2. Personality is diverse, original, and exclusive; Thought Adjusters are identical in nature.
3. Personality may be qualified by the nature of the material, mindal, or spiritual qualities of the organismal vehicle.

II. *REFERENCE*: Page 194, ¶5 - "Creature personality is..."

COMMENT

Personality is distinguished by:

1. Self-consciousness.
2. Relative free will.

III. *REFERENCE*: Page ¶194, ¶7 - "The relative free will..."

COMMENT

This is a list of things in which free will is involved.

The Universal Father bestows personality. Personality is not definable, but its components can be recognized. Personality is both unique and changeless. Personality is characterized by self-consciousness and free will. Personality recognizes the three basic mind realities of the cosmos.

9. REALITY OF HUMAN CONSCIOUSNESS

I. *REFERENCE*: Page 195, ¶4 - "The cosmic-mind-endowed..."

COMMENT

1. The cosmic-minded, Adjuster-indwelt person possesses innate recognition of:
    A. Energy reality—the fact of God.
    B. Mind reality—the law of God.
    C. Spirit reality—the love of God.
2. Human experience is validated by the unification of these reality responses.

II. *REFERENCE*: Page 195, ¶6 - "If mortal man fails..."

COMMENT

1. When mortal man fails to survive:
    A. Spiritual values survive in the Thought Adjuster.
    B. Personality values (but not identity) persist in the actualizing Supreme Being.
2. Personality identity survives in the survival of the soul.

III. *REFERENCE*: Page 196, ¶6 - "Self-consciousness is in essence..."

COMMENT

Four factors are inherent in human self-consciousness:

A. The quest for knowledge.
B. The quest for moral values.
C. The quest for spiritual values.
D. The quest for personality values.

The evolving soul has survival qualities. Civilizations perish, but science, morality, and religion survive. Only a God-knowing person can love another as he loves himself. The basis of worship.

DISCUSSION
MEANING OF SPIRIT AS USED IN THE BIBLE

1. **God is spirit. John 4:24.** *"God is spirit, and those who worship him must worship in spirit and truth."*

2. **The Creator Spirit—the Conjoint Actor. Gen. 1:2.** *"And the Spirit of God was moving over the face of the waters."*

   Ps. 104:30. *"When thou sendest forth thy Spirit, they are created."*

3. **The omnipresent spirit—the Infinite Spirit. Ps. 139.7.** *"Whither shall I go from thy Spirit?"*

4. **The mind spirit—mind gravity. Eph. 4:23.** *"And be renewed in the spirit of your minds."*

5. **Spirit—the breath of life. Job 27:3.** *"As long as my breath is in me, and the spirit of God is in my nostrils."* *(The domain of the Life Carriers.)*

6. **The indwelling spirit—Thought Adjusters. Zech. 12:1.** *"Thus says the Lord, who...formed the spirit of man within him."*

   Job 32:8. *"But it is the spirit in a man...that makes him understand."*

   Job 32:18. *"The spirit within me constrains me."*

   Ps. 31:5. *"Into thy hand I commit my spirit."*

   Prov. 20:27. *"The spirit of man is the lamp of the Lord."*

   Eccl. 12:7. *"And the spirit returns to God who gave it."*

   Note: This spirit symbolized. **See Matt. 3:16, Mark 1:10.** (Spirit decending on Jesus like a dove, following baptism.)

7. **The Holy Spirit. Ps. 51:11.** *"Take not thy holy spirit from me."*

   Acts 8:29. *"And the Spirit said to Philip, 'Go up and join this chariot.'"*

   In *The Urantia Book*, the Holy Spirit is the presence of the local universe Mother Spirit.

8. **Spiritual gifts. 1 Cor. 12:4.** *"Now there are varieties of gifts, but the same Spirit."*

   2 Sam. 23:2. *"The Spirit of the Lord speaks by me."*

9. **The fruits of the Spirit. Gal. 5:22.** *"But the fruit of the Spirit is love, joy, peace, patience, kindness, goodness, faithfulness, gentleness, self-control."*

10. **The seven adjutant spirits. Isa. 11:2.** *"The spirit of wisdom and understanding, the spirit of counsel and might, the spirit of knowledge and the fear of the Lord."*

    Ex. 28:3. *"Speak to all who have ability, whom I have endowed with an able mind."*

11. *One of the three factors of human personality.* **1 Thess. 5:23.** *"And may your spirit and soul and body be kept sound and blameless."*

12. *Used synonymously with personality.* **2 Kings 2:15.** *"They said, 'The spirit of Elijah rests upon Elisha.'"*

    Prov. 18:14. *"A man's spirit will endure sickness; but a broken spirit who can bear?"*

13. *Used as synonymous with temperament or disposition.* **Neh. 9:20.** *"Thou gavest thy good Spirit to instruct them."*

    Ps. 34:18. *"The Lord is near to the brokenhearted, and saves the crushed in spirit."*

    Ps. 51:10. *"And put a new and right spirit within me."*

    Prov. 16:18. *"Pride goes before destruction, and a haughty spirit before a fall."*

14. *Used to denote depression—despair.* **1 Kings 21:5.** *"'Why is your spirit so vexed that you eat no food?'"*

    Isa. 61:3. *"To give them...the mantle of praise instead of a faint spirit."*

    Prov. 15:13. *"By sorrow of heart the spirit is broken."*

    Luke 13:11. *"And there was a woman who had a spirit of infirmity for eighteen years."*

15. *Used to connote emotional enthusiasm.* **Acts 18:25.** *"And being fervent in spirit, he spoke and taught accurately."*

    Rom. 12:11. *"Never flag in zeal, be aglow with the Spirit."*

    1 Cor. 2:4. *"My speech and my message were...in demonstration of the Spirit."*

16. *Used to denote self-control.* **Prov. 16:32.** *"He who is slow to anger is better than the mighty, and he who rules his spirit than he who takes a city."*

17. *The Spirit of Truth.* **John 16:13.** *"When the Spirit of truth comes, he will guide you into all truth."*

    Prov. 1:23. *"Behold, I will pour out my thoughts to you."*

18. *Spirit assists in prayer and worship.* **Rom. 8:26.** *"Likewise the Spirit helps us in our weakness; for we do not know how to pray as we ought, but the Spirit himself intercedes for us."*

    1 Cor. 14:15. *"I will pray with the spirit and I will pray with the mind also."*

19. *Evil spirits.*

    A. Spirits in prison. **1 Peter 3:19.** *"He went and preached to the spirits in prison."* (Probably interned angels and midwayers.)

B. Wicked spirits. **Matt. 12:43.** *"And when the unclean spirit has gone out of a man."*

C. God sends evil spirits. **Judges 9:23.** *"And God sent an evil spirit."* **Note:** Early Hebrews believed that both good and evil spirits came from God.

   Ex. 31:3. *"And I have filled him with the Spirit of God."*

   1 Sam. 16:23. *"And whenever the evil spirit from God was upon Saul."*

20. **Used as characterizing the phenomena of mediumship, magic, etc.** (Tricks of the subconscious mind) **1 Kings 22:21, 22.** *"Then a spirit came forward …saying, 'I will entice him'…'I…will be a lying spirit.'"*

21. **Spirit as contrasted with the flesh.** **Matt. 26:41.** *"The spirit indeed is willing, but the flesh is weak."*

22. **To characterize the new birth.** **John 3:5.** *"Unless one is born of water and the Spirit, he cannot enter the kingdom of God."*

   Eze. 11:19. *"And I will give them one heart and put a new spirit within them."*

23. **To denote unity and perfection.** **Eph. 4:3.** *"Eager to maintain the unity of the Spirit in the bond of peace."*

24. **Angels are called spirits.** **Heb. 1:14.** *"Are they not all ministering spirits sent forth to serve?"*

25. **The seven spirits of revelation.** **Rev. 1:4.** *"The seven spirits who are before his throne."*

PAPER 17
The Seven Supreme Spirit Groups

PAPER 17
The Seven Supreme Spirit Groups

1. **THE SEVEN SUPREME EXECUTIVES**
2. **MAJESTON—CHIEF OF REFLECTIVITY**
3. **THE REFLECTIVE SPIRITS**
4. **THE REFLECTIVE IMAGE AIDS**
5. **THE SEVEN SPIRITS OF THE CIRCUITS**
6. **THE LOCAL UNIVERSE CREATIVE SPIRITS**
7. **THE ADJUTANT MIND-SPIRITS**
8. **FUNCTIONS OF THE SUPREME SPIRITS**

INTRODUCTION

I. *REFERENCE*: Page 197, ¶1,2 - "The seven Supreme Spirit groups..."

COMMENT

The first three groups are created by the Trinity and the last four by the Infinite Spirit or his associates.

1. THE SEVEN SUPREME EXECUTIVES

I. *REFERENCE*: Page 198, ¶4 - "These Supreme Executives do not originate..."

COMMENT

1. These executives do not originate policies; they are the over-all administrators of the Seven Master Spirits.

2. They also co-ordinate the policies of all rulers of the grand universe.

II. *REFERENCE*: Page 199, ¶3 - "Each Supreme Executive..."

COMMENT

Each Supreme Executive has two cabinets:

1. Children of the Infinite Spirit.

2. Mortals of Paradise attainment and trinitized sons of glorified mortals.

2. MAJESTON—CHIEF OF REFLECTIVITY

I. *REFERENCE*: Page 199, ¶7 - "This momentous transaction..."

COMMENT

1. When the Seven Master Spirits completed creation of forty-nine Reflective Spirits a new universe reaction occurred.

2. Majeston was created by:

    A. Seven Master Spirits.

    B. Paradise Trinity.
    C. Supreme Being.
    D. Deity Absolute.

II. REFERENCE: Page 200, ¶3 - "The creation of Majeston..."

COMMENT

1. Majeston was the first supreme creative act of the Supreme Being.

2. Majeston was the greatest factualization since Havona.

3. The Deity response in the creation of Majeston was vastly beyond all expectations.

3. THE REFLECTIVE SPIRITS

I. REFERENCE: Page 200, ¶5 - "The forty-nine Reflective Spirits..."

COMMENT

1. Though Reflective Spirits are of Trinity origin, each resembles one of the Seven Master Spirits.

2. To portray all Deity traits of the Father, Son, and Spirit it requires seven diverse Reflective Spirits.

3. Accordingly, each superuniverse has seven diverse Reflective Spirits.

II. REFERENCE: Page 201, ¶3 - "The Reflective Spirits are not..."

COMMENT

1. Reflective Spirits are retentive as well as transmitting personalities.

2. They produce seconaphim who also are retentive personalities.

III. REFERENCE: Page 201, ¶5 - "The reflectivity organization..."

COMMENT

The reflective system is in constant operation as both a news-gathering and a decree-disseminating mechanism.

4. THE REFLECTIVE IMAGE AIDS

5. THE SEVEN SPIRITS OF THE CIRCUITS

I. REFERENCE: Page 203, ¶4 - "The Circuit Spirits are…"

Comment

1. These spirits are related to Havona natives much as Adjusters are related to mortals.

2. But these Spirits never become a part of the Havona personality.

6. THE LOCAL UNIVERSE CREATIVE SPIRITS

II. REFERENCE: Page 203, ¶5 - "Much that pertains…"

Comment

There are six *known* phases of the universe Mother Spirits:

1. Initial Paradise Differentiation.
2. Preliminary Creatorship Training.
3. The Stage of Physical Creation.
4. The Life-Creation Era.
5. The Postbestowal Ages.
6. The Ages of Light and Life.
7. The Unrevealed Career.

7. THE ADJUTANT MIND-SPIRITS

8. FUNCTIONS OF THE SUPREME SPIRITS

I. REFERENCE: Page 205, ¶3 - "The seven groups of…"

Comment

1. These Spirits operate from the Trinity on Paradise to mortals on evolutionary worlds.

2. They unify descending administrative levels.

II. REFERENCES: Page 205, ¶4 - "Together with their…"

Comment

The vast host of ministering spirits are created by these Supreme Spirits.

III. *REFERENCE*: Page 205, ¶5 - "The seven Supreme "Spirit groups..."

COMMENT

1. These groups co-ordinate all inhabited creation—the grand universe.

2. The first group—the Seven Master Spirits—seems to co-ordinate the activities of God the Sevenfold.

PAPER 18
The Supreme Trinity Personalities

PAPER 18
The Supreme Trinity Personalities

1. **THE TRINITIZED SECRETS OF SUPREMACY**
2. **THE ETERNALS OF DAYS**
3. **THE ANCIENTS OF DAYS**
4. **THE PERFECTIONS OF DAYS**
5. **THE RECENTS OF DAYS**
6. **THE UNIONS OF DAYS**
7. **THE FAITHFULS OF DAYS**

INTRODUCTION

I. *REFERENCE*: **Page 207, ¶1 - "Supreme Trinity Personalities..."**

COMMENT

They are designed for specific work and function in seven groups.

II. *REFERENCE*: **Page 207, ¶3 - "Throughout the grand universe..."**

COMMENT

They are perfect administrators and represent the justice and *are* the executive judgment of the Paradise Trinity.

1. THE TRINITIZED SECRETS OF SUPREMACY

I. *REFERENCE*: **Page 208, ¶1 - "The Trinitized Secrets of Supremacy..."**

COMMENT

1. These Sons function as a council of ten as world rulers; they also function as individuals in charge of seven divisions of administration.

2. A group of three represent the Deities of the Trinity.

II. *REFERENCE*: **Page 208, ¶2 - "Although there is..."**

COMMENT

1. There is an over-all resemblance of these Secrets of Supremacy.

2. There is also a group characteristic distinguishing each company of ten. This is determined by the seven possible associations of the three Deities.

2. THE ETERNALS OF DAYS

I. *REFERENCE*: Page 208, ¶6 - "Each of the billion worlds..."

COMMENT

1. One billion Eternals of Days rule the worlds of Havona. They are created by the Trinity.

2. They eternally rule the one world of original assignment.

II. *REFERENCE*: Page 209, ¶2 - "The architecture..."

COMMENT

1. All structures and embellishment of each Havona world are original and unique.

2. Ascenders spend some time on each of these worlds.

3. Havona is inward from our world rather than upward.

3. THE ANCIENTS OF DAYS

I. *REFERENCE*: Page 209, ¶4 - "The Ancients of Days are..."

COMMENT

1. All Ancients of Days are identical. They disclose the unified nature of the Trinity.

2. They possess diverse personalities.

3. They provide a uniform direction of the otherwise seven different superuniverses.

II. *REFERENCE*: Page 209, ¶5 - "The Seven Master Spirits..."

COMMENT

1. The diverse Master Spirits determine the *nature* of their superuniverses.

2. The Ancients of Days provide the *administration*.

3. There is uniformity of administration in the presence of creative diversity.

III. *REFERENCE*: Page 209, ¶6 - "The Ancients of Days were..."

COMMENT

1. The Ancients of Days represent the beginning of the personality records of the universes.

2. The first entry on universe records pertains to the creation of the 21 Ancients of Days.

4. THE PERFECTIONS OF DAYS

I. *REFERENCE*: **Page 210, ¶4 - "There are just two hundred..."**

COMMENT

1. These beings rule the major sectors of the superuniverses.

2. They are the vicegerents of the Ancients of Days.

II. *REFERENCE*: **Page 211, ¶3 - "You will early see..."**

COMMENT

All ascenders contact these Sons; they administer pledges to the major sector graduates.

III. *REFERENCE*: **Page 211, ¶5 - "Although you are entered..."**

COMMENT

Ascenders pass through all ten of the major sectors in our superuniverse on the way to Havona.

5. THE RECENTS OF DAYS

I. *REFERENCE*: **Page 211, ¶6 - "The Recents of Days are the youngest..."**

COMMENT

1. They rule the minor sectors.

2. They were all trained by the Havona Eternals of Days.

II. *REFERENCE*: **Page 212, ¶3 - "You will all sometime know..."**

COMMENT

Urantians will meet the Recents of Days on Uminor the third, the capital of our minor sector of Ensa.

6. THE UNIONS OF DAYS

I. *REFERENCE*: **Page 212, ¶4 - "The Trinity personalities..."**

COMMENT

1. The orders of "Days" do not function as administrators below the superuniverse level.

2. The Unions of Days represent the Paradise Trinity to the rulers of the local universes.

3. They also in a special manner represent the Universal Father.

II. *REFERENCE*: Page 212, ¶8 – "A Union of Days is not..."

COMMENT

1. These Sons are not organically connected with the local universe governments, and act only on request.

2. They are ex officio members of all primary councils.

7. THE FAITHFULS OF DAYS

I. *REFERENCE*: Page 213, ¶3 – "These high Trinity-origin..."

COMMENT

1. These Sons are Paradise advisers to the constellation rulers—the Most Highs.

2. The reserve corps of these Sons is the Advisory Commission of Interuniverse Ethics and Self-government.

3. They rotate in service.

II. *REFERENCE*: Page 213, ¶7 – "The Faithfuls of Days..."

COMMENT

1. These Sons are the last link in the long advisory chain extending from Paradise to the local universes.

2. The two lower units of local universe administration (systems and inhabited worlds) are wholly in the hands of native beings.

BIBLE TEACHING ON THE JUDGMENT

1. *Judgment Day*—"Day of the Lord."

   2 Peter 2:9. *"And to keep the unrighteous under punishment until the day of judgment."*

   2 Peter 3:7. *"Have been stored up for fire, being kept until the day of judgment."*

   Matt. 11:24. *"It shall be more tolerable on the day of judgment for the land of Sodom."*

   John 12:31. *"Now is the judgment of this world."*

2.   ***Judgment Seat***—Throne

    Rom. 14:10. *"For we shall all stand before the judgment seat of God."*

    Ps. 9:7. *"He has established his throne for judgment."*

    Rev. 20:4. *"I saw thrones, and seated on them were those to whom judgment was committed."*

3.   ***The Ancients of Days***

    Dan. 7:9. *"Thrones were placed and one that was Ancient of Days took his seat."*

    Dan. 7:13. *"Then came one like a son of man, and he came to the Ancient of Days and was presented before him."*

    Dan. 7:22. *"Until the Ancient of Days came, and judgment was given for the saints of the Most High."*

    These are the only references to the Ancients of Days in the Bible.

    In **Dan. 7:10** it says: *"The court sat in judgment and the books were opened."*

    This recalls **Job 12:10**. *"In his hand is the life of every living thing."*

    The Moffatt translation reads: "In whose control lies every living soul, and the whole life of man."

4.   ***The Book of Life***

    Dan. 12:1. *"Your people shall be delivered, every one whose name shall be found written in the book."*

    Ps. 69:28. *"Let them be blotted out of the book of the living."*

    Rev. 20:12. *"Also another book was opened, which is the book of life."*

    Phil. 4:3. *"And the rest of my fellow workers, whose names are in the book of life."*

    Rev. 3:5. *"And I will not blot his name out of the book of life."*

5.   ***As You Judge***

    Matt. 7:2. *"For with the judgment you pronounce you will be judged."*

6. **According to Your Deeds**

   Eccl. 11:9. *"But know that...God will bring you into judgment."*

   Eccl. 12:14. *"For God will bring every deed into judgment, with every secret thing, whether good or evil."*

   Matt. 12:36. *"On the day of judgment men will render account for every careless word they utter."*

7. **God's Judgment Is Just**

   Job 34:12. *"And the Almighty will not pervert justice."*

   Isa. 30:18. *"The Lord is a God of justice."*

   Rom. 2:2. *"We know that the judgment of God rightly falls on those who do such things."*

   Rom. 11:33. *"How unsearchable are his judgments and how inscrutable his ways!"*

8. **The Righteous Are Judged First**

   1 Peter 4:17. *"The time has come for judgment to begin with the household of God."*

   Matt. 24:31. *"And he will send out his angels...and they will gather his elect."*

9. **Judgment of Fallen Angels**

   2 Peter 2:4. *"For if God did not spare the angels when they sinned, but cast them into hell and committed them to pits of nether gloom to be kept until the judgment."*

   Jude 6. *"And the angels that did not keep their own position...have been kept by him in eternal chains in the nether gloom until the judgment of the great day."*

10. **The Father Makes the Son Judge**

    John 5:22. *"The Father judges no one, but has given all judgment to the Son."*

    Rom. 2:16. *"On that day when...God judges the secrets of men by Christ Jesus."*

11. **The Saints Acting as Judges**

    Dan. 7:22. *"Until the Ancient of Days came, and judgment was given for the saints of the Most High."*

Luke 22:30. *"That you may eat and drink at my table in my kingdom, and sit on thrones judging the twelve tribes of Israel."*

1 Cor. 6:2,3. *"Do you not know that the saints will judge the world?... Do you not know that we are to judge angels?"*

PAPER 19

The Co-ordinate Trinity-Origin Beings

PAPER 19
The Co-ordinate Trinity-Origin Beings

1. **The Trinity Teacher Sons**
2. **The Perfectors of Wisdom**
3. **The Divine Counselors**
4. **The Universal Censors**
5. **Inspired Trinity Spirits**
6. **Havona Natives**
7. **Paradise Citizens**

INTRODUCTION

I. *REFERENCE*: Page 214, ¶1 – "This Paradise group..."

COMMENT

This is a mixed group of Trinity-origin beings with widely varying functions.

1. THE TRINITY TEACHER SONS

I. *REFERENCE*: Page 214, ¶3 – "Of all the high orders..."

COMMENT

1. While these Sons are of Trinity origin, they function in the realms of divine sonship.

2. They bridge the gulf between Trinity- and dual-origin personalities.

II. *REFERENCE*: Page 215, ¶1 – "In this connection..."

COMMENT

1. Teacher Sons are the supreme co-ordinators of Trinity origin.

2. In the universe two great dangers exist:

    A. The error of the circumscribed viewpoint.
    B. The evil of a segmentalized conception of reality and divinity.

III. *REFERENCE*: Page 215, ¶2 – "For example..."

COMMENT

1. Ordinarily the human mind craves to approach problems by proceeding from the simple to the complex.

2. This technique may reveal origins, but it reveals little about destiny.

IV. *REFERENCE*: Page 215, ¶4 - "When the human mind..."

COMMENT

Reasoning from the simple to the complex may involve four errors:

1. Failure to perceive the final goal.
2. Oversimplification of cosmic evolutionary reality.
3. Knowledge of causation does not necessarily indicate present status.
4. History does not reveal destiny. Ends are not shown in time beginnings.

V. *REFERENCE*: Page 215, ¶5 - "Therefore, because of these..."

COMMENT

The plan of *The Urantia Book* is to approach planetary problems by starting out with the infinite, the eternal, and the divine.

2. THE PERFECTORS OF WISDOM

I. *REFERENCE*: Page 215, ¶6 - "The Perfectors of Wisdom..."

COMMENT

These are the specialized Trinity beings who personify divine wisdom.

II. *REFERENCE*: Page 216, ¶2 - "Wherever and whenever..."

COMMENT

1. When these beings function, Trinity wisdom functions.
2. Perfectors of Wisdom do not *reflect* wisdom—they *are* wisdom.
3. They are fountains of discretion and wellsprings of discrimination to all.

III. *REFERENCE*: Page 216, ¶4 - "The Perfectors of Wisdom..."

COMMENT

1. Perfectors of Wisdom require the complement of experiential wisdom for administrative sagacity.
2. After becoming seventh stage spirits, Paradise finaliters may attain new heights of administrative wisdom in the ultimate universes of outer space.

3. THE DIVINE COUNSELORS

I. *REFERENCE*: Page 216, ¶6 - "These Trinity-origin beings..."

COMMENT

These Trinity-origin beings do not *reflect* divine counsel—they are that counsel.

II. *REFERENCE*: Page 217, ¶1 - "Divine Counselors are..."

COMMENT

1. From one to seven Counselors are associated with a Perfector of Wisdom and a Universal Censor.

2. All three orders serve throughout all divisions of the superuniverse government.

III. *REFERENCE*: Page 217, ¶3 - "One Perfector of Wisdom..."

COMMENT

1. A tribunal of Trinity divinity, the highest mobile advisory body in the universe, consists of:

    A. 1 Perfector of Wisdom.
    B. 1 Universal Censor.
    C. 7 Divine Counselors.

2. These advisers function as:

    A. Fact finders.
    B. Truth revealers.
    C. Problem solvers.

3. Their verdicts and decisions are equivalent to the adjudication of the Ancients of Days.

4. THE UNIVERSAL CENSORS

I. *REFERENCE*: Page 217, ¶7 - "There are exactly eight billion..."

COMMENT

1. These Censors *are* the judgment of Deity—the Paradise Trinity.

2. Ancients of Days do not sit in judgment without the Censors.

II. *REFERENCE*: Page 218, ¶3 - "Whenever and wherever..."

COMMENT

1. Censors render verdicts in association with Perfectors of Wisdom and Divine Counselors—their decisions represent the united wisdom, counsel, and judgment of the Trinity.

2. In this juridical trio—

 A. Perfector of Wisdom is — "I was."
 B. Divine Counselor is — "I will be."
 C. Universal Censor is — "I am."

III. *REFERENCE*: Page 218, ¶4 - "The Censors are..."

COMMENT

1. Censors are universe totaling personalities.

2. Regardless of the number of witnesses or the multiplicity of evidence—the Censor totals the whole.

3. There is no appeal from the verdict of a Censor.

IV. *REFERENCE*: Page 218, ¶6 - "But this is not..."

COMMENT

1. It is impossible to forecast the Censor's verdict.

2. It is possible to determine the Creator attitude and the creature experience, but Censor decisions are unpredictable.

3. The explanation: The Censors are probably in liaison with the Deity Absolute.

Note: Observation of a musical genius or a mathematical prodigy will afford some hint of how certain minds can almost automatically solve intricate mathematical problems. Recall how the seraphim knows the number of hairs on your head.

5. INSPIRED TRINITY SPIRITS

I. *REFERENCE*: Page 219, ¶3 - "I will be able..."

COMMENT

1. The Trinity Spirits are a wholly secret order of Trinity helpers.

2. Their number is probably not fixed.

II. *REFERENCE*: Page 219, ¶4 - "We fully understand..."

COMMENT

1. We understand little about these Spirits. Perhaps they are superpersonal spirits.

2. They operate over all known circuits and are almost independent of both time and space.

III. *REFERENCE*: Page 219, ¶6 - "The Melchizedeks..."

COMMENT

Inspired Trinity Spirits may sometime in the future function in place of Solitary Messengers, whose ranks are gradually being depleted.

IV. *REFERENCE*: Page 219, ¶7 - "The Inspired Spirits..." and Page 220, ¶2 - "I may relate..."

COMMENT

1. Solitary Messengers detect both qualitative and quantitative response when in the presence of Inspired Trinity Spirits.

2. Thought Adjusters produce only a qualitative response.

3. There appears to be a close relationship between Inspired Trinity Spirits and Thought Adjusters.

V. *REFERENCE*: Page 220, ¶5 - "We know that the..."

COMMENT

1. Trinity Teacher Sons are devoted to conscious enlightenment.

2. Inspired Trinity Spirits may be concerned with superconscious techniques of creature enlightenment.

3. There may be a liaison function of these two types of spiritual teachers.

6. HAVONA NATIVES

I. *REFERENCE*: Page 221, ¶4 - "The Havona natives are..."

COMMENT

Havona natives are created by the Paradise Trinity and are beyond the range of mortal conception.

II. *REFERENCE*: Page 221, ¶7 - "The status evolution..."

COMMENT

1. The population of Havona is being gradually depleted by infiltration into the various finaliter corps.

2. Will this sometime stop? Or, will the population of Havona undergo a change in the future ages?

3. Possible future inhabitants of Havona may be:

   A. Univitatia.
   B. Superuniverse mortals from worlds long settled in light and life.
   C. Spiritual aristocracy from the outer universes.

III. *REFERENCE*: Page 222, ¶2 - "We know that the Havona..."

COMMENT

1. Present-day Havona differs from the Havona of former ages.

2. The future may bring about still other changes.

3. The universe is nonstatic; only God is changeless.

7. PARADISE CITIZENS

REFERENCE: Page 222, ¶3 - "There are resident..."

COMMENT

There are more than three thousand orders of Paradise Citizens.

WISDOM IN THE BIBLE

1. *The Spirit of Wisdom*

   Isa. 11:2. *"And the Spirit of the Lord shall rest upon him, the spirit of wisdom and understanding, the spirit of counsel and might, the spirit of knowledge and the fear of the Lord."* The spirit of wisdom (the seventh adjutant spirit) is mentioned first.

2. *Wisdom Is the Gift of God*

   Ex. 28:3. *"You shall speak to all who have ability, whom I have endowed with an able mind."* (King James Version: "Have endowed with wisdom.")

   1 Kings 3:28. *"And they stood in awe of the king, because they perceived that the wisdom of God was in him."*

1 Kings 4:29, 30. *"And God gave Solomon wisdom and understanding beyond measure...so that Solomon's wisdom surpassed the wisdom of all the people of the east."*

Prov. 2:6. *"For the Lord gives wisdom."*

Eph. 1:17. *"That the God of our Lord Jesus Christ...may give you a spirit of wisdom."*

Jas. 1:5. *"If any of you lacks wisdom, let him ask God who gives to all men generously."*

3.   *Wisdom a Spiritual Bestowal*

Ex. 35:31. *"And he has filled him with the Spirit of God, with ability."* (Wisdom)

Deut. 34:9. *"And Joshua the son of Nun was full of the spirit of wisdom."*

4.   *Wisdom a Divine Attribute*

Job 12:13. *"With God are wisdom and might."*

Prov. 3:13. *"Happy is the man who finds wisdom."*

Eccl. 8:1. *"A man's wisdom makes his face shine."*

Dan. 2:21. *"He gives wisdom to the wise and knowledge to those who have understanding."*

5.   *Fear of God the Beginning of Wisdom*

Job 28:28. *"Behold, the fear of the Lord, that is wisdom."*

Ps. 111:10. *"The fear of the Lord is the beginning of wisdom."*

Prov. 9:10. *"The fear of the Lord is the beginning of wisdom, and the knowledge of the Holy One is insight."*

6.   *Wisdom the Chief of All Goals*

Ps. 90:12. *"So teach us to number our days that we may get a heart of wisdom."*

Prov. 4:5. *"Get wisdom; get insight."*

Prov. 16:16. *"To get wisdom is better than gold."*

7.   *The Folly of Worldly Wisdom*

1 Cor. 3:19. *"For the wisdom of this world is folly with God."*

Matt. 11:25. *"Jesus declared, 'I thank thee, Father...that thou hast hidden these things from the wise and understanding and revealed them to babes.'"*

8. **Spiritual Wisdom**

Luke 7:35. *"Wisdom is justified by all her children."*

Acts 6:3. *"Pick out from among you seven men of good repute, full of the Spirit and of wisdom."*

Col. 1:9. *"That you may be filled with the knowledge of his will in all spiritual wisdom and understanding."*

Jas. 3:17. *"But the wisdom from above is first pure, then peaceable, gentle, open to reason, full of mercy and good fruits."*

9. **Conceit Is Not Wisdom**

Prov. 3:7. *"Be not wise in your own eyes."*

Prov. 28:11. *"A rich man is wise in his own eyes."*

Note: Many "wisdom" passages in the King James Version are rendered "ability" or "intelligence" in the Revised Standard Version.

PAPER 20
The Paradise Sons of God

PAPER 20
The Paradise Sons of God

INTRODUCTION

I. *REFERENCE*: Page 223, ¶1 - "As they function..."

COMMENT

Functionally the Sons of God are divided into three groups—Descending, Ascending, and Trinitized.

1. THE DESCENDING SONS OF GOD

II. *REFERENCE*: Page 223, ¶3 - "All descending Sons..." and ¶4 - "The remaining four..."

COMMENT

1. These Sons are dedicated to helping evolutionary creatures ascend to Paradise to find the Father.

2. The first three groups are Paradise Sons, the last four are local universe Sons.

III. *REFERENCE*: Page 224, ¶2 - "The Paradise Sons..."

COMMENT

The Paradise Sons are of threefold origin:

1. Creator Sons—produced by the Universal Father and the Eternal Son.

2. Magisterial Sons—produced by the Eternal Son and the Infinite Spirit.

3. Trinity Teacher Sons—produced by the Father, Son, and Spirit.

III. *REFERENCE*: Page 224, ¶4 - "The Creator Sons..."

Comment

1. Creator Sons possess a spiritual endowment which they can bestow upon their creatures.

2. This is the Spirit of Truth which Michael bestowed upon Urantia mortals.

3. Creator Sons draw all spiritual values to themselves—like the Eternal Son.

2. THE MAGISTERIAL SONS

I. *REFERENCE*: Page 224, ¶7 - "Every time an original..."

Comment

1. Magisterial Sons are created by:

   A. Original and absolute concept of being on the part of the Eternal Son, and
   B. New and divine ideal of service on the part of the Infinite Spirit.

2. These Sons are closely related to all creative activities of the Michaels.

3. These Avonals are planetary ministers and magistrates.

II. *REFERENCE*: Page 225, ¶3 - "Avonals are the..."

Comment

1. The Avonals are the Paradise Sons of planetary service and bestowal.

2. They are often incarnated and sometimes born of evolutionary mothers.

III. *REFERENCE*: Page 225, ¶9 - "In all their work..."

Comment

1. Avonals are always backed up by the authority of the Creator Son of the universe where they are working.

2. The bestowal of an Avonal Son is just as effective as that of a Creator Son.

3. JUDICIAL ACTIONS

REFERENCE: Page 226, ¶2 - "When they sit..."

COMMENT

1. Avonals may decree the destinies of an age.

2. But all sentences are executed by the authorities of the superuniverse.

4. MAGISTERIAL MISSIONS

I. REFERENCE: Page 226, ¶5 - "Prior to the..."

COMMENT

1. A Magisterial Son usually precedes the bestowal Son on a planet.

2. A Magisterial Son on an initial visitation appears as a full-grown male.

3. During the incarnation the Magisterial Son is fully co-operative with all functioning spiritual forces.

II. REFERENCE: Page 227, ¶2 - "Urantia has never..."

COMMENT

If Urantia had followed the general plan, a Magisterial Son would have appeared sometime between Adam and the bestowal of Michael.

5. BESTOWAL OF THE PARADISE SONS OF GOD

I. REFERENCE: Page 227, ¶4 - "The Eternal Son is..."

COMMENT

1. The Eternal Son is the eternal Word of God.

2. When a Son of the Eternal Son is bestowed on a world, such an incarnated Son is the "Word made flesh."

II. REFERENCE: Page 227, ¶6 - "Some order of..."

COMMENT

1. The mission of a bestowal Son is a prerequisite for the general bestowal of Thought Adjusters.

2. The Thought Adjusters are not universally bestowed until after the coming of the Spirit of Truth.

III. *REFERENCE*: Page 228, ¶3 - "Understanding more about..."

COMMENT

Urantia is renowned in our local universe because it was the world on which our Creator Son executed his seventh and final bestowal.

6. THE MORTAL-BESTOWAL CAREERS

I. *REFERENCE*: Page 228, ¶6 - "The method whereby..."

COMMENT

The method of incarnation bestowal is a universe secret—known only to the bestowal Sons—and it is a waste of time to speculate.

II. *REFERENCE*: Page 229, ¶2 - "On a mortal-bestowal mission..."

COMMENT

1. On a mortal bestowal, a Paradise Son is always born of woman.

2. They live average mortal lives except that they do not beget offspring.

III. *REFERENCE*: Page 229, ¶6 - "When the bestowal Sons..."

COMMENT

1. When bestowal Sons die, they always reappear on the third day.

2. It is not required that they should experience a violent death, as occurred on Urantia.

3. Urantia is known in the local universe as "the world of the cross."

IV. *REFERENCE*: Page 229, ¶7 - "When bestowal Sons are not..."

COMMENT

1. When bestowal Sons are not put to death violently, they simply "lay down their lives."

2. But these deaths are not to satisfy the demands of the "divine wrath."

3. The bestowal is a universe necessity—death is just a part of such a bestowal life.

V. *REFERENCE*: Page 230, ¶2 - "Upon the completion..."

COMMENT

1. Subsequent to a final planetary bestowal, a Creator Son sends his Spirit of Truth to such a world.

2. The Spirit of Truth previously sent to all Avonal-bestowal worlds now changes to become more literally the spirit of Michael.

7. THE TRINITY TEACHER SONS

I. *REFERENCE*: Page 230, ¶3 – "These highly personal..."

COMMENT

These Paradise Daynal Sons are created by the Paradise Trinity.

II. *REFERENCE*: Page 230, ¶5 – "The Daynal order..."

COMMENT

1. Daynals are not a part of universe administration. They are neither judges nor rulers.

2. They are educators devoted to:
    A. Moral enlightenment.
    B. Spiritual awakening.
    C. Moral guidance.

8. LOCAL UNIVERSE MINISTRY OF THE DAYNALS

I. *REFERENCE*: Page 231, ¶1 – "The Paradise Spiritual Sons..."

COMMENT

1. These Trinity-origin Sons are almost wholly devoted to ministry to the dual-origin universes.

2. They are educational ministers to the mortal creatures and lower orders of spirit beings.

II. *REFERENCE*: Page 231, ¶3 – "The Teacher Sons compose..."

COMMENT

1. They supervise the entire educational system of a local universe.

2. They examine and certify a host of universe personalities.

3. They deal with both ascending mortals and ambitious angels.

9. PLANETARY SERVICE OF THE DAYNALS

I. *REFERENCE*: Page 231, ¶5 - "When the progress of events..."

COMMENT

1. When a world is ripe for a spiritual age, the Trinity Teacher Sons arrive.
2. Before such a time, they visit the worlds to formulate plans for the future deliverance from materialism.

II. *REFERENCE*: Page 232, ¶2 - "The Teacher Sons usually..."

COMMENT

1. A corps of Teacher Sons usually remains on the planet for one thousand years.
2. The Daynals do not incarnate or become visible. They contact mortals by the ministry of associated personalities.

III. *REFERENCE*: Page 232, ¶4 - "The Trinity Teacher Sons seem..."

COMMENT

The Teacher Sons are so identified with the scheme of mortal progression that it seems probable that they will remain associated in a future age.

10. UNITED MINISTRY OF THE PARADISE SONS

I. *REFERENCE*: Page 232, ¶6 - "The Paradise Sons are..."

COMMENT

1. The Paradise Sons portray the Paradise Deities to the domains of time and space.
2. They are devoted to helping the creatures of time attain the goals of eternity.

II. *REFERENCE*: Page 233, ¶2 - "In the local universes..."

COMMENT

1. The Paradise Sons collaborate to effect the revelation of the Paradise Deities:
   A. The Creator Sons—the Father.
   B. The Avonals—the Son.
   C. The Daynals—the Spirit.
2. They all contribute to the actualization of the Supreme Being.

PAPER 21
The Paradise Creator Sons

PAPER 21
The Paradise Creator Sons

INTRODUCTION

I. *REFERENCE*: Page 234, ¶1 - "The Creator Sons are..."

COMMENT

1. These Sons are the creators and rulers of the local universes.

2. These sovereigns are unique in nature and personality.

II. *REFERENCE*: Page 234, ¶2 - "In the vast work..."

COMMENT

1. In perfecting and evolving the local universes, these Creator Sons enjoy the full support of the Universal Father.

2. This profound affection of Father and Son is the wellspring of human affection.

1. ORIGIN AND NATURE OF CREATOR SONS

I. *REFERENCE*: Page 234, ¶6 - "When the fullness of..."

COMMENT

1. Creator Sons are produced by the Father and the Son when:

   A. Fullness of absolute spiritual ideation in the Son encounters
   B. Fullness of absolute personality concept in the Father.

2. These original Sons of the perfect ideal and the powerful idea are only-begotten Sons.

II. *REFERENCE*: Page 235, ¶2 - "Each Creator Son is..."

COMMENT

1. Each Creator Son is the absolute of the united deity concepts of his origin.

2. Such Sons are the only-begettable offspring of such eternal and perfect minds.

3. Each Son is the final and eternal expression of the infinite potential of the concept of his origin.

III. *REFERENCE*: Page 235, ¶4 - "I do not know..."

COMMENT

1. There are more than 700,000 Creator Sons in existence.

2. Michael Sons continue to be created.

3. The destiny of Creator Sons above the 700,000 is not revealed.

2. THE CREATORS OF LOCAL UNIVERSES

I. *REFERENCE*: Page 235, ¶5 - "The Paradise Sons..."

COMMENT

1. Michael Creators are designers, creators, and administrators of local universes.

2. They choose the cosmic sites for their universes.

3. These Sons, before undertaking creative work, undergo long special training.

II. *REFERENCE*: Page 236, ¶2 - "The departure of a..."

COMMENT

Creator Sons are limited by the following:

1. Energy-matter is dominated by the Infinite Spirit.
2. Creature types are controlled by the Eternal Son.
3. Personality is bestowed by the Universal Father.

III. *REFERENCE*: Page 236, ¶5 - "When such a perfect..."

COMMENT

1. Materialization is effected by the liaison of Creator Sons and the Daughters of the Infinite Spirit.

2. Subsequent to physical creation they produce their universe family of living creatures.

3. Now the local universe Mother Spirit assumes the qualities of personality.

IV. *REFERENCE*: Page 236, ¶6 - "Notwithstanding that all..."

COMMENT

1. Michaels are unique, diverse, and exclusive in nature and personality.

2. This insures that local universes will also be unique and diverse.

V. *REFERENCE*: Page 237, ¶3 - "The personal presence..."

COMMENT

The smooth running of a local universe does not require the personal presence of the Creator Son.

3. LOCAL UNIVERSE SOVEREIGNTY

I. *REFERENCE*: Page 237, ¶4 - "A Creator Son is given..."

COMMENT

1. The leasehold of a local universe is granted by the Trinity and one of the Seven Master Spirits.

2. The Creator Son earns his complete sovereignty by his seven bestowals.

3. Before earned sovereignty, the Michael Son reigns as vicegerent of the Father.

II. *REFERENCE*: Page 237, ¶5 - "A Creator Son could assert..."

COMMENT

At any time a Michael could assert full sovereignty regardless of bestowals, but such action would deprive him of his Paradise advisers.

III. *REFERENCE*: Page 237, ¶6 - "The fact of creatorship..."

COMMENT

No Michael is known who ever asserted his sovereignty before completing his seven bestowals.

IV. *REFERENCE*: Page 237, ¶7 - "The sovereignty of a Creator Son..."

COMMENT

There are seven stages of a Creator Son's sovereignty, as follows:

1. Initial vicegerent sovereignty.
2. Conjoint vicegerent sovereignty.
3. Augmenting vicegerent sovereignty.
4. Supreme sovereignty.
5. Augmenting supreme sovereignty.
6. Trinitarian sovereignty.
7. Unrevealed sovereignty.

V. *REFERENCE*: Page 238, ¶6 - "The technique of obtaining..."

COMMENT

Local universe supreme sovereignty involves seven experiential steps, starting with seven bestowals, each dedicated to a different will of Deity, and culminating in a new and higher relationship with the Supreme Being.

4. THE MICHAEL BESTOWALS

I. *REFERENCE*: Page 239, ¶7 - "There are seven groups..."

COMMENT

There are seven groups of bestowal Creator Sons—depending on the number of their bestowals.

II. *REFERENCE*: Page 239, ¶8 - "Avonal bestowals are..."

COMMENT

1. Michael bestowals differ from the Avonal bestowals.

2. Michael bestowals portray the seven primary expressions of the nature and will of Paradise Deity on seven different creature levels.

5. RELATION OF MASTER SONS TO THE UNIVERSE

I. *REFERENCE*: Page 240, ¶4 - "The power of a..."

COMMENT

The sovereignty of a Master Michael is supreme because it embraces both the sevenfold Deity viewpoint and a sevenfold creature attitude and synthesizes the two.

II. *REFERENCE*: Page 241, ¶5 - "The Master Sons seem..."

COMMENT

1. Master Sons maintain contact with their bestowal worlds—also with worlds of the Avonal bestowals.
2. Chief of this contact technique is the Spirit of Truth.
3. Michaels have unbroken connection with the Eternal Son.
4. Their sympathetic reach extends from the Paradise Father to the lowly mortals.

6. DESTINY OF THE MASTER MICHAELS

I. *REFERENCE*: Page 241, ¶6 - "No one may..."

COMMENT

1. Each Paradise Michael is the *absolute* of the dual concepts of his origin.
2. The work of the Michaels in the finite local universes does not afford expression for their full potentials.
3. The Michael superfinite capacities must pertain to the universes of a future age.
4. But no one really knows what the future work of the Michaels may be.

II. *REFERENCE*: Page 242, ¶3 - "It is highly probable..."

COMMENT

1. The Michaels are probably destined to service in the now mobilizing universes of outer space.
2. Master Sons and seventh stage Creative Spirits may attain absonite levels of new things, meanings, and values.
3. This absonite service could be on the transcendental levels of the Ultimate.

III. *REFERENCE*: Page 242, ¶4 - "Just as the Deity..."

COMMENT

1. As the Supreme Being is actualizing by experience, so the Michaels may be in preparation for future augmented service.
2. Said Jesus: "I am the way, the truth, and the life."

3.   The Michaels are blazing the path that leads from supremacy through ultimate absonity to eternal deity finality.

WHAT THE BIBLE
TEACHES ABOUT THE SON OF GOD

Throughout the New Testament Michael, our Creator Son, is confused with the Eternal Son of Paradise—the Second Person of Deity and a member of the Trinity.

1.   *The Divinity of Jesus*

Mark 1:1. *"The gospel of Jesus Christ, the Son of God."*

John 17:5. *"Father, glorify thou me...with the glory which I had with thee before the world was made."*

Col. 2:9. *"For in him the whole fulness of deity dwells bodily."*

Matt. 26:64. *"I tell you, hereafter you will see the Son of man seated at the right hand of Power."*

John 10:30. *"I and the Father are one."*

Mark 8:29. *"Peter answered him, 'You are the Christ.'"*

1 Cor. 1:24. *"Christ the power of God and the wisdom of God."*

Matt. 12:8. *"The Son of man is lord of the sabbath."*

Matt. 9:6. *"That you may know that the Son of man has authority on earth to forgive sins."*

John 5:26. *"He has granted the Son also to have life in himself."*

John 11:25. *"Jesus said to her, 'I am the resurrection and the life.'"*

Heb. 2:14. *"That through death he might destroy him who has the power of death."*

John 10:17. *"I lay down my life, that I may take it again."*

2.   *The Humanity of Jesus*

John 1:14. *"The Word became flesh and dwelt among us."*

Matt. 8:20. *"And Jesus said to him: 'Foxes have holes, and birds of the air have nests; but the Son of man has nowhere to lay his head.'"*

Heb. 5:8. *"Although he was a Son, he learned obedience through what he suffered."*

Mark 9:12. *"That he should suffer many things and be treated with contempt."*

Heb. 2:18. *"He himself has suffered and been tempted."*

Mark 14:34. *"And he said to them, 'My soul is very sorrowful, even to death.'"*

John 11:35. *"Jesus wept."*

Heb. 4:15. *"One who in every respect has been tempted as we are, yet without sinning."*

3. *Sovereignty of Jesus*

1 Tim. 6:15. *"Blessed and only Sovereign."*

1 Cor. 15:25. *"For he must reign until he has put all his enemies under his feet."*

Col. 2:10. *"Him, who is the head of all rule and authority."*

1 Cor. 15:27. *"For God has put all things in subjection under his feet."*

Eph. 1:22. *"And he has put all things under his feet and has made him head over all things."*

Acts 8:10. *"'This man is that power of God which is called Great.'"*

Matt. 28:18. *"And Jesus…said to them: 'All authority in heaven and on earth has been given to me.'"*

Mark 14:62. *"'And you will see the Son of man sitting at the right hand of Power.'"*

John 18:37. *"Jesus answered, 'You say that I am a king. For this I was born, and for this I have come into the world.'"*

Rev. 17:14. *"The Lamb will conquer them, for he is Lord of lords and King of kings."*

Mark 13:26. *"And then they will see the Son of man coming in clouds with great power and glory."*

4. *Jesus as the Atonement Sacrifice*

John 10:11. *"The good shepherd lays down his life for the sheep."*

1 Peter 2:21. *"Christ also suffered for you."*

Heb. 2:17. *"To make expiation for the sins of the people."*

1 Peter 3:18. *"For Christ also died for sins once for all."*

John 1:29. *"'Behold the Lamb of God, who takes away the sin of the world.'"*

2 Cor. 5:21. *"For our sake he made him to be sin who knew no sin, so that in him we might become the righteousness of God."*

Gal. 1:4. *"Who gave himself for our sins."*

Matt. 20:28. *"'Even as the Son of man came...to give his life a ransom for many.'"*

1 Peter 1:18. *"You know that you were ransomed...with the precious blood of Christ."*

Eph. 1:7. *"We have redemption through his blood."*

1 John 1:7. *"And the blood of Jesus his Son cleanses us from all sin."*

Rom. 8:34. *"Is it Christ Jesus...who indeed intercedes for us?"*

5. **The Kingdom of Heaven**

   A. **Jesus' Gospel**
      Luke 12:32. *"Fear not, little flock, for it is your Father's good leasure to give you the kingdom."*
      John 18:36. *"My kingship is not of this world."*
      Matt. 4:23. *"And he went about all Galilee...preaching the gospel of the kingdom."*
      Luke 24:47. *"And that repentance and forgiveness of sins should be preached in his name to all nations."*
      Mark 12:30, 31. *"'You shall love the Lord your God with all your heart...you shall love your neighbor as yourself.'"*
      Note: In the religion of Jesus the gospel of the kingdom was: The Fatherhood of God and the Brotherhood of Man. Peace, forgiveness, liberty, and eternal life were the results of that faith which accepted the salvation of the gospel.

   B. **The Apostolic Gospel** (The religion *about* Jesus)
      Acts. 2:32, 33, 38. *"This Jesus God raised up, and...Being therefore exalted at the right hand of God...has poured out this which you see and hear....And Peter said to them, 'Repent, and be baptised every one of you in the name of Jesus Christ for the forgiveness of your sins.'"*
      Acts 20:24. *"The ministry which I received from the Lord Jesus, to testify to the gospel of the grace of God."*

Eph. 1:13. *"You...who have heard the word of truth, the gospel of your salvation, and have believed in him."*

Eph. 6:15. *"And having shod your feet...with the gospel of peace."*

Mark 1:1. *"The beginning of the gospel of Jesus Christ, the Son of God."*

Rom. 2:16. *"On that day when, according to my gospel, God judges the secrets of men by Christ Jesus."*

6. *Jesus and the Lucifer Rebellion*

Luke 9:1. *"And he called the twelve together and gave them power and authority over all demons."*

Luke 10:18. *"And he said to them, 'I saw Satan fall like lightning from heaven.'"*

John 16:11. *"The ruler of this world is judged."*

7. *Michael in the Bible*

Michael as the name of human beings occurs about a dozen times in the Old Testament. As applied to supermortals, it is found in five passages.

Dan. 10:13. *"But Michael, one of the chief princes, came to help me."*

Dan. 10:21. *"There is none who contends by my side against these except Michael, your prince."*

Dan. 12:1. *"At that time shall arise Michael, the great prince who has charge of your people."*

Jude 9. *"But when the archangel Michael, contending with the devil, disputed about the body of Moses."*

Rev. 12:7. *"Michael and his angels fighting against the dragon."*

PAPER 22
The Trinitized Sons of God

PAPER 22
The Trinitized Sons of God

INTRODUCTION

REFERENCE: **Page 243, ¶1 - "There are three groups..."**

COMMENT

Origin determines the division into three groups of the Trinitized Sons, one group being unrevealed.

1. THE TRINITY-EMBRACED SONS

I. *REFERENCE*: **Page 243, ¶3 - "All Trinity-embraced sons..."**

COMMENT

There are seven orders of Trinity-embraced sons, all of whom were originally of single or dual origin.

II. *REFERENCE*: **Page 244, ¶1 - "*The Trinitized Sons of Attainment...*"**

COMMENT

Trinitized Sons of Attainment are Adjuster-fused mortals, but no longer are they finaliters.

III. *REFERENCE*: **Page 244, ¶2 - "*The Trinitized Sons of Selection...*"**

COMMENT

1. Trinitized Sons of Selection are recruited from the seraphim and midwayers, and from certain Spirit-fused and Son-fused mortals.

2. These Sons are assigned to the courts of the Ancients of Days.

IV. *REFERENCE*: Page 244, ¶3 - "*The Trinitized Sons of Perfection...*"

COMMENT

1. Trinitized Sons of Perfection are twice-trinitized sons. They are the creature-trinitized sons of Paradise-Havona personalities or mortal finaliters.

2. After creature-trinitized sons have served with the Supreme Executives and the Trinity Teacher Sons, they may be embraced by the Trinity.

V. *REFERENCE*: Page 244, ¶6 - "Apparently the Trinity-embraced..."

COMMENT

For the present universe age, these Trinity-embraced sons have been assigned to the services of the superuniverses.

2. THE MIGHTY MESSENGERS

I. *REFERENCE*: Page 245, ¶1 - "Mighty Messengers belong..."

COMMENT

Mighty Messengers are trinitized, rebellion-tested, ascendant mortals.

II. *REFERENCE*: Page 245, ¶2 - "With such personal records..."

COMMENT

These loyalty-tested mortals are first mustered into the Finaliter Corps and then Trinity embraced.

III. *REFERENCE*: Page 245, ¶6 - "I am a Mighty Messenger..."

COMMENT

This Mighty Messenger's earthly companion is his present associate.

IV. *REFERENCE*: Page 246, ¶2 - "Mighty Messengers are..."

COMMENT

Mighty Messengers are fully conscious of their entire ascendant careers, and therefore very helpful to other ascendant creatures.

3. THOSE HIGH IN AUTHORITY

REFERENCE: **Page 246, ¶3 - "Those High in Authority..."**

COMMENT

These are the trinitized, Adjuster-fused mortals of superior administrative ability.

4. THOSE WITHOUT NAME AND NUMBER

I. *REFERENCE*: **Page 246, ¶7 - "Those Without Name and Number..."**

COMMENT

These are the Trinitized ascendant souls who have extraordinary skills of worship.

II. *REFERENCE*: **Page 247, ¶7 - "You mortals who read..."**

COMMENT

Even Urantia mortals may become trinitized sons of any of these orders and act as revealers of truth.

5. THE TRINITIZED CUSTODIANS

I. *REFERENCE*: **Page 247, ¶8 - "The Trinitized Custodians are..."**

COMMENT

These are the selected ascendant seraphim and midwayers.

II. *REFERENCE*: **Page 248, ¶2 - "Trinitized Custodians are ascendant..."**

COMMENT

These ascendant angels and midwayers have become finaliters and been embraoed by the Trinity, and then are assigned to the Ancients of Days.

6. THE TRINITIZED AMBASSADORS

I. *REFERENCE*: **Page 248, ¶7 - "Trinitized Ambassadors are the second..."**

COMMENT

These sons are recruited from the ascendant Spirit-fused and Son-fused mortals and are then assigned to the Ancients of Days.

7. TECHNIQUE OF TRINITIZATION

I. *REFERENCE*: Page 249, ¶2 - "I cannot fully unfold..."

COMMENT

The technique of trinitization is one of the secrets of Vicegerington, known only to participants.

II. *REFERENCE*: Page 249, ¶3 - "Aside from the Deities..."

COMMENT

Those who may trinitize:

1. The Deities.
2. Paradise-Havona citizens.
3. Certain finaliters.

III. *REFERENCE*: Page 249, ¶6 - "If two mortal finaliters..."

COMMENT

1. Permission for finaliters to attempt trinitization is granted by the Master Architects.
2. Trinitization consists in the attempt to idealize and actualize an original concept, not theretofore trinitized.
3. Final activation is granted by Master Spirit Number Seven.

IV. *REFERENCE*: Page 250, ¶2 - "When a new and original..."

COMMENT

1. When Deity trinitizes, the parents are unchanged.
2. When two creatures trinitize, the participants undergo unique personality modifications.
3. This change is called bi-unification. It may persist until the Supreme Being is finally personalized.

V. *REFERENCE*: Page 250, ¶4 - "While these parents..."

COMMENT

1. United parents of trinitized sons continue to function as two beings on the finaliter roll call.
2. But during the present universe age such parents are inseparable for assignment.
3. Mixed types of trinitization parents forgather in a special corps.

8. THE CREATURE-TRINITIZED SONS

I. *REFERENCE*: Page 251, ¶5 - "In addition to the..."

COMMENT

There are numerous unrevealed groups of trinitized sons, all endowed with personality by the Universal Father.

II. *REFERENCE*: Page 251, ¶6 - "When new ascender-trinitized..."

COMMENT

1. At first young trinitised sons serve with the Supreme Executives on the worlds of the Infinite Spirit.

2. Later they serve with the Trinity Teacher Sons in the local universes.

III. *REFERENCE*: Page 251, ¶8 - "The Teacher Sons..."

COMMENT

1. Teacher Sons may nominate their creature-trinitized wards for Trinity embrace.

2. Subsequent to Trinity embrace, they enter the service of the Ancients of Days.

IV. *REFERENCE*: Page 252, ¶2 - "Excepting the Trinitized Sons..."

COMMENT

Excepting Trinitized Sons of Perfection and those forgathering on Vicegerington, all creature-trinitized sons enter the Corps of Trinitized Finaliters.

9. THE CELESTIAL GUARDIANS

REFERENCE: Page 252, ¶6 - "The Celestial Guardians are..."

COMMENT

These twice-trinitized sons assist the Ancients of Days as court officers.

10. HIGH SON ASSISTANTS

I. *REFERENCE*: Page 253, ¶4 – "The High Son Assistants..."

COMMENT

1. These are the superior twice-trinitized sons of ascendant mortals and Paradise-Havona personalities.

2. They are assigned to superuniverse service as personal aids to the high sons of the government—private secretaries.

II. *REFERENCE*: Page 253, ¶6 – "Can you not see..."

COMMENT

These personalities representing a single supreme concept are of great value to superuniverse administrators.

III. *REFERENCE*: Page 254, ¶5 – "They are touchingly..."

COMMENT

They are supremely wise regarding a single idea, but eagerly seek knowledge on everything else.

Note:

Papers 23 through 30 inclusive are **not** abstracted since they so largely deal with work and ministrations of numerous groups of universe personalities.

The next paper presented will be No. 31 - "The Corps of the Finality" - which is the last paper in Part I of *The Urantia Book*.

PAPER 31
The Corps of the Finality

PAPER 31
The Corps of the Finality

1. **THE HAVONA NATIVES**
2. **GRAVITY MESSENGERS**
3. **GLORIFIED MORTALS**
4. **ADOPTED SERAPHIM**
5. **GLORIFIED MATERIAL SONS**
6. **GLORIFIED MIDWAY CREATURES**
7. **THE EVANGELS OF LIGHT**
8. **THE TRANSCENDENTALERS**
9. **ARCHITECTS OF THE MASTER UNIVERSE**
10. **THE ULTIMATE ADVENTURE**

INTRODUCTION

I. *REFERENCE*: Page 345, ¶4 - "During the present..."

COMMENT9

1. Finaliters serve in all seven superuniverses.

2. Thus they gain the sevenfold concept of the Supreme Being.

II. *REFERENCE*: Page 345, ¶6 - "We have no idea..."

COMMENT

The corps is wholly a self-governing body.

1. THE HAVONA NATIVES

I. *REFERENCE*: Page 346, ¶2 - "Many of the Havona natives..."

COMMENT

1. Millions of Havoners register to join the Mortal Finaliter Corps.

2. They provide the viewpoint of one born in perfection.

II. *REFERENCE*: Page 346, ¶4 - "The inhabitants of the..."

COMMENT

1. Only one Havoner may join a company of 1000.

2. A company of mortal finaliters includes:

   A. 997 Ascendant beings.
   B. 1 Havona Native.
   C. 1 Gravity Messinger.
   D. 1 Temporary member.

2. GRAVITY MESSENGERS

I. *REFERENCE*: Page 346, ¶7 - "Wherever and whenever..."

COMMENT

1. Gravity Messengers are directed by Grandfanda—assigned only to the Mortal Corps of the Finality.

2. Messengers attached to the other corps are not personalized—they are absonitized.

II. *REFERENCE*: Page 347, ¶2 - "Gravity Messengers hail from..."

COMMENT

1. Gravity Messengers are modified and personalized Adjusters.

2. Finaliters cannot ignore time and space, but the Messengers can.

III. *REFERENCE*: Page 347, ¶3 - "Gravity Messengers may be..."

COMMENT

Only one Messenger belongs to a finaliter company, but unlimited numbers may be attached.

3. GLORIFIED MORTALS

I. *REFERENCE*: Page 347, ¶5 - "Ascendant Adjuster-fused..."

COMMENT

1. The Corps contains more mortals than seraphim.

2. Mortals and seraphim make up all but one per cent of each finaliter company.

II. *REFERENCE*: Page 347, ¶6 - "We of Uversa..."

COMMENT

1. Finaliters for the time being serve in the Corps of Light and Life assigned to the superuniverses.

2. Future destiny—probably outer space.

4. ADOPTED SERAPHIM

REFERENCE: **Page 348, ¶7 – "Many of the faithful..."**

COMMENT

Ascendant seraphim are attached to nonmortal finality corps—but in larger numbers to the mortal corps.

5. GLORIFIED MATERIAL SONS

REFERENCE: **Page 349, ¶2 – "There is provision..."**

COMMENT

Some mortal finaliter companies contain Adamic Sons.

6. GLORIFIED MIDWAY CREATURES

REFERENCE: **Page 349, ¶6 – "The midway creatures..."**

COMMENT

All midway creatures ascend to one of the finality corps, but the secondaries always go into the *mortal* corps.

7. THE EVANGELS OF LIGHT

I. *REFERENCE*: **Page 349, ¶7 – "At the present time..."**

COMMENT

Each finaliter company has 999 permanent members, the last place being filled by a temporary Evangel of Light.

II. *REFERENCE*: **Page 349, ¶8 – "Any celestial personality..."**

COMMENT

Any celestial being assigned to the company on a temporary basis may be called an Evangel of Light.

8. THE TRANSCENDENTALERS

REFERENCE: **Page 350, ¶5 - "Part of the perfected..."**

COMMENT

Finaliters must associate with more than one thousand groups of transcendental supercitizens of Paradise.

9. ARCHITECTS OF THE MASTER UNIVERSE

REFERENCE: **Page 351, ¶3 - "The Architects of the..." and ¶4 - "The sixteenth proscription..."**

COMMENT

The Master Architects total 28,011 personalities and function on seven levels of the absonite:

1. Paradise Level—the senior Architect.
2. Havona Level—3 Architects.
3. Superuniverse Level—7 Architects.
4. Primary Space Level—70 Architects.
5. Secondary Space Level—490 Architects.
6. Tertiary Space Level—3,430 Architects.
7. Quartan Space Level—24,010 Architects.

10. THE ULTIMATE ADVENTURE

I. *REFERENCE*: **Page 352, ¶8 - "The senior Master Architect..." and Page 353, ¶2 - "Each of these destiny corps..."**

COMMENT

1. These seven Corps of the Finality are under the general direction of the senior Architect.

2. Grandfanda, the first ascendant mortal, is the head of the Supreme Council of Destiny, consisting of the seven heads of the finaliter corps.

II. *REFERENCE*: **Page 354, ¶5 - "As we view this..."**

COMMENT

There is impressive evidence that the perfected ascendant mortals who have become finaliters are destined for a glorious future in outer space.

ULTIMATE DESTINY IN THE BIBLE

1. *God's Eternal Purpose*

   Eph. 3:11. *"This was according to the eternal purpose which he has realized in Christ Jesus our Lord."*

   Deut. 33:27. *"The eternal God is your dwelling place, and underneath are the everlasting arms."*

2. *Survival in the Old Testament*

   In early times, among the Hebrews, survival was very hazy. There were seven heavens and also Sheol and Hades. Belief in the resurrection was slow in appearing—became general only shortly before the times of Christ. During the days of Jesus, the Sadducees did not believe in the resurrection.

   To the Jews, survival meant the biologic survival—survival of the Hebrew race or nation.

3. *Immortality*

   Among the Jews the concept evolved slowly from Moses to Daniel.

   During the times of Jesus the doctrine of immortality was born full-fledged.

   A. *Man Is Not Naturally Immortal.*
   Deity alone has immortality.
   1 Tim. 6:16. *"Who alone has immortality and dwells in unapproachable light, whom no man has ever seen or can see."*

   B. *Eternal Life Is the Gift of God*
   Luke 18:30. *"Who will not receive manifold more in this time, and in the age to come eternal life."*
   John 3:15. *"That whoever believes in him may have eternal life."*
   John 6:40. *"For this is the will of my Father, that every one who sees the Son and believes in him should have eternal life."*
   John 6:47. *"Truly, truly, I say to you, he who believes has eternal life."*
   John 10:28. *"And I give them eternal life, and they shall never perish."*
   John 17:3. *"And this is eternal life, that they know thee the only true God."*

Rom. 2:7. *"To those who by patience in well-doing seek for glory and honor and immortality, he will give eternal life."*

Rom. 6:23. *"For the wages of sin is death, but the free gift of God is eternal life."*

1 Tim. 6:12. *"Fight the good fight of faith; take hold of the eternal life."*

1 John 2:25. *"And this is what he has promised us, eternal life."*

1 John 5:13. *"I write this to you who believe in the name of the Son of God, that you may know that you have eternal life."*

4. *Heaven*

The Jews believed in seven heavens.

   A.   ***Heaven of the Old Testament***
        Deut. 10:14. *"Behold, to the Lord your God belong heaven and the heaven of heavens."*
        1 Kings 8:49. *"Then hear those in heaven thy dwelling place their prayer and their supplication."*
        2 Chron. 2:6. *"But who is able to build him a house, since heaven, even highest heaven, cannot contain him?"*
        Job 22:12. *"Is not God high in the heavens?"*

   B.   ***Jesus'Teaching about Heaven***
        Luke 10:20. *"But rejoice that your names are written in heaven."*
        Luke 15:7. *"There will be more joy in heaven over one sinner who repents than over ninety-nine righteous persons who need no repentance."*

   C.   ***Paul and the Apostles***
        Col. 1:5. *"Because of the hope laid up for you in heaven."*
        2 Tim. 4:18. *"The Lord will rescue me from every evil and save me for this heavenly kingdom."*
        Heb. 12:23. *"And to the assembly of the first-born who are enrolled in heaven…and to the spirits of just men made perfect."*
        1 Peter 1:4. *"And to an inheritance which is imperishable, undefiled, and unfading, kept in heaven for you."*

5. **Hell**

    A. ***Hell in the Old Testament***

        Old Testament ideas about hell were very indefinite, being centered about the concepts of Sheol and Hades.

        Deut. 32:22. *"For a fire is kindled by my anger, and it burns to the depths of Sheol."*

        Ps. 18:5. *"The cords of Sheol entangled me, the snares of death confronted me."*

        Ps. 9:17. *"The wicked shall depart to Sheol, all the nations that forget God."*

        Prov. 23:14. *"If you beat him with the rod you will save his life from Sheol."*

        Amos 9:2. *"Though they dig into Sheol, from there shall my hand take them."*

    B. ***Hell in the New Testament***

        Matt. 5:22. *"Whoever insults his brother...and whoever says, You fool shall be liable to the hell of fire."*

        Matt. 23:33. *"You brood of vipers, how are you to escape being sentenced to hell?"*

        Luke 10:15. *"And you Capernaum...you shall be brought down to Hades."*

        Luke 16:23. *"And in Hades, being in torment, he lifted up his eyes, and saw Abraham far off."*

        Heb. 10:26,27. *"For if we sin deliberately after receiving the knowledge of the truth, there no longer remains a sacrifice for sins, but a fearful prospect of judgement, and a fury of fire which will consume the adversaries."*

        Jas. 3:6. *"The tongue is a fire. The tongue is an unrighteous world...setting on fire the cycle of nature, and set on fire by hell."*

        2 Peter 2:4. *"For if God did not spare the angels when they sinned, but cast them into hell and committed them to pits of nether gloom to be kept until the judgment."*

The Jews had very hazy ideas regarding punishment in either Sheol or Hades. In general, they believed that both rewards and punishment were received during their mortal lives on earth. Justice among the Jews pertained to restitution and retaliation—a life for a life. They had no prisons.

Jer. 21:14. "*I will punish you according to the fruit of your doings, says the Lord.*"

Lam. 3:39. "*Why should a living man complain, a man, about the punishment of his sins?*"

Eze. 14:10. "*And they shall bear their punishment—the punishment of the prophet and the punishment of the inquirer shall be alike.*"

B. **Punishment in the New Testament**

Matt. 25:46. "*And they will go away into eternal punishment, but the righteous into eternal life.*"

Note: The good have eternal life. The bad get eternal punishment.

Rev. 21:8. "*Their lot shall be in the lake that burns with fire and brimstone, which is the second death.*"

Note: While such punishment is spoken of as "everlasting punishment," at the same time it is referred to as the "second death." It is the result—not the duration—of the punishment which is *eternal*—even eternal death.

Obad. 16. "*They shall drink, and stagger, and shall be as though they had not been.*"

Matt. 25:46. "*And they shall go away into eternal punishment, but the righteous into eternal life.*"

Note: 1. The righteous to eternal life.

2. The wicked to eternal death.

Notice again - **2 Thess. 1:9.** "*They shall suffer the punishment of eternal destruction and exclusion from the presence of the Lord.*"

Once more: It is the result which is *eternal*—not the *duration* of the punishment.

Heb. 12:29. "*For our God is a consuming fire.*"

6. **Punishment**

   A. **Punishment in the Old Testament**

      Fire is a figure of speech which suggests that all of sin and
      iniquity will be consumed by fire—divinity.

      2 Peter 2:9. *"The Lord knows how...to keep the unrighteous under
      punishment until the day of judgment."*

      Note: Here is the suggestion of pre-judgment punishment.

      FIRE has many meanings in the Bible:

      1. Purification.
      2. Divinity.
      3. Metaphysical—refining.
      4. Discipline.
      5. Punishment.
      6. Destruction.

      See Heb. 1:7. *"Of the angels he says, 'Who makes his angels winds,
      and his servants flames of fire."*

7. **Redemption**

   A. **Redemption in the Old Testament**

      There are two meanings of redemption in the Bible:

      (1) Man's act—like redeeming land.

      (2) God's act-the plan of salvation.

      Deut. 21:8. *"Forgive, O Lord, thy people Israel, whom thou hast
      redeemed."*

      Job 33:24. *"And he is gracious to him, and says, 'Deliver him from
      going down into the Pit, I have found a ransom."*

      Ps. 19:14. *"O Lord, my rock and my redeemer."*

      Ps. 103:4. *"Who redeems your life from the Pit, who crowns you with
      steadfast love and mercy."*

      Ps. 130:7. *"With him is plenteous redemption."*

      Isa. 43:14. *"Thus says the Lord, your Redeemer."*

      The Old Testament presented God as a vindicator, redeemer,
      deliverer. and avenger.

   B. **Redemption in the New Testament**

      Matt. 20:28. *"Even as the Son of man came...to give his life as a
      ransom for many."*

      John 10:15. *"And I lay down my life for the sheep."*

      Rom. 3:24. *"Yet now God his gracious kindness declares us not guilty.
      He has done this through Christ Jesus, who has freed us by taking away
      our sins."*

Eph. 1:7. *"In him we have redemption through his blood."*

1 Tim. 2:6. *"Who gave himself as a ransom for all."*

Heb. 9:12. *"He entered once for all into the Holy Place, taking... his own blood, thus securing an eternal redemption."*

1 John 3:16. *"That he laid down his life for us."*

Throughout the New Testament Paul's doctrine of the atonement is supported.

8. *The Resurrection*

   A. *Resurrection in the Old Testament*

      The resurrection doctrine was a gradual growth among the Jews. It was becoming general by the times of Daniel. But even in Jesus' time the Sadducees did not believe in the resurrection. The hebrew concept of survival was the continuance of the race—the nation. It was a reproach to be childless. **Gen. 30:23.** *"She conceived and bore a son, and said, 'God has taken away my reproach."*

      Ps. 17:15. *"When I awake, I shall be satisfied."*

      Ps. 73:24. *"Thou dost guide me with thy counsel, and afterward thou wilt receive me to glory."*

      Dan. 12:2. *"And many of those who sleep in the dust of the earth shall awake, some to everlasting life, and some to shame and everlasting contempt."*

   B. *Resurrection in the New Testament*

      Matt. 22:23. *"The Sadducees came to him, who say there is no resurrection."*

      Acts. 24:15. *"Having a hope in God...that there will be a resurrection of both the just and the unjust."*

      Luke 14:14. *"You will be repaid at the resurrection of the just."*

      Rev. 20:5. *"This is the first resurrection."*

   C. *Paul and the Resurrection*

      Acts 26:8. *"Why is it thought incredible by any of you that God raises the dead?"*

      Acts. 24:21. *"With respect to the resurrection of the dead I am on trial before you this day."*

1 Thess. 4:16. *"For the Lord himself will descend from heaven…And the dead in Christ will rise first."*

1 Cor. 15:52. *"For the trumpet will sound, and the dead will be raised imperishable, and we shall be changed."*

1 Cor. 15:35. 38. *"'How are the dead raised? With what kind of body do they come?'…God gives it a body as he has chosen."*

Rom. 6:5. *"For if we have been united with him in a death like his, we shall certainly be united with him in a resurrection like his."*

D. *Jesus and the Resurrection*

Matt. 22:31. *"And as for the resurrection of the dead, have you not read what was said to you by God."*

John 11:25. *"Jesus said to her, 'I am the resurrection and the life.'"*

Mark 12:25. *"When they rise from the dead, they…are like angels in heaven."*

Luke 20:36. *"They…are sons of God, being sons of the resurrection."*

John 5:28, 29. *"The hour is coming when all who are in the tombs will hear his voice and come forth, those who have done good, to the resurrection of life, and those who have done evil, to the resurrection of judgment."*

NOTES

Printed in the United States
1218900003B/1-21